FREEDOM OF CONSCIENCE

FREEDOM OF CONSCIENCE

A
Baptist/Humanist Dialogue

Edited by
Paul D. Simmons

Prometheus Books
59 John Glenn Drive
Amherst, New York 14228-2197

Published 2000 by Prometheus Books

Freedom of Conscience: A Baptist/Humanist Dialogue. Copyright © 2000 by Paul D. Simmons. All rights reserved. No part of this publication may be reproduced, stored in a retrieval system, or transmitted in any form or by any means, electronic, mechanical, photocopying, recording, or otherwise, without prior written permission of the publisher, except in the case of brief quotations embodied in critical articles and reviews.

Inquiries should be addressed to
Prometheus Books, 59 John Glenn Drive, Amherst, New York 14228–2197.
VOICE: 716–691–0133, ext. 207.
FAX: 716–564–2711.
WWW.PROMETHEUSBOOKS.COM

04 03 02 01 00   5 4 3 2 1

Library of Congress Cataloging-in-Publication Data

Freedom of conscience : a Baptist/humanist dialogue / Paul D. Simmons, editor and contributor.
    p.   cm.
Includes bibliographical references.
ISBN 1–57392–766–X (cloth)
    1. Christian ethics—Baptist authors—Congresses. 2. Humanistic ethics—Congresses. I. Simmons, Paul D.
BJ1275 .F74 2000
261.7'2—dc21   99–047757
                                                                                  CIP

Printed in the United States of America on acid-free paper

CONTENTS

Introduction: Thank God for Humanism!
    Paul D. Simmons   9

PART I: RELIGIOUS FREEDOM: A CONSTITUTIONAL MANDATE

1. The Wall of Separation
    Joe Barnhart   29

2. Humanism and the Idea of Freedom
    Paul Kurtz   34

3. Jefferson and the Danbury Baptists: The Interaction between Baptists and the Nation's Founders
    Robert S. Alley   41

4. James Madison, the Baptists, and Religious Liberty
    Paul D. Simmons   50

5. The Dangers of Being Tolerant of the Intolerant
    George H. Shriver   74

6. Bootleg Baptists?
    Robert M. Price   80

PART II: ACADEMIC FREEDOM: CONSCIENCE IN THE CLASSROOM

7. Academic Freedom
   Vern L. Bullough — 87

8. The Anatomy of Academic Freedom and Religiously Oriented Institutions of Higher Learning in the United States: A Selected Look
   George H. Shriver — 91

9. Academic Freedom in the Seminary: The Myth, the Reality, and the Future
   Paul D. Simmons — 106

10. Truth against Freedom
    Bernard C. Farr — 133

11. The Liberal Arts, Time, and Truth: A Last Lecture
    Arthur J. Slavin — 156

PART III: REASON, REVELATION, AND RELIGION

12. The Believing Biblical Scholar and Enlightenment Humanism
    Dan O. Via — 169

13. Inerrancy: The New Catholicism? Biblical Authority vs. Creedal Authority
    Robert M. Price — 175

14. Must Humanism Be Secular?
    E. Glenn Hinson — 182

15. Spiritual Formation: Humanity As Unfinished Presence
    Molly Marshall — 194

PART IV: FREEDOM OF CONSCIENCE IN THE PUBLIC ARENA

16. Strange Bedfellows: Mormon Polygamy and Baptist History
    George D. Smith — 207

17. Stephen Carter, the Christian Coalition,
    and the Civil Rights Analogy
    David McKenzie 217

18. Religious Liberty and Abortion Policy: *Casey* As Catch-22
    Paul D. Simmons 240

19. In Defense of Freedom of Conscience:
    A Cooperative Baptist/Secular Humanist Declaration
    Joint Statement 263

Contributors 271

INTRODUCTION

THANK GOD FOR HUMANISM!

Paul D. Simmons

With apologies to Shakespeare and Julius Caesar, I have not come to bury humanism but to praise it. It was a privilege to participate in the dialogue at the University of Richmond as a Baptist Christian and I thank God for those who brought us together for a "Baptist-Humanist Dialogue." The conference on October 6 and 7, 1995, was made possible by the leadership of humanists like Dr. Paul Kurtz and Dr. George Smith, and, on the Baptist side, Dr. David Burhans, chaplain, and Dr. Robert Alley, professor emeritus at the University of Virginia.

Both organizers and participants saw the occasion as an opportunity to discuss important issues in a context of openness and honesty. Baptists were free to be confessional; the humanists felt free to express their conscientious beliefs. Participants held common interests in such values as academic freedom, religious liberty, ethical values in the moral community, and the contributions of the Enlightenment to religious thought and the American ethos. The conference provided not only a framework for better understandings across ideological divisions, but an appreciation for a certain heritage we hold in common. Fresh from the bloodletting among Baptists, I felt a strong sense of gratitude to God for such an occasion and those who made it possible.

Even so, I recognize the irony in saying that I thank God for humanism, and more particularly, for certain humanists. I intend no offense to those who are not theists—to those who may feel some objection to my invocation of deity. At the same time, I do not hesitate to identify my own frame of reference—my own commitment to a belief in God as revealed most supremely in Jesus Christ.

A BAPTIST/HUMANIST DIALOGUE

The conference was designed to explore issues of vital mutual interest. These topics are not simply interesting to discuss as abstract philosophical issues, they touch the nerve of everyday life and affect the institutions that provide protections for universal human liberties. The discussions were straightforward and direct and touched a nerve among both Baptists and humanists. Regardless of the (religious) affections of the presenters, each recognized that every person's life is affected for good or ill by the ways in which these particular issues are resolved. They further recognized that such issues are at the heart of intense controversies in American society.

Inevitably, a point of reference in the "dialogue" was the Religious Right, though no representatives from that coalition participated in the conference. The Christian Coalition has extensively altered the Southern Baptist Convention (SBC) and has its sights set on American society. Both humanists and Baptists at the conference see the coalition on the Right as a threat to good morals, civil community or political values, and vitality in religion.

The Baptists present were committed to the historic freedoms that have defined and refined the Baptist witness in America. Baptists have historically been champions of religious liberty, which is foundational for all political and social freedoms.[1] The First Amendment embodies Baptists' most significant contribution to political science. Virginia Baptists had united efforts with humanists like James Madison and Thomas Jefferson, thus making possible that distinctive American institution of the separation of church and state.

But the witness of Baptists to religious liberty has hardly been uniform. In a speech on the east steps of the Capitol in Washington, D.C., the late George Truett declared that "Baptists have one consistent record concerning religious liberty throughout all their long and eventful history. They have never been a party to oppression of conscience. They have forever been the unwavering champions of liberty both religious and civil."[2] That was in 1920. More recently, W. A. Criswell, Truett's successor at First Baptist in Dallas, Texas, declared publicly that "the notion of separation of church and state was the figment of some infidel's imagination."[3] Criswell was also a leader in the new coalition on the Right and a contributor to the new directions of the SBC.

That shift represents a significant revisionism at work in Baptists' historical witness and sense of identity.[4] The largest Protestant denomination in America now seems more like the establishmentarians against whom Baptists once rebelled. The shift in the direction and commitments of the SBC could be traced to that fundamental but all-important shift in loyalty away from religious liberty as a defining belief. A theocratic agenda emerged with political alliances with the Republican Party and New Right organizations.

This brief foray into SBC politics helps to define those Baptists whose story is told in these pages or who have contributed to this collection of articles. Conference participants are not the Baptists of rightwing politics identified with the Christian Coalition. Rather, they are leading the effort to preserve the traditional Baptist witness by distancing themselves from the SBC and its social/theological agenda, and developing alternative seminaries and structures for association. Contributors like Drs. Glenn Hinson, Dan Via, George Shriver, Molly Marshall, Joe Barnhart, and myself represent thousands who have felt the sharp edge of intolerance for diversity in the SBC. Their experiences of divisiveness, oppression, broken covenants, and betrayal at Southeastern Seminary in Wake Forest, North Carolina, Southern Seminary in Louisville, Kentucky, and elsewhere helped to shape the perspectives shared at the conference. They found the dialogue a welcome retreat from the angry invectives and false accusations to which they were subjected from the fundamentalists who took control of seminary boards of trustees.

The conference provided an opportunity to explore issues of importance to all Americans, believers and unbelievers alike, and to do so from a perspective informed by experience, a sense of history, and an awareness of the struggles in early America and its European background.

A joint statement was one of the highlights that grew out of the conference. "In Defense of Freedom of Conscience: A Cooperative Baptist/Secular Humanist Declaration" is a statement of principled commitments to which both Baptists and humanists could append their signatures. It is the final chapter in this book. To be sure, it is a consensus statement, not one that everyone agrees with in every detail. The disagreements are of secondary importance to the broad areas of agreement outlined, however. Thank God for such general working agreements on topics of profound importance for the future of democratic governance and liberties, both religious and civil, that all Americans should enjoy.

Beyond the joint statement, there were certain insights gleaned from the conference that merit isolation and emphasis. The dialogue around specific topics (viz., academic freedom, religious liberty, biblical studies, and political participation) revealed certain commitments that serve to unite an extremely diverse group. Religious thinkers need the leavening influence of those who do not share their faith assumptions. Insights are gained from the mirror held up by thoughtful persons who are not part of the majority. We are reminded of truths that tend to be neglected or rejected for want of a wider dialogue. Six uniting truths that emerged were: (1) we are all concerned about ethics and the moral community; (2) theistic beliefs are no assurance of good morals; (3) defining "the human" is important for humanists and Baptist Christians alike; (4) Jesus is of interest to people far beyond the boundaries of organized religion; (5) religious liberty is for believers and unbelievers alike; and (6) there is an ever-present need for a prophetic criticism of misguided religion. These might even be proposed as moral action guides in a pluralistic society. They certainly characterized participants on both sides of the aisle at Richmond. Areas of agreement as well as points of tension in perspective can thus be identified.

A MUTUAL REGARD FOR ETHICS AND THE MORAL COMMUNITY

Ethics is a common ground for discussions between Baptists and humanists. The Roger Williams tradition among Baptists provides a sympathetic and at times compatible, if not always consistent, point of interest and identification with humanism. Broad areas of agreement can be established even if we differ significantly about the images, principles, and ground-of-meaning beliefs which shape our perspectives. Ethical humanism's basic orientation is moral rather than theological. It is concerned about the human problem and the various patterns of actions and attitudes that exist among people. In spite of crucial differences between us, concerns about the moral community provide a fruitful area of exploration and a common point of reference.

Two things become obvious as one studies humanism and the history of Christian thought. One is that theism is not a prerequisite to being moral. Christians relate their moral witness to faith commitments, which provide strong incentives and guidance for ethical wisdom and behavior. But they have no monopoly on morality. At times Christians come off looking rather shabby when compared to certain humanists of high ethical or moral character.

The second insight is that neither Christians nor humanists have a monopoly on virtue. We all struggle with the problems of moral fault in the human family. There is enough in the human story of rape and pillage, murder and intrigue, duplicity and deceit to embarrass any person who takes moral values seriously. Baptist Christians appropriate a doctrine of sin to provide a way to name the problem and deal with its complex consequences for individuals and society. Humanism tends to explain moral fault in terms of a person's lacking intelligence or rational capacity. While we might agree that such insights are true, Christians would insist they do not go far enough. The human problem is not simply a matter of incomplete education or moral intention; it goes to the core of being human. From a Christian perspective, what is required is not resolve and reform but conversion and redemption.

The Meaning of Being "Human"

Even so, one cannot help but be impressed by humanism's continued stress on the importance and even the indispensability of the "human" as a standard for measuring the moral acceptability of actions, intentions, dispositions, and public policies. The humanist has a high standard of what it means to be human, and the excellence of character to which every person should aspire. No metaphysical explanation is needed to know that people are special. The uniqueness of being human lies in the capacity for discerning the difference between permitted and prohibited actions. We need no laws imposed from eternity to know that we cannot abuse and injure one another and claim to be moral. We need no rule handed down from Sinai to know that we cannot despoil our environment and maintain human survival. If we are to survive as a society, we must appeal to the things that unite us in a common endeavor, rather than be willing to kill one another over doctrines that ultimately make little if any difference. Without the irreverent sense of humor found among humanists, such as Mark Twain, that casts doubt on the importance of abstract metaphysical speculation, theologians would likely take themselves far too seriously. For the humanist, it is enough to know that we should do right, and that people are creatures of intelligence and conscience that should be decent and fair in their relations to one another.

Humanism's concern for ethics puts to shame many of those who are zealous followers of God or who would kill in the name of Jesus. The meaning of the "human" thus provides a point of dialogue between humanists and those of the Judeo-Christian tradition concerning the nature and possibilities of being human. The essay by Glenn Hinson explores the issue insightfully. Humanists remind us of the dignity inherent in being human. Christian thought is often quite negative about human nature in a way that denies human dignity in God's creative and redemptive activity.

The Psalmist held a rather exalted view of humanity *imago dei* ("in

God's image"). He declared that God had "made human beings a little less than God/and had crowned them with glory and honor./People have been given dominion over God's works/and all things were placed under their feet/all sheep and oxen, and also the beasts of the field,/the birds of the air, and the fish of the sea,/whatever passes along the paths of the sea" (Ps. 8:5–8). The passage recapitulates the Creation narrative in which God is portrayed as promising dominion over all creation to Adam and Eve, the primeval pair (Gen. 1:28). The point of the Psalm, however, is not to exalt human existence, but to praise God. All creation, the apex of which is in human beings, points to the greatness of God. The amazing thing is that God would give people the abundant life of shared glory, especially the life able to relate to the living God in celebration and worship. Thus, Christians can join the Psalmist's doxology: "O Lord, our Lord, how majestic is your name in all the earth!"

The Christian understanding of human beings *imago dei* is a strong statement of the dignity of being human and the respect due each person, which were also basic emphases in the Enlightenment. Two things underscore a strong Christian humanism. First, the love of God is universally directed toward all people. Every person, regardless of race, gender, or ethnic origin, is the object of divine love and grace. All people are invited to become the people of God, responding to the divine initiative and accepting their place in the covenant community. The incarnation of God in Christ is the second powerful support for a positive Christian view of human nature. God chose a human being as the supreme embodiment of the Eternal Creator/Redeemer. Humanity was the highest expression of the creative work of God and in Christ became the vehicle of God's supreme revelation of the nature of the divine transcendence that empowers and directs the future of the world. But we know our humanity in Christ as truly or fully man. Humanism has no definitive model or norm for what it means to be human. In spite of our mutual regard for being human, therefore, we have plenty of room for discussion of differences.

Jesus is Larger than Institutional Religion

The place and importance of Jesus in Christian theology and for the world also came into focus. It was a telling moment to discover again that many humanists have a profound appreciation for Jesus, but not in the same sense as those who are Christian believers. Christians are devoted to Jesus Christ as the center of faith and the one by whom we understand what it means to be human, the nature of God, and the reality of evil. The humanists are fascinated by Jesus, but they stop short of attributions of divinity or special revelation which are so basic to Christian perspectives. But Jesus' teachings are of great interest to humanists, who hold them among the finest and richest moral insights ever given the world. They admire and frequently follow what Jesus had to say while rejecting the Resurrection and Ascension as mythological fantasy. Or, much as Gandhi once said, they love Jesus but cannot stand Christianity.

Thomas Jefferson, for instance, had his own version of the New Testament. Using a type of canonical criticism, he decided only certain portions of Scripture could be acceptable to morally serious but rational people. The result was what he called "an octavo of forty-six pages of pure and unsophisticated doctrines such as were professed and acted on by the *unlettered* Apostles, the Apostolic Fathers, and the Christians of the first century."[5] Jefferson was no enemy of Jesus but was an opponent of bad morals and irrational beliefs. He regarded his summation not only as a more "beautiful" and "precious morsel of ethics" than any he had ever seen, but as "proof" that he was "*a real Christian*" (emphasis his). He said those Christians who called him infidel were charlatans.[6] "[T]hey draw all their characteristic dogmas from what its author never said nor saw. . . ." Jefferson believed that had Jesus' teachings been preached purely, "the whole civilized world would now have been Christian."[7]

Baptists and many humanists appreciate Jesus, therefore, but have quite different perceptions of his work and place in history. Humanists appreciate Jesus as one who embodied the human excellencies; Baptist Christians revere him as unique in God's redemption of the world.

Moral Discernment in the Human Community

God is also to be thanked for those humanists who are people of keen insight into human nature and who have no small intellectual grasp of the critical issues facing the human race. They remind us all of our indebtedness to the Enlightenment, a point made in the chapter by Paul Kurtz and affirmed by Dan Via's essay on biblical scholarship. The list of secular humanists from whom we have all learned is impressive and extensive, drawing on the world of politics, philosophy, and literature. They include Samuel Clemens (Mark Twain), Thomas Jefferson, James Madison, Alexander Hamilton, Abraham Lincoln, Ralph Waldo Emerson, Henry David Thoreau, Bertrand Russell, Mahatma Gandhi, and William Macneile Dixon. Writing as Mark Twain, Samuel Clemens tweaked the nose of what he regarded as pompous but preposterous religion.

Bertrand Russell found strong arguments for atheism in the outlandish and totally immoral acts of people claiming to be Christian. In *Why I am Not a Christian*, he asked the embarassing question of why supposedly good people do such terrible things. He found abundant evidence to question the morality of the religious. Jews slaughtered two hundred thousand Greeks in Cyrene and even more on Cyprus. Muslims and Hindus regularly face off in bloody battles in India and Pakistan. Christians waged war on one another, not to mention the Muslims and Jews, over a four-hundred-year period we call the Inquisition. Hundreds of thousands were killed because they were tried and found wanting. They failed the basic tests for orthodoxy.

Religion, for all its grandeur and mystery and its promise for special relationships to ultimate reality, is also the occasion for the most subtle of temptations—distorting the very message it is called to share by focusing more on power than on God's truth in Christ. There is more than enough guilt to go around. Accusations that humanists cannot be moral because they do not believe in God flies in the face of solid evidence to the contrary. Bertrand Russell fought for peace against a religious and political fanaticism that seemed willing if not eager to incinerate the world with nuclear weapons. But polemical charges that Christians have no redeeming features suffer the same fallacy of judging the many by the few whose morals very few admire.

Most everyone is interested in being moral, but people seem to be more capable of *intending* truth than achieving integrity. Hurling accusations at the others as if they are the source of all social problems is both misguided and counterproductive. We will do well to begin with a mutual acknowledgement of moral faults and an attempt to assist one another in creating the moral community we all desire.

RELIGIOUS FREEDOM IS FOR EVERYONE

Staunch support for religious freedom is found both among humanists and Baptists. The corollary to everyone's enjoyment of that fundamental human right is that the state must be secular. But the very notion of the secular state is anathema to those who are still trying to declare America a Christian nation. The theocrats and church-over-staters we will have with us always. The fact that the First Amendment was included in the Bill of Rights has not settled the question of the proper relation of church and state and the terms for protecting and exercising the prerogatives of a free people.

The dialogue at Richmond was a reminder that religious liberties are not just for the religious, which gives meaning to the notion of a secular government. Religious liberty is for believers and nonbelievers alike, a point explored below in part I. This important ground for democratic governance is openly rejected by right-wing evangelical coalitions. Baptists have historically championed "soul" freedom as a universal human right. Nonbelievers have the freedom to reject religious belief and practice, just as believers have the freedom to believe as they will and engage in services of worship consistent with their particular traditions. Humanists are to be as free to reject religion as believers are to accept and practice religion.

Early Baptists saw that to threaten anyone with coercion in matters of religious belief or practice was to undermine the principle of voluntarism so vital to biblical faith. Religious freedom involves freedom *of* religion, freedom *from* religion, and freedom *for* religious groups to pursue their mission in the world. But the power of the state was never to enforce the evangelistic or educational mission of any faith group. Minority religious groups like nonbelievers are to be protected against the simple rule of the majority in using public policy to reflect any sectarian belief. Jefferson put it strongly in rejoicing that this was a "blessed country of free enquiry and belief, which has surrendered its creed and conscience to neither kings nor priests. . . ."[9]

Men like Jefferson and Madison teach us something of abiding importance about religion and politics. These outstanding political leaders were men who showed a deep affection for Jesus but a critical detachment from zealotic religion. The problem is not religion, but that religion that seeks to dominate and to limit the freedoms of others. Politicians can be religious, but should not adopt the agenda of nor submit to the intimidations of those who wish to tear down the wall separating church and state. Politicians, in short, are to be representatives of *all* the people and preserve those freedoms that assure the well-being of nonbelievers as well as the religious. That leaves plenty of room for a politician's open and personal expressions of religious affections.

Jefferson and Madison both had a profound appreciation for Jesus and his teaching but grew impatient with the clergy who sought to establish theocracy or Christian dominance through public policy. We can thank God that the framers of the Constitution had the good sense and moral fortitude to keep the powers of the institutional church at bay. They were educated in the classics and knew only too well the excesses caused by religious imperialism in Europe. They happened also to be the politicians most targeted by religious zealots who expect public servants to be submissive to religious leaders in all things. Politically involved fundamentalists like Jerry Falwell, Pat Robertson, and James Dobson do not take kindly to criticism. Nor do such preachers like to tolerate "insubordination." When they speak they expect others to jump—to follow their dictates to the letter. John Calvin, John Cotton Smith, and Cotton Mather are still alive in the assertiveness and authoritarianism of the Religious Right. The sign of the Puritan preacher thundering orders to magistrates and the faithful in the pew are everywhere apparent on the current scene. It is important to take them seriously as sincere opponents of the liberties, both religious and nonreligious, that belong to all Americans.

THE PROPHETIC CRITICISM OF MISGUIDED RELIGION

The excesses of religious zeal are egregious violations of basic moral values, and certainly a threat to the social contract of toleration and forbearance among people of widely differing views. Humanists and Baptists find a common cause in raising concerns about and criticizing the excesses of misguided religion. Karl Barth once said that "the first object of prophetic religion is the criticism of bad religion." There is enough false faith to go around these days, challenging the critical intellectual and moral faculties of both humanists and religious leaders.

The loss of civility in public discourse, for instance, is an example of intolerance toward persons who disagree about public policy and personal choices.[10] When reason and open debate cannot settle an issue, hardliners have turned to uncivil behavior, including heckling, sit-in demonstrations, and other efforts to coerce the public into accepting dubious solutions to complex issues. Bombing clinics, shooting abortion providers, and creating mayhem around clinics, for instance, show the belligerent intolerance at work in an effort to substitute coercion for consensus. Civility in social manners and political dialogue would be a far superior ethic to what true believers call the list of moral or "family" values they attempt to legislate. Religious zealotism has a poorly informed sense of ethics, a twisted and distorted vision of what constitutes morality. Legislating their social agenda would create an oppressive society where freedom would be little more than a figment of the imagination.

Baptist Christians think it incongruous to say such actions stem from the teachings of Jesus. Religious dogmatism in morals is irreconcilable with the morality necessary in a pluralistic political setting. Arrogant judgmentalism is also in conflict with the teachings of Jesus. Jesus taught an ethic of common sense in the tradition of Wisdom,[11] at least in part because he saw through the pretensions and false piety of religious dogmatists (cf. Matt. 23:1–15). Rigid rules, or rigid interpretations and applications of even very good rules, are contrary to the spirit and teachings of Jesus. In his story of the Good Samaritan (Luke 10), Jesus emphasized an ethic that transcended the moral requirements of orthodox theists. The

Samaritan did what was right; the priest and Levite avoided doing good and did the predictable, namely, what their religious roles demanded. They kept to their temple and synagogue schedules; the Samaritan kept to his moral compass in helping the wounded and dying Jew.

Jesus commended the Samaritan's action as an example of what God approves and love requires. He linked moral or ethical action to the nature and character of God. There are some things God just does not do and does not will that people do to one another. Nothing less than the integrity of God is at stake in the claims people make about the actions to which God has led them. There is a story of two farmers talking about the tragic death of a bright and talented young farmer in a farm accident. One surmised sadly that God must have had a good reason for killing such a fine person! To which the other responded strongly, "Dammit, Clyde, you know God would not do something like that!" The story embodies a significant dimension to Jesus' approach to ethics. Pious claims that God does unethical things vilifies God.

Jesus' ethic also served to increase the circle of those who reflect the very mind of God. God's kind of people are not to be defined by some formal test or formula for belonging to the insider's group. The standard for belonging is both simple and demanding: Discern and implement the demands of love for neighbor.[12] It is a commonsense approach; there are no secret societies or special knowledge (*gnosis*) at work. The task is to show beneficence toward one another, that is, to love one another, just as one would like to be loved. Jefferson considered himself "a Christian in the only sense in which [Jesus] wished anyone to be, sincerely attached to his doctrines in preference to all others, ascribing to himself every *human* excellence, and believing he never claimed any other. . . ."[13]

Right-wing evangelical Christians are adamantly opposed to such inclusiveness. They are devoted to doctrinal orthodoxy as a test of both good morals and true faith. John Calvin, their spiritual father, became so preoccupied with the sovereign power of God that he wound up with a loveless and harsh legalism. In that spirit, he imposed or approved harsh penalties through the Consistory at Geneva. He had his own adopted son and daughter-in-law executed for adultery, and Servetus was put to the pyre for challenging Calvin's notion of predestination. Such dogmatic legalism shows nothing of the spirit of Christ nor any serious commitment to following Jesus' explicit teachings.

The current interest in creationism by certain segments of the Christian community is an odd continuation of the church's oppressive battle against science in the name of "truth." That struggle has persisted at least since Copernicus and Galileo were condemned for findings in science that were thought "dangerous to the faith." Creation science advocates seem anachronistic in a world informed by scientists who are as much impressed by mystery as they are by the relativism of physics or the vastness of the universe. Even more disturbing is the egregious grab for power and authority, as if religion knows exactly how science should teach the beginnings of life on earth and in the universe.

A faith tied simply to correct propositional statements is no faith at all. It is a quest for the undoable, for a rationalistic structure of the universe that defies the human imagination and perverts the nature of the biblical revelation. Why is there a need among God's people for some notion of special creation, as the creationists insist? Why should people be isolated from the rest of God's creative activity? Are they alone the objects of divine love? Is the creative, redemptive activity of God in both nature and history limited only to human beings? Some seem to think the rest of creation must be vilified before God can be glorified or people be saved.

The humanist, whether Christian or secular, brings an insight to such nonsense. A tempering, leveling perspective is needed to reduce the glare of ignorance and increase commonsense wisdom. People have a unique place in the scheme of life and history, but they are not the special aim of either creation (nature) or history. They are privileged to share in this vast scheme and to wonder at its magnificence and depth. But they are not the reason for its existence. In the grand scale of the cosmos, people are a tiny bit of space dust. Their dignity consists in the fact that they know it and may become aware of their relative place in time and space. Knowing the connection of human life to all other components of the life drama and reflecting upon the greatness and grandeur of it all may help to effect its interconnectedness and relatedness. Thank God for such humanism that reminds us of our place in a larger frame of reference.

Humanists often get a bad rap among religious leaders on the extremist Right. They are vilified, misrepresented, and demonized by enemies who distort the nature, aims, and goals of humanism. Two groups are especially aggressive toward humanists. The first is comprised of those who prefer dubious doctrine to a reasoned and reasonable faith. For them, the "true [religious] believer"[14] is one profoundly committed to doctrinal expressions of faith and a zeal that substitutes energy for credibility. An incredible faith requires incredulity in belief. Like those of the Middle Ages, they seem to believe that the profundity of one's faith is in direct proportion to their ability to suspend critical judgment. "The more incredible the doctrine the more pious to believe" was the slogan that inspired simplicity in faithful followers and evoked ever more incredible postulations on the part of their religious leaders. Notions proliferated about how many angels could dance on the head of a pin; or the idea that Mary's virginity was preserved in spite of her having numerous children.

The will to believe is strong on the contemporary scene. People believe the most amazing and incredible things. Large groups of people gather near Cincinnati to watch a statue of the Virgin Mary weep. Others gather around a woman in Georgia who claims visitation from the Virgin mother, who has given her a message for the faithful. The message is invariably some version of "Be faithful and wait in hope." Not much new there. But the amazing thing is that people are actually expecting such visitations and for statues to weep! In India, millions have been rushing to temples where it is reported that the elephant-headed Lord Ganesha has started drinking the milk poured on its head by the faithful.[15] Surely miracles are in the eyes of the beholder.

Macneile Dixon once observed that "so numerous are the illusions, frenzies, hallucinations afloat in the world that some thinkers have been of [the] opinion that our planet was the asylum of the universe for disordered minds. It is not merely the things [people] say, and they are fantastic enough, it is the proposals they seriously advocate, the proceedings in which they actually engage."[16] Gandhi, for all his prominence and moral influence in the cause of justice, had corners of his mind that allowed the morally atrocious. He once said that "he would die" before killing rats! Holiness is hardly consistent with being willing for vermin to carry typhus or other germs that cause the death and misery of millions of people. We need only to be reminded of the Waco inferno, the Jim Jones massacre, and the Heaven's Gate suicides to know how religion can be distorted into an ugly and demonic changeling.

The current popularity and prominence of fundamentalism is an equally amazing phenomenon. With Alice, of *Alice in Wonderland* fame, I find it one of those incredible things I am asked to believe before breakfast each day. One should think that whatever makes for the rigidity of mind and the fossilization of spirit that characterizes that movement would long ago have turned thoughtful people away in dismay and disgust. Many thoughtful people have, of course, but that leaves many who are angry and fearful, the unthinking and unreflective who comprise this movement. The Nazi extremism of Hitler was also enthusiastically supported by millions of otherwise decent religious people.

Fundamentalist/evangelical Christians do not take such criticism lightly, of course. They are adept at demonizing their critics, which is a favorite and effective tool of religious demogogues. The words "secular humanist" and "liberal" are spit out with contempt and disgust as if these were the source of all moral maladies and the root of all evil. The best defense for the fundamentalists is an uncivil offense against a fabricated enemy. David Ehrenfield[17] criticized "humanism" as the belief that utopian goals are possible by human ingenuity alone and that technology is an entirely good thing. But few humanists embrace the utopianism he condemns and most are also concerned about the impact of unbridled technology on the environment. Ehrenfield feeds the appetite for an enemy that exists in the paranoia of the Right. But his definitions are fuzzy and so general they could apply as well to technologism as to humanism. Thinking people aware of the ecological crisis confronting humanity are against misdirected and all-powerful applications of technology. They all feel a bit powerless to slow the momentum toward disaster and the near-total control of human life by ever more sophisticated technological wizardry.

Fundamentalists vehemently attack anyone, humanist or fellow believer, who disagrees with their precious beliefs or "moral" postures. They become especially enraged against anyone who criticizes or questions their lack of ethical seriousness or insight. But that is an area in which they are particularly vulnerable. Jefferson once said of such people: "From the clergy I expect no mercy. They crucified their Saviour, who preached that their kingdom was not of this world; and all who practice on that precept must expect the extreme of their wrath. The laws of the present day withhold their hands from blood; but lies and slander still remain to them."[18]

There is no love lost in either direction, of course. Humanists are quite adept both at defending themselves and have been perennial critics of fundamentalist Christianity. Humanists typically sneer at the so-called articles of faith that fundamentalists claim as basic to Christian faith. Harold Bloom regarded fundamentalists as "know-nothings" who claimed to have the absolute truth about nearly everything. He mocked their claim regarding biblical inerrancy and infallibility as little else than a clever political ploy.[19] Tragically for the Southern Baptist Convention, it was also effective, far more so than even the fundamentalists expected. No few critics of the Religious Right saw the claim about inerrancy and infallibility as a way to place respectability on their own misguided opinions on social and theological issues. The so-called rationalism of fundamentalism is simply intellectually vacuous to the humanist. Jefferson called its first cousin a "monkish ignorance and superstition."[20]

Humanists like Jefferson provide a welcome retreat into a world of sanity and common sense from the world of religious zealotism. They invite us to think and think rightly about the tough issues confronting the democracy we call America. New-Right religion has lost both soul and mind in its zeal for the Holy Grail of political power. But its threat to liberties that belong to all of us is real and should be taken with the utmost seriousness. Humanists and people of good faith help assure us that the world is not completely mad, that sobriety in religious thought is not completely absent. Thank God for the humor, good grace, wit, and intelligent insights which combine to put a mockery to the excesses of religion gone mad on its own extremism.

CONCLUSION

There are two strong hopes behind this collection of essays. One is that they will be informative and inspirational to readers who take the time to think along with us about some of the crucial issues of our time. The second is that the reader will join the dialogue and offer further insight as to sources that might be consulted or guidelines that might be adopted to make of America a better place in which to live. The conviction shared by these writers is that America will be *better* only as it strives to be inclusive of all people and assures basic human rights to all groups regardless of racial, ethnic, gender, or religious differences.

The structure of the book reflects the four areas of interest that were addressed in the conference at the University of Richmond. The themes discussed above were interwoven with the presentations on particular topics. The articles in part I deal with religious liberty and the separation of church and state from perspectives informed by both Baptists and humanists. Part II continues the quest for freedom of conscience into the classroom. The issue of academic freedom is particularly acute in religious circles. Part III explores the importance of reason and the tools of historical and literary criticism for biblical and theological scholarship. Three Baptist scholars show that faith and reason are hardly incompatible. Part IV examines issues pertaining to pluralism in America and political actions and goals on the part of Christian activists and how those actions might affect unbelievers. The crucial question is how religious liberty commitments serve as a moral action guide to Christians' political activity.

Both common concerns and basic differences between Baptists and humanists have been exposed and explored. But we have embraced an ethic we believe basic to human survival, namely, a respect for one another. That respect may be based on Jesus' call to "love one another" or on an appreciation for human dignity, as the humanists insist. In either case, it is the clue for a unity within diversity that goes to the very question of human and social survival.

NOTES

1. See Charles W. Deweese, ed., *Defining Baptist Convictions: Guidelines for the Twenty-first Century* (Franklin, Tenn.: Providence House Publishers, 1996); and Walter B. Shurden, *The Baptist Identity: Four Fragile Freedoms* (Macon, Ga.: Smyth & Helwys, 1993).

2. George W. Truett, "Baptist and Religious Liberty," in *A Sourcebook for the Baptist Heritage* (Nashville: Broadman, 1990), p. 469.

3. Cited by Shurden, *Baptist Identity*, p. 52.

4. See two volumes by H. Leon McBeth, *The Baptist Heritage* (Nashville: Broadman, 1987) and *A Sourcebook for Baptist Heritage* (Nashville: Broadman, 1990). A later work by McBeth that detailed the rewriting of the Baptist history and the rejection of historical defining points for Baptists was purchased by Broadman/Holman, who then refused to publish it. That repressive attitude toward dissent and disagreement now pervades the SBC. See Paul D. Simmons, "The Politics of Silencing the Enemy," *Baptists Today*, May 21, 1998, pp. 18–19.

5. Thomas Jefferson, *Jefferson Himself: The Personal Narrative of a Many-Sided American*, ed. Bernard Mayo (Charlottesville: University of Virginia, 1942), p. 322.

6. Jefferson was not speaking of *all* Christians. He had great affinity for Baptists because of their commitment to religious freedom. But he heaped scorn on those who sought political privilege and pushed for the elimination of the First Amendment and the nullification of any separation of powers between church and state. Jefferson called them "the loudest, the most intolerant of all sects, the most tyrannical and ambitious; ready at the word of the lawgiver, if such a word could now be obtained, to put the torch to the pile and to rekindle in this virgin hemisphere, the flames in which their oracle Calvin consumed the poor Servetus." From a letter to William Short, April 13, 1820, cited in D. W. Adams, ed. "Jefferson's Extracts from the Gospels," in *The Papers of Thomas Jefferson*, 2d ser. (Princeton: Princeton University, 1983), p. 393. See also Robert Alley's article on "Jefferson and the Danbury Baptists," in this volume.

7. Jefferson, *Jefferson Himself*, p. 323.

8. Bertrand Russell, *Why I am Not a Christian* (London: National Secular Society, 1970).

9. Jefferson, *Jefferson Himself*, p. 323.

10. See R. J. Mouw, "Religious Conviction and Public Civility," in *Ethics, Religion and the Good Society*, ed. J. Runzo (Louisville: Westminster/John Knox, 1992).

11. See Marcus J. Borg, *Jesus: A New Vision* (San Francisco: Harper & Row, 1987), esp. chap. 6.

12. See John Hick, "The Universality of the Golden Rule," in *Ethics, Religion and the Good Society*.

13. Jefferson, *Jefferson Himself*, p. 231.

14. See the classic by Eric Hoffer, *The True Believer* (New York: Harper & Row, 1951).

15. *Courier-Journal*, September 22, 1995, p. A-8.

16. William Macneile Dixon, *The Human Situation* (New York: Oxford University Press, 1958), p. 96.

17. David Ehrenfield, *The Arrogance of Humanism* (Oxford: University Press, 1981).

18. Jefferson, *Jefferson Himself*, p. 231.

19. Harold Bloom, *The American Religion: The Emergence of the Post-Christian Nation* (New York: Simon & Schuster, 1992), p. 232.

20. Jefferson, *Jefferson Himself*, p. 345.

PART I
RELIGIOUS FREEDOM: A CONSTITUTIONAL MANDATE

The various meanings of and intellectual groundings for religious liberty in America are explored by the articles in this section. The writers appeal to historical and theological perspectives as well as stories from the early days of the American republic to gain insight and provide guidance for current debates.

Joe Barnhart's introduction to the section criticizes the evangelical notions of Christocracy or theonomy as in Rousas John Rushdoony's Reconstuctionism. His hope rests with a pluralistic view of freedom for all Americans advocated by Baptists like Roger Williams and John Leland.

Paul Kurtz emphasizes freedom as basic to what it means to be a humanist, a point with which Baptists should be able readily to identify. Kurtz is an internationally recognized expert on humanism and has written widely on the subject. His *Forbidden Fruit: The Ethics of Humanism* and *Eupraxophy: Living Without Religion*[1] are major contributions to the world of humanist and ethical thought. Kurtz does a splendid job of showing the various dimensions of freedom (academic, political, and human rights) and the historic and philosophical grounds for opposition to authoritarianism, whether in the classroom or the political arena.

Bob Alley explores the relation of Baptists to the founders of the nation, Thomas Jefferson and James Madison. He puts special attention on the importance of Jefferson's letter to the Baptists of Danbury, Connecticut, which contained the phrase regarding the "wall of separation" between church and state. That metaphor has been crucial in court interpretations of First Amendment issues. Alley strongly defends Jefferson's principle against attacks from Christian Coalition founder Pat Robertson and, more recently, from within the Library of Congress.

My essay shows that James Madison fought battles in Virginia and as president that have a contemporary ring. Prayer in the public schools, further Constitutional amendments to assure religious liberties, and special favoritism for church groups through public policy are sure to generate intense heat but often shed little light on the church-state issues involved. I argue that Madison's thoughts and actions should provide guidance for current debates.

George Shriver cautions against tolerating the intolerable and points to the radical intolerance manifested among leaders for the religious and political Right in America. The efforts by leaders in the Christian Coalition to exclude secularists from the political table simply underscores the need to keep America secular; that is, open to all persuasions and basing public policy on reasons both theists and atheists can understand and support.

A sermon by Robert Price goes to the heart of the issue in terms of what it means to be a Baptist. He contends not only that schisms can only be overcome by a generous inclusiveness toward persons who disagree with one another, but that the Baptist identity is related to the freedom to be different.

NOTE

1. Paul Kurtz, *Forbidden Fruit: The Ethics of Humanism* (Amherst, N.Y.: Prometheus Books, 1988); *Eupraxophy: Living without Religion* (Amherst, N.Y.: Prometheus Books, 1989).

CHAPTER 1

THE WALL OF SEPARATION
Joe Barnhart

In 1968, former Ambassador George W. Ball publicly described Richard M. Nixon as "a man without principle." One of Nixon's friends fired back:

> I reacted strongly to a below-the-belt statement against my long-time friend Richard Nixon. Mr. Ball reflected on Mr. Nixon's character and personal integrity. I've known Richard Nixon intimately for 20 years. I can testify that he is a man of high moral principle. I have not seen one thing in my personal relationship with him that would give any indication that he is tricky.[1]

The friend who defended Nixon was frequently introduced as "God's man with God's message." He had earlier invited Nixon to contribute "A Nation's Faith in God" as an article for *Decision* magazine. Later the article appeared in an anthology of evangelical apologists that included such notables as C. S. Lewis and Charles Spurgeon.[2] Nixon's friend was Billy Graham, who became disillusioned with the politician rather belatedly.

For several decades, Dr. Graham appeared to view himself as a prophet to America called by God to give the divine interpretation of international events. In 1973, however, Graham made it clear he was not an Old Testament prophet but a New Testament evangelist. During the Vietnam War, the noted preacher seemed to grow disillusioned with his ability as a prophet.

Interpreting international events had proven to be a precarious venture. A prophet who has to revise and correct his pronouncements and predictions gives the appearance of being pretty much like the rest of us—fallible and subject to error. Graham's inability to discern Nixon's habit of using and deceiving him made the evangelist appear human, overly trusting, and perhaps a little too eager to imitate his favorite prophet, Daniel. According to the biblical story, Daniel had influenced King Darius to send out a decree in every language throughout the world that everyone in the royal domains would "fear and revere the God of Daniel" (Dan. 6:25).

Over the decades, Graham has wandered off in a variety of directions on the issue of church-state relations. At one period of his life, he spoke of his vision of America as a "Christocracy." He hoped to bring such a rule of Christ about by the democratic process, by which he meant majority rule. If enough Christians, as Graham understood the term "Christian," could win the majority of votes, they would, he hoped, enact Christian principles and laws legally binding on all citizens.

Graham did not always specify which new laws would be passed in a Christocracy. He made several suggestions, however, including stricter laws on divorce, restraints on freedom of publication, and promotion of some form of state-sponsored prayer and Bible reading in the public schools. He even offered hints that the death penalty should be established as fitting punishment for adultery.[3]

Other evangelicals, primarily those called Reconstructionists, appear eager to pass laws against witches, idolators, and blasphemers. The long shadow of Governor John Winthrop, the early seventeenth-century Puritan theocrat, falls across one wing of the evangelicals and some Roman Catholics in the United States. In a 1994 interview, Graham called himself a conservative rather than a right-winger, although he did not make clear the line of demarcation between the two.

At the end of the continuum opposite John Winthrop stands another New England Christian. Trained for the Church of England clergy, Roger Williams identified with the seventeenth-century Baptists for a season and called himself a Seeker. Williams made it clear to Winthrop and the theocrats that their attempts to use the state's power to enforce belief in a set of religious doctrines succeeded in promoting not righteousness, but hypocrisy. True religion, he argued, could thrive only in a setting of liberty of conscience. Without such liberty, religion was "soul rape."

In many ways, Roger Williams, with his notion of "natural freedom" and "soul liberty," may be viewed as a forerunner of the Enlightenment. His libertarian view of government directly challenged the magistrates who set themselves up as the voice of heaven in determining what individuals should or should not believe. For him, government served primarily to protect individuals from threat of intrusion on their person and property. For Williams, no doctrine or belief had any claim on the state to receive protection from criticism. Only individuals had the legal right to be protected not from criticism, but from those who would use force to prevent them from propagating their views or from learning from whomever they chose.

In examining the controversy over Salman Rushdie, Michael Ignatieff made the following keen observation: "In theocratic States like Iran, the law guarantees the inviolability of certain sacred doctrines. In free societies, the law does not protect doctrines as such; it protects individuals."[4] This is precisely the point Roger Williams spent most of his adult life explicating and embodying. For him, liberty meant the right to believe or to disbelieve. Without the option to disbelievee, believing is mere hypocrisy.

Baptist historian Edwin S. Gaustad in his book, *Liberty of Conscience*, offers a highly readable and insightful account of Roger Williams's battle with the theocrats and others who sought to use the state to give special government privileges to their doctrines and to deny individuals the right to propagate rival beliefs.[5] In a forthcoming book on Thomas Jefferson, Gaustad will, among other things, show how Jefferson carried the torch of freedom and advanced the early Baptist doctrine of the wall of separation between church and state.[6] Humanists and other heirs of the Enlightenment owe a profound debt of gratitude to those courageous seventeenth-century Baptists, in particular because of their radical position that the state and church only corrupted one another when they became partners.

John Bunyan, a Baptist and author of *Pilgrim's Progress*, was frequently incarcerated in England. His high crime was that of preaching without seeking the state's approval or license. The U.S. constitutional protection of citizens against government agents entering uninvited into private dwellings grew, in part, out of the early English and Dutch Baptist emphasis on local autonomy and congregationism. Private property, as it turned out, proved to be a strong foundation upon which to build freedom of speech.

While John Winthrop and some of the other New England Puritans were labeling Native Americans as Canaanites, Roger Williams made friends with them and learned their language. He charged that while professing a desire to convert the natives, King Charles and the Massachusetts magistrates in fact stole the natives' land. Far from serving as model Christians or a city set on a hill as a light to the pagans, the Massachusetts magistrates and clergy had, Roger Williams argued, dishonored their religion and proved to be more the cinder of hypocrisy than the jewel of morality.

With his friend John Milton, Williams contended that no religion had a moral claim on the purse strings of the state's treasury. Over a century later, another Baptist, John Leland, a personal friend of Thomas Jefferson, rejoiced that the federal Constitution ruled out religious affiliation as a requirement for holding public office. Leland followed Williams's earlier counsel to inquire of ship captains not their religious affiliation, but their ability and skill in commanding the ship. Like Williams before him, Leland called on his fellow Christians to show where Jesus so much as intimated that "the civil powers... ought to force people to observe the rules and doctrine of the Gospel." This same Leland, again following the earlier lead of Williams, denounced slavery as a "violent deprivation of the rights of nature and inconsistent with the republican government...."[7] In his impassioned way, Williams wrote: "Millions of innocent men, women, and childen, since the introduction of Christianity, have been burnt, tortured, fined, imprisoned, yet we have not advanced one inch toward uniformity. What has been the effect of coercion? To make one half the world fools, the other half hypocrites."[8]

I will not here explore the connection between the early Baptists and James Madison, since Bob Alley has examined it with greater depth and insight than I could hope to give. I will close, rather, with a quotation from Jefferson, one of the foremost voices of the Enlightenment. That the quotation echoes the libertarian thoughts and sentiments of Roger Williams will be readily noted: "The legitimate powers of government extend to such acts only as are injurious to others. But it does me no injury for my neighbor to say there are twenty gods, or no God. It neither picks my pocket nor breaks my leg."[9]

NOTES

1. Quoted in *Dallas Morning News*, September 30, 1968, p. 5A. Used by permission of United Press International.

2. See Sherwood E. Wirt and Mavis R. Sanders, *Great Readings from Decision* (Minneapolis: World Wide Publications, 1970), pp. 356–60.

3. Cort R. Flint, ed., *The Quotable Billy Graham* (Anderson, S.C.: Drake House, 1966), pp. 101 f.

4. Michael Ignatieff, "The Value of Toleration," in *The Rushdie File*, ed. Lisa Appignanesi and Sara Maitland (Syracuse, N.Y.: Syracuse University Press, 1990), p. 256.

5. Edwin S. Gaustad, *Liberty of Conscience: Roger Williams in America* (Grand Rapids: William B. Eerdmans Publishing Co., 1991).

6. Forthcoming book to be published by Eerdmans.

7. For an excellent study of the contribution of the early Baptists to a free society, see William R. Estep, *Revolution Within the Revolution: The First Amendment in Historical Context, 1612–1789* (Grand Rapids: William B. Eerdmans Publishing Co., 1990).

8. See Roger Williams, *The Bloudy Tennent of Persecution*, a book the English Parliament publicly burned in the very year that its members were at war with King Charles, who had denied them their full religious liberty. For a treatment of the emerging views of Roger Williams and his adventurous life, see Linda Kraeger's historical novel, *Trust and Treachery* (Lewiston, N.Y.: Mellen University Press, 1995). The follow-up novels on Williams, coauthored by Kraeger and J. E. Barnhart, have recently been completed and are in need of an aggressive publisher. It is highly significant that Roger and Mary Williams named their second daughter *Freeborn*—in Puritan New England in 1635.

9. Thomas Jefferson, *Notes on Virginia*, in vol. 2 of *The Writings of Thomas Jefferson*, ed. Albert Ellery Bergh (Washington, D.C.: Thomas Jefferson Memorial Association of the United States, 1905), pp. 221–22.

CHAPTER 2

HUMANISM AND THE IDEA OF FREEDOM

Paul Kurtz

A dialogue between Baptists and humanists is long overdue. In a multicultural society such as America, it is important that people from diverse religious and nonreligious traditions engage in discussion to define any differences and, more meaningfully, to discover any common ground.

As a secular humanist, I am often asked, "What does the term 'humanism,' or indeed 'secular humanism' mean?" These terms have been attacked by religious fundamentalists on the Right for well over a decade. How shall we define "humanism"?

I

The term "humanism" means different things to different people. For some, it has been simply identified with the study of the "humanities." For others, it has been used synonymously with "humanitarianism." Its critics have condemned it as a mere form of "godless atheism." Some have considered humanism to be a new religion, and others a new form of antireligion. Yet even critics would not consider themselves "antihuman" or "antihumanistic." Like "peace," "motherhood," or "virtue," it has been all things to all men and women.

Is there any way out of this impasse? Humanism is not "an ideal essence," laid up in some Platonic heaven of abstract meanings. On the contrary, in unraveling its meaning, we see that it has been used primarily to refer to a set of moral principles. And in this linguistic controversy there is a central idea that emerges strongly—namely, the idea of *freedom*. I submit that throughout its long tradition of usage, the term "humanism" has embodied the sense of freedom. This may surprise many Baptists who share a commitment to freedom of conscience and defended this value in the early days of the American republic.

Humanism has had a long career in human history. Indeed, it is one of the oldest and deepest intellectual traditions of Western civilization. From the great philosophers, scientists, poets, and artists of the Greek and Roman world, through the Renaissance and the Protestant Reformation, to the development of the new science in the sixteenth century, the discovery of the New World, and the democratic revolutions of the modern era, the basic humanist value of *liberty* has inspired the noble deeds and passions of countless men and women.

The first principle of humanism, thus is its commitment to the idea of freedom. But what does that mean? First, freedom of conscience within the inward domain of thought and belief; second, the free expression of ideas; and third, freedom of choice in the moral domain. This latter ideal may trouble many Baptists, but humanists believe that it is implied in the very idea of freedom.

The above ideas have been central to American democracy and were among the most cherished principles embraced by the Founding Fathers. Thomas Jefferson, the author of the Declaration of Independence, affirmed his opposition to any tyranny over the human mind. And James Madison, chief architect of the Constitution and the Bill of Rights, affirmed that government should make no law abridging freedom of speech or press, or prohibiting the free exercise of religion. American democracy protects all forms of belief. Similarly, many American patriots have defended individual moral freedom, though it must be allied with moral responsibility.

Humanism and libertarianism are thus indelibly intertwined. Humanists in the modern world have been the chief critics of the authoritarian or totalitarian state. John Stuart Mill, John Dewey, Karl Popper, Sidney Hook, and others have provided a powerful case in defense of democracy. Indeed, it may surprise many Baptists, but the first intellectual opponents of fascism and communism are humanists who have defended the open society.

What is often overlooked in this debate is that liberty may be endangered by other powerful institutions within society which de facto tend to limit the inward domain of conscience, freedom of expression, and moral freedom. I have in mind many established churches, temples, or mosques which may seek to deny the most fundamental of all human rights: primacy of conscience and the right to believe or—especially important for humanists—the right *not* to believe. This is especially evident in Muslim countries today, where there is no separation between church and state, and theocracies repress human freedom. In the name of Allah, Salman Rushdie, an avowed secular humanist, was condemned to death by the Iranians as a blasphemer, as was Taslima Nasrin in Bangladesh; no one is permitted to dissent from prevailing Islamic doctrines. Extremist Muslim fundamentalists do not simply excommunicate, they seek to execute! In the history of religious persecution, the Roman Catholic Inquisition no doubt stands out as an infamous illustration of the worst-case scenario: the use of state power to enforce religious orthodoxy. But even where there is a separation of church and state, churches may have powerful influences on adherents, demanding absolute obedience. The threat of excommunication, the censorship of publications, or the limits imposed on professors are unfortunate illustrations of the power of some churches seeking to enforce discipline in a community. Does a church in a free society have a legal right to do that? Does it have a moral right, particularly in a pluralistic democracy? A similar question can be asked of powerful economic forces: the coercive sanctions imposed by a corporation or a company town on its employees, or perhaps a union on its members.

In his famous work, *On Liberty*, John Stuart Mill presents a set of arguments as to why the rights of the minority need to be respected, including the rights of heretics, dissenters, or iconoclasts. For Mill, the real question is, How do you deal with the tyranny of the majority? Namely, if a majority of people in the community fervently believe that something is true, do they have a right to exercise coercion, whether subtle or overt, in order to demand conformity to the prevailing orthodoxy? Mill argues that people who deny freedom imply that they are infallible and/or that they have a monopoly on truth or virtue. But who can say with assurance that his or her beliefs have reached their final formulation, and that they alone have the absolute truth? For the humanist, truth is a product of the give-and-take of a free marketplace of ideas, and it depends upon criticism and on response to that criticism if it is to prevail. One should always leave open the possibility that one may be mistaken. Surely the very premise of democracy is that we have something to learn from those who disagree with us. But, said Mill, even if we believe we have the absolute truth, not to allow it to be contested by dissenters would mean that it would degenerate into a mere habit of thought. It would lose all conviction and vitality for succeeding generations—unless it were allowed to be challenged. Those who would deny freedom of inquiry perhaps mask a hidden fear that if there were really an open debate, they would lose out in the end. The censor or inquisitor thus seeks to unfairly impose his or her views by insisting on conformity by everyone.

The point is, quasi-public institutions, such as the church, corporation, university, or even public opinion, may be as powerful as the government, and individuals should have the right to dissent in the face of such power. Perhaps the strongest argument in favor of freedom of conscience and free expression is that these freedoms will, in the long run, contribute to the public good and to the progressive development of knowledge, for they allow for the emergence of creativity and the uncovering of new dimensions of truth. By closing the parameters of dissent, the quest for knowledge is restricted. Given the great problems that humankind constantly faces, it is essential that new avenues for the discovery of knowledge be encouraged.

The most awesome attack on freedom in recent time was in Marxist-Leninist-Stalinist societies. During the long night of communism, a reign of ideological terror prevailed, and anyone who disagreed with or defied the doctrine of dialectical materialism was severely punished. If Salman Rushdie stands as the symbol today of the idea of freedom in the Islamic world, so Andrei Sakharov, who was a great exponent of secular humanist ideals, symbolizes the yearning for freedom in Soviet society. In American society today many humanists fear that sincere and devout Baptists who believe in inerrancy have become part of an oppressive coalition that will seek to use the state to impose their doctrines of belief and morality on dissenters.

II

Permit me to apply the idea of freedom very briefly to three areas that need exploration. First, to the question of academic freedom in the university; second, to the scientific investigation of religion; and third, to the area of women's rights.

The university is a unique institution in society, for it has a double function. On the one hand, it is interested in transmitting to students the best knowledge available within civilization and in cultivating an appreciation for the quest for knowledge. This is known as *Lernfreiheit*; that is, it is the right of students to learn and to be able to engage in free inquiry. Students at a university are thus placed in contact with the best minds and the best literature in many domains of human experience and knowledge. They have a right to cultural freedom without censorship or prohibition.

The university, however, is especially unique because it is the primary institution committed not only to teaching but to research. Here we need to distinguish the college from the multiversity, though I would argue that similar considerations should apply to colleges and seminaries—if they are to achieve intellectual excellence. What is preeminent is that institutions devoted to learning are not only repositories of wisdom and truth in many fields of human endeavor, but that they provide fertile soil where professors and researchers can come together and explore cooperatively the quest for knowledge. This is why *Lehrfreiheit* (the right of teachers and professors to do research) presupposes, as its basic principle, academic freedom. Thus institutions of higher learning seek to appoint to their faculties the best qualified minds who are competent in their fields and recognized by peers. And they must give to their faculties the freedom to pursue research, to reach conclusions which, on the basis of their considered judgments, seem to be true, and this entails the right to speak out and publish the results. Any effort by the corporate body to censor or to prohibit is to deny *Lehrfreiheit* and this is a betrayal of the very idea of learning itself. Academic freedom has a long and distinguished career, and the great universities—from Oxford, Cambridge, and the Sorbonne to Harvard, Stanford, and state universities—respect this right. This not only applies to secular but increasingly to religious institutions as well.

Authoritarian institutions fear new ideas; they persecute intellectuals and they seek to deny tenure to their professors. Is there a necessary contradiction between an ecclesiastical institution and a university such that an ecclesiastical institution need not permit *Lehrfreiheit*? If this is the case, then a viable university no longer can be said to exist, and the university has become a place for indoctrination; it is not receptive to the quest for truth, nor does it respect the right of dissent. Humanists, of course, will not compromise on this point. To declare than an institution is devoted to higher learning in some sense must entail academic freedom untrammeled by the threats of a grand inquisitor.

This leads to the question, What should be the extent or limits placed on freedom of inquiry in regard to religious doctrines? It is again the conviction of the humanist that every domain of human interest, whether economics or politics, the social sciences, natural or biological sciences, history, literature, philosophy, the arts, or religion, should be amenable to critical investigation. This means that there should be no blocks placed on free inquiry. It means that the Koran, the Bible, or the Book of Mormon should be read like other books, by using the best tools of scientific, linguistic, and scholarly research; and that any claims made in these books can be examined critically and evaluated cognitively.

Now there are those who are opposed to this, and who believe that this kind of free inquiry would endanger faith, upset dogma, or imperil the body of church doctrines. That may or may not be the case. Surely, if one has little hope that an analysis of belief will survive critical scrutiny, or if one believes that questioning beliefs would lead to their destruction, then so much the worse for the beliefs. If we are truly convinced that our beliefs are true, we ought to permit them to be challenged. And that is why in the area of biblical or Koranic or Mormon criticism, the most advanced tools of scientific, historical, and scholarly analysis should be employed.

The third area for discussion is the question of human rights, and in particular, to what extent should they be extended to women? Are not women equal in dignity and value? Do not the interests and needs of women deserve equal consideration with those of men? Or should the role of women in the various institutions of society be relegated to a submissive position, and should women obey men? It is clear that patriarchal attitudes have long dominated our social institutions. The battle of the suffragist movement for the vote gave women political equality. Similarly for the great battles in the economy and in institutions of higher learning today where there is a need to allow women to achieve positions of responsibility. The real question is, Do not the *same* considerations apply to religious institutions? There are some religions today that believe that women should serve in the pulpit to the same extent as men; that the viewpoints of women are entitled to be heard, that their freedoms should be protected and encouraged. Other religions deny this. Is God the Father a male and is sexist language tolerable in a religious context? Humanists agree with the feminist indictment, and indeed many of the outstanding leaders of the feminist movement worldwide have been humanists, such as Betty Friedan, Gloria Steinem, and Simone de Beauvoir. Hence, the cause of women for liberation is continuous with the cause of freedom, and this means that biblical language and practice need to be revised in the light of these considerations.

III

The concluding point that I wish to raise briefly is the commitment of humanists to rational inquiry. Humanists believe that it is essential that we encourage the tools of critical thinking in society. Belief should not simply be a question of faith or dogma, emotion or intuition, custom or authority, but should be guided by informed judgment, an appeal to evidence and logic, and tested in practice. Humanists maintain that there are areas of reliable knowledge that we share, and that truth is not established by authoritarian declaration but by objective justification. This is particularly the case in institutions committed to inquiry, for they are based on the idea that debate, discussion, and dialogue are the very essence of freedom.

Thus the idea of freedom as a humanist value is concomitant with the idea of reason, and humanism may also be defined by its commitment to methods of rational inquiry. It is our conviction that we ought to engage in a dialogue with those with whom we disagree, and that we ought not seek to impose our views on others by power of force, but we ought to listen in a fair and impartial way to claims made in the free marketplace of ideas, and we ought to try to work out as best we can what seems most likely true on the basis of cooperative, rational inquiry. This is why a dialogue between Baptists and humanists is so important.

CHAPTER 3

JEFFERSON AND THE DANBURY BAPTISTS

The Interaction between Baptists and the Nation's Founders

Robert S. Alley

The gathering in Richmond, which Paul Kurtz has called historic, was a gratifying step toward honest exploration of ideas in the spirit of mutual understanding. For far too long the power of dogmatism and the abuse of history have created unnatural barriers between persons of goodwill. Baptists and humanists share a commitment to a republican democracy that was shaped with the enthusiastic cooperation of the two traditions. The roots for this common ground lie in the conflict with a theocratic mentality that consumed seventeenth-century Puritanism. Roger Williams devised a system of governance in Rhode Island that united Baptists and humanists in a common cause. A century later Baptist ministers in Virginia, incarcerated by the religious establishment, ignited the spirit of religious liberty in the young James Madison. It remained a central passion for him for his whole life. In 1785, combating the effort to provide public funds for religious education, Madison joined with Baptists throughout the new state to defeat the assessment bill that would have provided state funds for religious education by the churches. The affinity between Baptists and humanists seems best defined by that single concept—religious freedom.

As we gathered on the campus of the University of Richmond in 1995, that common cause was in evidence. And it was an emotional moment because the Baptists themselves were beset with controversy. Even as Virginia Baptists celebrated that heritage of freedom, a scant 150 miles south the Southern Baptist Convention had destroyed the integrity of a fine theological seminary, Southeastern in North Carolina. Participants were saddened and angered by the stumbling corpse of a school, laid low by a fundamentalist mentality that has now engulfed the entire Convention. But our meeting made clear that the heritage of the Baptist tradition has not been lost. It lives on in the lives of thousands of Baptists who hold dear to their history against the tide of arrogance, intolerance, and denial of simple freedoms.

Traditionally, Baptists have a natural affinity for humanism, for they stand on the tradition of individual competency in devising one's opinions respecting the Bible. William O. Carver, professor at Southern Baptist Seminary in Louisville during the first half of this century, was fond of saying, "an open mind and an open Bible makes a Baptist." The humanist would put it differently—an open mind and evidence from nature make a humanist; but it is that common appeal to reason—the open mind—that links the two traditions in their affirmations of freedom. Traditionally, the natural antagonism toward externally imposed theological authority applies equally respecting secular authority when it comes to matters of conscience.

Common ground for Baptists and humanists can be found in the words of Thomas Jefferson:

> *Well aware that the opinions and beliefs of men depend not on their own will, but follow involuntarily the evidence proposed to their minds;* that Almighty God hath created the mind free; *and manifested his supreme will, that free it shall remain by making it altogether insusceptible of restraint;* that all attempts to influence it by temporal punishments or burthens, or by civil incapacitations, tend only to beget habits of hypocrisy and meanness, and are a departure from the plan of the Holy author of our religion, who being Lord both of body and mind, yet chose not to propagate it by coercions on either, as was in his Almighty Power to do; *but to extend it by its influence on reason alone;* . . .[1]

If these words sound unfamiliar, there is a reason. When, in 1777, Jefferson wrote his Bill for Establishing Religious Freedom in Virginia, his preamble read as quoted above. The same bill was first introduced into the House of Delegates in 1779 where it died for lack of a third reading. It was not until 1785 that James Madison brought the bill to the floor once again and the Virginia General Assembly passed it in December, but not before striking the italicized words noted in the quotation above. In a letter of January 22, 1786, Madison explained this to Jefferson.

> The preamble was sent up again from the H[ouse] of D[elegates] with one or two verbal alterations. As an amendment to these the Senate sent

down a few others; which as they did not affect the substance though they somewhat defaced the composition, it was thought better to agree to than to run further risks, especially as it was getting late in the Session and the House growing thin. The enacting clauses past [sic] without a single alteration, and I flatter myself [to believe that we] have in this Country extinguished for ever the ambitious hope of making laws for the human mind.[2]

Why did the Senate tamper with the text? The editors of *The Papers of James Madison* note, ". . . Jefferson's philosophical preamble met opposition in both Houses." Madison saw their complaint as "frivolous" but rather than lose the bill he agreed to the deletion of "some of the more sweeping statements about the supremacy of reason. . . ."[3] Of that bill, Baptist historian Robert Semple wrote in 1810: "The law for assessment did not pass; but, on the contrary an act passed explaining the nature of religious liberty. This law, so much admired . . . was drawn by the venerable Mr. Thomas Jefferson."[4] The Baptist General Committee in Virginia had sent its own memorial on the subject to the General Assembly on August 13, 1785. It read in part, ". . . should the legislature assume the right of taxing the people for the support of the gospel, it will be destructive to religious liberty."[5] Actively involved in this activity was a young Baptist minister from the valley, John Leland.

When Madison, as a member of the Virginia General Assembly, became the leader of the opposition to the "assessment" bill, which would have provided state support for teachers of the Christian religion, he was supported by both separate and regular Baptists in the state. One of Madison's strongest supporters was John Leland of Orange County, an ardent advocate of religious freedom. Indeed, his commitment to freedom also led him to champion the passage of a Baptist General Committee resolution "[t]hat slavery is a violent deprivation of the rights of nature, and inconsistent with a republican government."[6]

Leland surfaced again in 1789 when James Madison, writing to George Washington concerning the recently adopted Bill of Rights, noted that "[o]ne of the principal leaders of the Baptists lately sent me word that the amendments had entirely satisfied the disaffected of his Sect, and that it would appear in their subsequent conduct."[7]

It was this series of events in history that led to a discussion with Paul Kurtz at a Mormon/humanist dialogue in Salt Lake City in 1993, where we decided to engage in a similar conference with Baptists in Richmond.

How strong was the link between the founders of the nation and the growing Baptist population? Let me transport the reader back to the year 1774, when James Madison first felt an urge to become involved in Virginia political life. He was energized by observing the imprisonment of

Baptist ministers in Orange and Culpeper county jails. The spectre of those ministers jailed for affirming their religious beliefs burned itself into Madison's mind and memory. It so affected him that he became a lifelong champion of religious freedom. Indeed, it established a bond between the Baptists and Madison that lasted until his death in 1836.

What we know of Madison's religious sentiments is quite limited, yet his biographer, Ralph Ketcham seems on the mark in noting that

> Madison saw that in the final analysis he could not demonstrate with assurance the logical rectitude of his religious views, any more than he could accept the claims of theologians of other persuasions that they had absolutely proved the validity of their doctrines. Madison insisted rather, that religious sentiments were based on dispositions and inclinations of the human mind and spirit. To apply state power in support of these kinds of experiences was obviously absurd.[8]

In such thinking Madison was in harmony with prominent Baptists of his day.

In 1834, two years prior to his death, Madison wrote these telling words about the nation's first half-century: "... the lapse of time now more than 50 years since the legal support of Religion was withdrawn sufficiently prove that it does not need the support of Govt. and it will scarcely be contended that Government has suffered by the exemption of Religion from its cognizance, or its pecuniary aid."[9] In that view he was consistently supported by the Baptists.

Yet, no matter how remarkable a political leader Madison was, he has been dead now for over 160 years. We should not quote him because he was a founder, but rather because reason tells us he was right and his principles apply in our own current experiences.

A special moment in the life of Madison's closest friend, Thomas Jefferson, is also instructive and interesting. I construe Jefferson's deism and reliance upon human reason as a valid proof of his fundamentally ethical humanist sentiments. If that judgment is fair, then one may explore a Baptist/humanist dialogue in the correspondence between Jefferson and a group of Baptists in Danbury, Connecticut.

The common ground that exists on these shores between Baptists and humanists is nowhere better illustrated than on the occasion when the Danbury Baptists wrote a letter to Mr. Jefferson in the year of his first inauguration, 1801. Jefferson, who would construct his own New Testament with scissors and paste, had little theological common ground with the dedicated, biblically based Baptists of Connecticut. What he and they shared equally was a belief in the importance of human freedom.

Because that critically important exchange between a president and his constituents has been so brutally distorted by a Virginia neighbor, Pat

Robertson, it is appropriate to use his critique as a means of establishing the historical record on the matter. On February 22, 1995, Robertson remarked that the separation of church and state "was never in the Constitution. However much the liberals laugh at me for saying it, they know good and well it was never in the Constitution. Such language only appeared in the constitution of the Communist Soviet Union."[10] Thirteen years earlier Mr. Robertson, in a 1982 appearance before the Senate Committee on the Judiciary, testified on behalf of the Reagan school prayer amendment. On that occasion he asserted that separation of church and state was more compatible with the constitution of the Soviet Union than that of the United States. In order to support that claim, Robertson sought to discredit the 1802 Jefferson letter of response to the Danbury Baptist Association, in which President Jefferson described the First Amendment as "building a wall of separation between church and state." Robertson, without a single shred of evidence, said the letter resulted from the Danbury Baptists having "aroused [Jefferson's] ire by criticism of one of his policies." In his oral testimony to the Senate, Robertson spoke of Jefferson having "some pique, because of criticism."[11] The conclusion to be drawn was that the separation metaphor resulted from anger, and was thus to be dismissed. Implicit in Robertson's harangue was the notion that Jefferson was merely telling the Baptists to leave him alone since the First Amendment separated him from the need to listen to their criticism. Because of his powerful network, Robertson is heeded by millions. Thus, it is imperative to establish that Robertson's entire premise seems a fabrication, demonstrating a complete contempt for history, the Constitution, and the founders.

Anyone who has read the letter from the Danbury Baptist Association can categorically state that there is not a single shred of criticism of Mr. Jefferson in the entire letter. It begins by expressing "our great satisfaction in your appointment to the chief Majestracy in the United States." Quickly the writers moved to assert: "Our Sentiments are uniformly on the side of Religious Liberty—That Religion is at all times and places a matter between God and individuals—That the legitimate Power of civil government extends no further than to punish the man who *works ill to his neighbor....*" Turning from that ideal, the letter calls attention to Connecticut laws made at the time of the Revolution and asserts: "Religion is considered as the first object of Legislation; and therefore what religious privileges we enjoy (as a minor part of the State) we enjoy as favors granted, and not as inalienable rights...."[12]

Respecting the Connecticut state legislators, the Baptists note:

> It is not to be wondered at therefore; if those, who seek after power & gain under the pretense of *government & Religion* should reproach their

fellow men—should reproach their chief Magistrate [President Jefferson] as an enemy of religion Law & good order because he will not, dare not assume the prerogatives of Jehovah and make Laws to govern the Kingdom of Christ.[13]

They concluded: "[O]ur hopes are strong that the sentiments of our beloved President, which have had such genial affect already, like the radiant beams of the Sun, will shine and prevail through all these States and all the world till Hierarchy and Tyranny be destroyed from the Earth." The writers expound on their hopes by asserting: "May God strengthen you for the arduous task which providence & the voice of the people have cald you to sustain and support you in your Administration against all the predetermined opposition of those who wish to rise to wealth & importance on the poverty and subjection of the people."[14]

This message to the new president reflected the sentiments of most Baptists in Connecticut where the "Standing Order," the established Congregational ministers, dominated the political scene in the state. Most established clergy of Connecticut were firmly opposed to Jefferson's election in 1800. The Connecticut establishment survived until 1818, when the following words were included in the State constitution: "That the exercise and enjoyment of religious profession and worship without discrimination, shall forever be free to all persons in this State. . . ."[15]

It is no wonder that President Jefferson, who received the letter on December 30, 1801, replied on January 1, 1802: "The affectionate sentiments of esteem and approbation you are so good as to express towards me, on behalf of the Danbury Baptist Association, give me the highest satisfaction."[16] Then Jefferson turned to the association's concerns, stating:

> Believing with you that religion is a matter which lies solely between man and his God, that he owes account to none other for his faith or his worship, that the legislative powers of government reach actions only, and not opinions, I contemplate with sovereign reverence that act of the whole American people which declared that their legislature should "make no law respecting an establishment of religion, or prohibiting the free exercise thereof," thus building a wall of separation between Church and State.[17]

Modern critics of "separation" frequently insist that Jefferson dashed this letter off in haste, as Justice Rehnquist claimed in *Wallace v. Jaffree* (1985) when he called it ". . . a short note of courtesy."[18] The evidence is totally to the contrary. Jefferson received the Danbury letter on December 30, 1801. On January 1, 1802, he sent the letter, a draft of his response, and a request to Attorney General Levi Lincoln. Jefferson wrote:

The Baptist address, now enclosed, admits of a condemnation of the alliance between Church and State, under the authority of the Constitution. It furnishes an occasion, too, which I have long wished to find, of saying why I do not proclaim fastings and thanksgivings, as my predecessor did. The address, to be sure, does not point at this, and its introduction is awkward. But I foresee no opportunity of doing it more pertinently. I know it will give great offense to the New England clergy; but the advocate of religious freedom is to expect neither peace nor forgiveness from them. Will you be so good as to examine the answer and suggest any alterations which might prevent an ill effect, or promote a good one, among the people?"[19]

Mr. Lincoln replied on the same day with the suggestion that Jefferson alter his comments on proclamations because, with the exception of Rhode Island, the other New England states were used to "proclamations from their respective executives." He went on: "This custom is venerable, being handed down from our ancestors . . . [and] they regretted very much the late conduct of the legislature of Rhode Island on this subject." Based on Lincoln's advice, Jefferson excised from his text the portion that said "Congress thus inhibited from acts respecting religion and the Executive authorized only to execute their acts, I have refrained from prescribing even those occasional performances of devotion." Explaining his decision, Jefferson wrote in the margin of the original draft that "[t]his paragraph was omitted on the suggestion that it might give uneasiness to some of our republican friends in the eastern states where the proclamation of thanksgivings etc. by their Executive is an antient habit and is respected."[20]

What a remarkable story this is. In 1801, Baptists in Connecticut were still persecuted under a "mild" establishment. Jefferson, as president, could do nothing about the state laws except to anticipate seeing "the progress of those sentiments which tend to restore to man all his natural rights, convinced he has no natural right in opposition to his social duties." In their hearts the Baptists knew that and so stated when they wrote:

> [W]e are sensible that the President of the United States, is not the national legislator, and also sensible that the national government cannot destroy the Laws of each State; but our hopes are strong that the sentiments of our beloved President . . . will shine and prevail through all these States and all the world till Hierarchy and Tyranny be destroyed from the Earth.[21]

These letters and events together reflect how seriously Mr. Jefferson approached the plight of fellow citizens, and, when understood in that context, make the separation metaphor profoundly significant. It was born out of human suffering, not rational abstraction. How Mr. Robertson, with such disdain for facts, could callously violate the dedication and commitment of those Connecticut Baptist citizens is difficult to fathom.

I am satisfied by observation and research that there is a natural commonality between humanists and Baptists. Both reject the abandonment of reason, seeing that as a mortal threat both to our secular democracy and to the Baptist principle of free exercise of conscience, unhindered and undirected by civil authority. Madison's words are an ending and a beginning for us.

> Who does not see that the same authority which can establish Christianity, in exclusion of all other Religions, may establish with the same ease any particular sect of Christians, in exclusion of all other Sects? that the same authority which can force a citizen to contribute three pence only of his property for the support of any one establishment, may force him to conform to any other establishment in all cases whatsoever?[22]

NOTES

1. Julian P. Bond, ed., *The Papers of Thomas Jefferson*, vol. 2 (Princeton: Princeton University Press, 1950), p. 545. This is the wording of Jefferson's original bill of 1777. The words in italics were removed by vote of the Virginia General Assembly in 1785–86. The amended bill became law in 1786. See also Thomas Jefferson, *Jefferson Himself*, ed. Bernard Mayo (Charlottesville: University of Virginia Press, 1942), p. 86.
2. Robert B. Semple, *A History of the Rise and Progress of Baptists in Virginia* (Richmond: John O'Lynch Printer, 1810), p. 72.
3. James Madison, "Letter to Rev. (Jasper) Adams of South Carolina in 1833," The Writings of James Madison, vol. 9, ed. Gaillard Hunt (New York: G. P. Putnam, 1910), p. 486.
4. Semple, *History of the Rise and Progress*, p. 72.
5. Ibid.
6. Ralph L. Ketcham, "James Madison and Religion: A New Hypothesis," in *James Madison on Religious Liberty*, ed. Robert S. Alley (Amherst, N.Y.: Prometheus Books, 1985), pp. 192–93.
7. Ibid.
8. Ketcham, "James Madison and Religion," p. 193.
9. Madison, "Letter to Rev. Adams," p. 486.
10. Pat Robertson, address to a symposium on "How Much God in the School?" sponsored by the Marshall/Wythe School of Law, William and Mary University, Williamsburg, Va., February 22, 1995 (unpublished).
11. Pat Robertson, "Voluntary Prayer: Prepared Statement of M. G. 'Pat'

Robertson," *Hearings Before the Committee on the Judiciary, United States Senate* (submitted August 18, 1982), p. 265.

12. See the Danbury letter in "The Papers of Thomas Jefferson" on microfilm in the Madison Building of the Library of Congress. For a full discussion of this exchange of letters see Robert S. Alley, "Public Education and the Public Good," in *William and Mary Bill of Rights Journal* 4, no. 1 (summer 1995): 309–16.

13. Ibid.

14. Ibid.

15. See Steven Green, annotator, *Stars in the Constitutional Constellation: Federal and State Constitutional Provisions on Church and State* (Washington, D.C.: Americans United, 1993), p. 19.

16. See the Danbury letter, p. 312.

17. Robert S. Alley, ed. *The Constitution and Religion: Leading Supreme Court Cases on Church and State* (Amherst, N.Y.: Prometheus Books, 1999), p. 208.

18. *Wallace v. Jaffree*, 105 S.Ct. 2479 (1985).

19. See the Danbury letter, p. 312.

20. Ibid., p. 313.

21. Ibid.

22. James Madison, *Memorial and Remonstrance*, Memorial #3, quoted by Robert S. Alley, "On Behalf of Religious Liberty: James Madison's Memorial and Remonstrance," in *This Constitution*, "A Bicentennial Chronicle," No. 12 (fall 1986): 29.

CHAPTER 4

JAMES MADISON, THE BAPTISTS, AND RELIGIOUS LIBERTY

Paul D. Simmons

The focus of this essay is on James Madison, the Baptists, and the struggle for religious liberty. Madison's relation to the Baptists of early America is of special interest, as are Baptist attitudes toward religious liberty on the contemporary scene. The questions Madison faced in Virginia have a contemporary ring. He was one of the great champions of religious liberty as the country's Constitution and Bill of Rights were being shaped. Interestingly, there is significant similarity between the issues he faced and those that continue to pose questions as to the proper relationship between the institutions of church and government. I want to call attention to certain reasons for Madison's commitment to religious liberty, the insights he brought to the political debate, and the solutions he offered for securing the liberties proper to both religious and nonreligious citizens.

I. MADISON, BAPTISTS, AND RELIGIOUS LIBERTY

James Madison (1743–1826) was one of those heroes who led in the struggle to keep religious belief and practice free from the intrusive and coercive powers of the state. The task is not only to praise him, but to understand, to be reminded of the heritage that was established, and to be committed to preserving that for future generations. We are to consider again "the rock from which we have been hewn" as Americans, and thus receive inspiration and guidance for facing the challenges of our day. Madison was influential as one of the founders and framers of the Constitution and Bill of Rights.

Baptists also played a significant role in helping fashion the great American experiment in religious liberty. Roger Williams was among the first leaders in the colonial era who envisioned governance without collusion with a religious establishment. He showed the way in Rhode Island. He was the first to establish a genuinely free church within a free state among the Colonies. He was briefly a Baptist before declaring himself a Seeker, but he was a Baptist long enough to establish a long line of followers who think he had it right.

Williams thought it an odious and repugnant idea that there could be anything like a Christian nation. In *The Bloudy Tennent of Persecution* (1644) he argued that the world had seen enough of people who tried to wrap the mantle of Christ around their greed for political power. There was, he thought, a great gulf fixed between Christianity and Christendom, the latter being a despicable word that pointed to everything that had gone wrong with Christianity since the fourth century. Christendom pertains to politics and empires; to persecuting bishops and slashing swords; it is the enemy of Christianity and genuine faith; it reeks of heresy and blasphemous actions; it substitutes an idolatrous worship of the state for the truth of Christ; it is a sugarcoated, emasculated version of the Gospel which goes down easily but neither purifies nor redeems, but corrupts and destroys.[1]

To be sure, there were other Baptists, like Isaac Backus in New England and John Leland, who worked with Madison and Jefferson in Virginia to disestablish religion and then to pass what became the First Amendment to the Bill of Rights: "Congress shall make no law respecting an establishment of religion nor prohibiting the free exercise thereof." The greatest contribution Baptists have made to political science has been an emphasis on religious liberty as the first and foremost human right. They sought soul liberty not only for themselves, but for everyone.

The fundamental principle involved was articulated by Thomas Helwys in his pamphlet, "The Mistery of Iniquity" (1612), which was addressed to King James I. Helwys, like other dissenters, had suffered imprisonment and fines at the hand of the king for their unwillingness to accept the doctrinal and ecclesiastical standards of the Anglican Church. He wrote to King James that "the king might punish any person for temporal offenses; but for spiritual error, Let them be heretikes, Turkes, Jews or whatsoever, it appertynes not to the earthly power to punish them in the least measure."[2] For him, God alone is lord of the conscience; no king can stand in judgment of a person's religious convictions, or, as he made clear, even for having no religious affections. The king had Helwys thrown into Newgate prison where he remained until his death.

On the American scene, James Madison managed to effect public policy safeguarding the liberties of conscience for which people like Helwys had died. In his *Memorial and Remonstrance* (1785), Madison articulated several factors that are involved in the First Amendment protections and how they came to be implemented. First, he set forth the difference that should characterize the American states and their European background. Second, he argued strongly for the profound need for separation of church and state in pluralistic America. Third, Madison revealed the sources of his passionate commitment to religious freedom.

His writings reveal a person deeply invested emotionally, spiritually, and intellectually in the separation of church and state. He wrote passionately, in part at least because of his awareness of European history that had been besmirched and bloodied by the heavy hand of despotic religion in collusion with misguided politics. He was determined that such egregious errors as the Inquisition should never take place in America.

When he was twenty-two years of age, Madison found himself outraged by neighboring Anglicans who indulged in what he called that "diabolical, hell-conceived principle of persecution."[3] Six of his neighbors had been jailed for proclaiming their religious opinions, which were contrary to the Anglican governance. It was an injustice and outrage he would not soon forget. From that point on, Madison was unreservedly and unswervingly committed to religious liberty.

But the notion of religious freedom was hardly universally supported. What seemed of inherent and obvious benefit to all parties with the birth of a federal union was vehemently opposed by powerful groups and individuals. Madison's home state of Virginia, for instance, was a cauldron of ferment fueled by the vitriol and meanness that only bad religion can create in the human spirit. Jefferson, Hamilton, and Madison were all made the object of vitriolic attacks. The most vicious attacks came from clergy who demonized them and consigned their souls to a special place in perdition. Ideology and power made a heady and dangerous mix on this issue, as many others. Madison saw that the very notion of religious liberty hang precariously by a thread. "Pity me, and pray for liberty of conscience to all," he wrote.

To a friend in Philadelphia, he wrote of the contrast between the openness and freedom of conscience experienced in Pennsylvania and the oppression and intolerance in Virginia.

> The Sentiments of our people of Fortune & fashion on this subject are vastly different from what you have been used to. That liberal catholic and equitable way of thinking as to the rights of Conscience, which is one of the Characteristics of a free people and so strongly marks the People of your province but little known among the Zealous adherents to our Hierarchy.[4]

Madison even attributed the economic prosperity in Pennsylvania to "the good effects of their religious as well as Civil Liberty." In clinging to the establishment, Virginians, he charged, ". . . abuse dissenters, and dampen our natural genius." He argued that "Religious bondage shackles and debilitates the mind and unfits it for every noble enterprize, every expanded prospect."[5]

Beyond such passionate appeals, Madison gave clear, distinct, and reasoned support to the value and need for religious liberty as a Constitutional guarantee. His efforts in the colonial context provide helpful guidance for the disturbing parallels in our own time. For instance, Madison led the effort to defeat a proposal to declare Christianity the religion of the United States.

As recently as 1996–1997 there was a strong campaign to change the wording of the Constitution to read: "under God *as revealed in Jesus Christ.*" The effort was led by fundamentalist leaders of New Right groups including Ralph Reed, director of the Christian Coalition (now replaced by Donald Hoden and Randy Tate); Pat Robertson, founder of the Coalition; Jerry Falwell, head of the Moral Majority; and R. J. Rushdoony, leader of the Christian Reconstructionism movement, which seeks to impose the laws of the Old Testament theocracy upon the United states. The net effect of Rep. Ernest Istook's proposed constitutional amendment to assure religious liberty in America was also intended to secure Christianity as the dominant religion in America.

The distressing irony is that the battle is still raging in Virginia, the state in which Jefferson and Madison had succeeded with an amendment to disestablish religion in January 1787, two years before the First Amendment was added to the Constitution. The Bill of Rights became law in December 15, 1791. Jerry Falwell is, of course, a Baptist with a Puritan background. His spiritual forbears, unlike Roger Williams, never made the break from their Puritan overlords. Falwell is more the son of John Cotton; he is no spiritual relative of Roger Williams. Falwell is constantly trying to get public funding for his Liberty University, which is heavily in debt. He has been defeated in the courts by Americans United for Separation of Church and State.

Pat Robertson, founder of the Christian Coalition and chancellor of his own university in Virginia Beach, constantly pressures evangelical Christians to become politicized. It seems to many of us a brazen effort to enhance his own political power after his failed effort to gain the Republican nomination for president in 1987. He also wants to pass a constitutional amendment favoring Christianity. He wants another amendment declaring fertilized ova persons, so as to outlaw abortion. Finally, he favors allowing public funding of sectarian schools. Like Falwell, he speaks both out of vested interest and ideological bias.

Madison's involvement in the battle for religious liberty was the occasion of his *Memorial and Remonstrance*. The bill to support the establishment of Christianity was led by Patrick Henry and other tidewater people. Henry's bill was called "Establishing a Provision for Teachers of the Christian Religion." It had a seductive appeal for traditional but insecure leaders in the dominant Anglican or Episcopal church, who were chafing under their lost prestige from efforts to disestablish.

Henry's measure was opposed by backcountry Baptists led by John Leland. The Baptists aimed for "every grievous yoke be broken." Presbyterians also joined the opposition, saying the legislators should recognize that it would violate (1) Virginia's own declaration of rights, and (2) their own limits as temporal leaders, namely, they had no "Supremacy in Spirituals."[6]

Madison's powerful statement, personal stature, and persuasive rhetoric in his *Memorial and Remonstrance* led to the defeat of Henry's popular bill. Madison saw it as a "dangerous abuse of power." One of his strongest and most insightful arguments was: "Who does not see that the same authority which can establish Christianity, in exclusion of all other Religions, may establish with the same ease any particular sect of Christians, in exclusion of all other Sects?"

Efforts like those of Patrick Henry and Pat Robertson seem never to disappear from the American political forum. The phenomenon is something of a curiosity since the experiment has been so successful in America. Why is so much effort expended to alter the First Amendment?

Madison reflected on this question from his retirement in Montpelier. He wondered as to why the public is led to press for public support of religion. What fears or concerns fuel this movement? He began by setting it in historical perspective. Prior to the American experiment, he wrote in 1819, it seemed a "universal opinion . . . that civil Government could not stand without the prop of a religious establishment, and that the Christian religion itself would perish if not supported by a legal provision for its clergy." In other words, fears that Christianity would diminish and some other religion emerge as a dominant power added to the natural affections and commitments that many Christians had made.

Madison argued that Christianity is not threatened by disestablishment. The opinion that Christianity will fade away without public support had been disproved, he said. He pointed to Virginia at the state level and to America at the federal level.[7] Separation had caused both the nation and the churches to flourish in ways they had never done under collusion.

Madison was distressed to note that some parts of the country still maintain "a strong bias towards the old error, that without some sort of alliance or coalition between Govt & Religion neither can be duly supported." Efforts to return to the old way were a "danger [that] cannot be too carefully guarded against." The only ultimate protection for religious liberty in a free and open country like ours, he argued, is public opinion: a firm and pervading opinion that the First Amendment works. He thus felt strongly that "[e]very new & successful example therefore of a perfect separation between ecclesiastical and civil matters is of importance."[8]

Madison's second basic premise of religious liberty was that the only legitimate support of religion is reason, not coercive power. Reason, for the secularist or humanist, is a close corollary to the Baptist principle of the voluntarism of faith in religious belief and affections. The concern of both groups is the tendency by religious leaders to turn to political power to compensate for the failures of doctrinal or dogmatic formulations to win allegiance from the people. Madison put it strongly. For him, reason, not coercion, must prevail because we hold it for a fundamental and undeniable truth, "that Religion or the duty which we owe to our Creator and the manner of discharging it, can be directed only by reason and conviction, not by force or violence."

The right of every person to exercise conviction and conscience as they may dictate is the issue at stake. Baptists regard it as an unalienable right, one given by God as Creator and Redeemer. The religious convictions of people cannot follow the dictates of others, whether politician or priest.

Every person is first a subject of the Governor of the Universe, Madison argued, so that "... in matters of Religion, no man's right is abridged by the institution of Civil Society and that Religion is wholly exempt from its cognizance."

A third principle articulated by Madison was that of freedom *from* religion. Religious liberty does not mean the freedom of a religious sect or a combination of groups to organize for a political takeover and impose religious beliefs or requirements upon minorities. This limitation on political power seems terribly impious to many evangelical or fundamentalist Christians. Right-wing religious leaders attempt to organize politically to destroy the wall of separation. But that separation of power is important to persons who hold no theistic faith or who resent the power of the state being used to expose them to religious confessions, prayers, and ceremonies or even to coerce them to participating, however passively, in such exercises. The rationale for the state, of course, is that they are catering to a large segment of the voting public. The rationale for the religious is that whatever religious exposure the atheist or agnostic or other simple unbeliever gets is probably good for them in the end. The truth is that efforts to force religious exercises upon unbelievers is totally counterproductive to any affection toward religion such persons might finally have. Coercion is insulting in the extreme, and bad feelings are created that cause resistance and anger toward all religion as such.

The second problem is more theoretical. Abandoning the principle of voluntarism in religious faith seems to be behind the effort to get government to do what religious groups have been unwilling to do. The mission of the church is to convert the unbeliever by persuasion and compassion, not by coercion and anger. Efforts to get government to do the mission of the church is to confess impotency and laziness; Christian zealots have been woefully unwilling to go into the difficult areas to win the lost. But they want the government, nonetheless, to force such people to pray!

The third mistake of the theocrats is the assumption that Christianity should lead to Christendom. They embrace the totally discredited notion of Constantine's embrace of and establishment of Christianity as the favored religion, as if that benefited either. It gave a type of public-relations boost to Christians who thought they needed it, but resulted in a perversion of the Christian message from which the church and various nations have yet to recover. In Reconstructionism and the Christian Coalition, we see again a connection between Caesar and Christ that is a perversion of Christianity and a distortion of democratic governance.

Knowing a bit about the history of the church's efforts to dominate politics makes total sense of those strong efforts by the Founding Fathers to establish safeguards that such mistakes would never happen in the United States. It is as important to protect people from religion as it is to protect religion for the people. Madison put it well:

> [We] assert for ourselves a freedom to embrace, to profess and to observe the Religion which we believe to be of divine origin, we cannot deny an equal freedom to those whose minds have not yielded to the evidence which has convinced us. If this freedom be abused, it is an offence against God, not against man. . . .[9]

Madison's friend Thomas Jefferson agreed. He felt that state-protected, state-coerced religion succeeds only in making "one half the world fools, and the other half hypocrites." Insightful as his comment was, it became ammunition for his religious opponents during his race for the presidency. But he was right. As he noted, the legitimate powers of government "extend to such acts only as are injurious to others. But it does me no injury for my neighbor to say that there are twenty gods, or no God. It neither picks my pocket nor breaks my leg."[10]

The careful "delineation of powers" outlined by Madison puts a lie to the contention made by right-wing religious leaders that only the enemies of religion support limits on provisions of government financial support for religious groups. That is simply untrue. Many of their opposition comes from religious groups who feel strongly that faith enterprises should be supported by the adherents or followers of the particular sect or denomination, not the general public. Government should not be in the religion business any more than religion should be in the business of government. Politicians can be religious without trying to politicize religion.

Madison made still a further point that supports religious liberty. He maintained that religion suffers more from its zealous defenders than from its determined critics. Those who advocate public support for clergy or religious enterprises have not come to terms with the corrupting and enervating effect of governmental protectionism. Madison pointed to the powerlessness of government to protect the purity and efficacy of religion. Actually, efforts to protect lead to the corruption and weakening of religion by the civil powers. He argued, for instance, that "pride and indolence in the Clergy, ignorance and servility in the laity, in both, superstition, bigotry and persecution" are the predictable results.[11] For him, the most vigorous, appealing, and effective religious movements typically and historically are those most independent of government association or protectionism. They have more vitality and power because they know their mission is from God and they depend upon the blessings of God, not the largesse of government.

A final argument from Madison was that religious domination of the state leads to an uncivil society. The lack of civility in American political and social life in the last quarter of the twentieth century is ample proof of his insight. Madison put it in historical perspective:

> ... in some instances they have been seen to erect a spiritual tyranny on the ruins of the Civil authority; in many instances they have been seen upholding the thrones of political tyranny: in no instance have they been seen as the guardians of the liberties of the people.[12]

To the contrary, the "liberties" they seek are usually self-serving. They organize to achieve an aggrandizement of sectarian privilege. They are hardly the advocates of general public liberties. When Falwell, Robertson, Reed, and Dobson speak of freedom of religion, they mean freedom to do as they please. Adopting the freedoms of the democratic process, they seek a coalition of evangelicals to impose religious perspectives on others. But they are unwilling for others to do likewise. They embrace a narrow and self-serving definition of religious freedom.

Americans will do well to recall Madison's warning that preferential treatment generates divisiveness and incivility among the various groups in American life. Using public funds for religious groups, he said, "will destroy that moderation and harmony which the forbearance of our laws to intermeddle with Religion has produced among its several sects." He added, "Torrents of blood have been spilt in the old world, by vain attempts of the secular arm to extinguish Religious discord, by proscribing all difference in Religious opinion."[13]

The American experience has shown that equal liberties tend to diminish the spirit of malignancy and vehemence that often exists between and among the various groups. Religious liberty and the separation of church and state have proven of benefit to both civil society and the spiritual strength of the various religions.

II. THE BAPTIST WITNESS TO RELIGIOUS LIBERTY

Baptists were of considerable help to Madison in defeating bills to establish religion. They made a team of like-minded witnesses to the evils of church-state collusion and the benefits of separating the powers.

Advocates of strong First Amendment rights have a profound sense of grief about the reversal of the Southern Baptist Convention from its historic posture as champion of religious liberties. A terrible irony is apparent. Until the last two decades, Southern Baptists were rather unequivocal in holding and proclaiming virtually unanimous support for the principles outlined in Madison's *Remonstrance*.

The great theologian E. Y. Mullins had given solid guidance to Southern Baptists. He was president of the Southern Baptist Theological Seminary and once served as president of the Convention. His book, *The Axioms of Religion*,[14] set forth classic theological reasons for religious freedom.

First, Mullins said, is the religio-civic axiom which proclaims and requires "a free church in a free state." From his vantage point in 1908, he thought the separation of powers was virtually self-evident and beyond threat. He wrote that it is "so well understood and is accepted . . . so generally and so heartily" that it needed little defense or elaboration. He asserted strongly that there had never been a time when Baptists had ever "wavered in their support" for that principle. Unfortunately, Mullins's statement can no longer be held without considerable qualification.

The convention that once followed Mullins now follows a theocratic leadership. The group that once led the fight against public monies for religious schools now leads the effort to raid the public till and impose religious exercises on all Americans. Those issues were also alive in Mullins's time, and he addressed them in a way that has enormous contemporary relevance. Mullins regarded using public money for sectarian schools a "flagrant violation" of the principle of separation and condemned it without qualification. It would represent a major step toward the establishment of one or more denominations and thus totally contradict the First Amendment.

The second issue Mullins addressed was Bible reading in public schools. He declared that "Baptists very generally and consistently oppose the public reading of the Bible in the schools, because they respect the consciences of all others." That public and political sentiment was based upon a religious conviction about the freedom of religious convictions for *all* people. It is a human right, not to be bartered on the altar of political expediency.

Baptists held steadfastly to the principle that no one should be coerced by state power in religious matters until 1979. In that year, Ronald Reagan launched his presidential campaign from Dallas, Texas. A large group of Baptist pastors joined him on the dais, representing a number of leaders within the Convention who were co-opted by the Republican National Committee to elect Ronald Reagan and, more broadly, to support Republican causes. Two Southern Baptists, Rev. Paige Patterson and Paul Pressler, an appeals court judge, masterminded the takeover of the Convention and the linkage to the Republicans. As Pressler put it, he provided the political strategies and Patterson provided names for the religious leadership.[15] Being an elected official gave Pressler not only political know-how, but ties to the national Republican Party and its operatives. The "conversion" of the Southern Baptist Convention to Republicanism was as effective, if not more, than the effort by the Christian Coalition to dominate the platform, agenda, and direction of the Republican Party.

In 1980, 67 percent of all Baptist pastors were registered as Democrats. By 1985, sixty-seven percent of all Baptist pastors were registered as Republicans. Operatives from the Reagan White House wrote resolutions for the annual Southern Baptist Conventions, which were herded through to passage by leaders supportive of Reagan policies. Reagan wanted religious backing for such things as strong foreign policy support for Israel. Baptist pastors yielded to the siren song of political power. Jerry Falwell, at the time leader of the political action group the Moral Majority, was active among Southern Baptists and persuaded support for his social and political agenda, which had also been adopted by the Republican platform. With Pat Robertson, Falwell organized a grassroots movement to dominate and control the Republican Party, with no little success.

The shift for Southern Baptists was dramatic and far-reaching. Historically, they had been apolitical, maintaining a distance from politics as a danger to spiritual and ethical purity. They are now deeply involved in the politics of the far-right, with its opposition to First Amendment guarantees for all Americans.

The liaison with Republicans made possible a new political leverage for Baptists. Self-interest made that possibility seem desirable and attractive. They had begun establishing their own private schools, K–12 and beyond. They now saw the opportunity to obtain government funding to finance these operations, a tactic they once strongly opposed. Such schools began among independent Baptist circles which were fundamentalistic, cultish, and racist. The racial factor was extensive. Baptists draw their primary constituency from the South, and racial integration threatened many of the cultural values that had characterized so much of southern and Baptist life. The appeal to their own schools won the loyalty and mind of Southern Baptists. Such schools had once been opposed as "the Catholic way." Now Baptists and evangelicals (fundamentalists) have become deeply involved in right-wing political activities and vote consistently to secure vouchers for private school education. Being interpreted, that means *their* private schools. Blatant self-interest has won out over a principled posture deriving from the axiom of a free church in a free state.

Mullins had likened the church-state struggle in the Middle Ages to one between an eagle, which represented the church, and a serpent, which stood for the state. The serpent frequently dragged the eagle down into the dust and mud, where it coiled around the noble bird, said Mullins. But the eagle "would rise heavily into the air, only to be dragged down again. At length, the eagle, with beak and talons dripping with the blood of her slain foe, mounts upward and builds her nest on a lofty crag, forever beyond the serpent's reach." That happened, Mullins said, when Roger Williams founded the commonwealth of Rhode Island where all people had freedom to pursue and believe religious convictions of their own persuasion. He mentioned Madison, "along with a few other great minds" in whom this "novel and far-reaching conception [had] taken root."

His comfort with the thought of this self-evident axiom of religious and political truth sounds a bit naive today. Baptists have so retrenched on the issue of separation they sound more than a bit like those establishmentarians they once fiercely opposed. The nation is locked in a bitter battle for the mind and spirit of Americans over whether to retain the principle of freedom from coercion basic to the First Amendment.

The possibility that political power would become the arm of religious intolerance and favoritism was a loathsome and repugnant idea to Mullins, as it had been to separationists like Madison, Jefferson, Williams, and Leland. But it is now embraced as desirable and necessary by the likes of the Christian Coalition and their allies in the political arena, comprised primarily of Republicans but also including certain Democrats. The American experiment in religious liberty is under severe pressure from two primary and powerful dynamics.

Self-interest is perhaps the primary motive, since large amounts of money are at stake in the battle for public funding of private schools. But the second dynamic behind the assault on the wall of separation is ideological. There are large constituencies in the United States who still believe strongly in some form of theocracy. Traditional Roman Catholics, evangelicals in the Puritan tradition, Anglican traditionalists, and, more recently, Christian Reconstructionists led by Rousas John Rushdoony, are strong advocates of church-state collusion. The most vocal coalition is in right-wing extremism as seen in the Christian Coalition and leaders such as Pat Robertson, Jerry Falwell, and Ralph Reed. When Reed resigned as chair of the Christian Coalition to head a lobbying group, he was succeeded for a time by Donald Hodel and Randy Tate, longtime Republican activists. Robertson placed his mantle and blessing on them and outlined three objectives for the near future: (1) to double the number of Christian Coalition activists; (2) to train twice as many political candidates; and (3) to double the number of initiatives favoring their agenda in Congress and state legislatures.

The Coalition and its new leaders were endorsed at that time by House Speaker Newt Gingrich, Majority Leader Trent Lott, Phyllis Schlafly of Eagle Forum, and other Religious Right hard-liners. The concern with developments in this area is at the point of blending of religious extremism with the Republican Party platform at both state and federal levels. Pat Robertson, who now openly heads the Christian Coalision, and others are seeking to develop what they regard as a "Christian Republican Party."

From the beginning of the American republic, there have been opponents of the separation of church and state. Establishmentarians were not converted by the passage of the Bill of Rights. Contemporary theocrats would like to see the notion of a free church in a free state pass from the political and social scene. The evidence is everywhere apparent: The acrimony of debate over so-called family values; the constant effort by various coalitions of religious groups to obtain favored treatment through public funding; and the open declarations by public officials like Gov. Fob James and religious leaders like Pat Robertson that "there is no wall of separation between church and state." Such comments are a declaration of open war against those liberal minds that fashioned "the first freedom."[16]

In Alabama, Fob James threatened the use of the National Guard and state police to defend religious practices in courtrooms. Judge Roy Moore of Etowah County uses clergy in court to lead prayers and prominently displays a large, handcrafted Protestant version of the Ten Commandments, in defiance of Supreme Court decisions.[17] Thank God for Circuit Judge Charles Price, who ordered Moore to stop using his court to promote his religion.[18] Critics should note that Judge Price is not antireligious. He openly admits his Christian commitments. What he is opposing is the heresy of coerced religion which the governor and others are trying to make public policy in Alabama, and in America.

Opponents of separation have seized upon one of the paradoxes in American political life. There is a tension between democratic governance as a process involving majority rule and the protection of religious liberty and other human rights which are protected for minorities. The separation of church and state, if submitted strictly to a majority vote, would likely not survive in the current climate. The majoritarian vote approach is precisely what lies behind organizations such as Falwell's now-defunct Moral Majority. The hope is that sufficient numbers of fundamentalist and evangelical Christians can be enlisted to outvote those who defend separation. Justice Antonin Scalia voiced a preference for the majoritarian vote solution in his opinion in *Smith v. Oregon* (1990). He argued that criticisms of the Supreme Court stem from its refusal to subject issues to the political process, that is, to a vote by the people. He went on to say in this landmark case, which punished Native Americans for using a controlled substance (peyote) in a religious ceremony, that "absolute religious liberty is a concept this country cannot afford."

More recently in a 5–4 Supreme Court decision, *Agostini v. Felton* (1997), government programs of instructional aid to religious schools were approved. Publicly funded teachers (Title I) will go into Roman Catholic and other religious schools to offer remedial classes.

The majority opinion was written by Sandra Day O'Connor, who said bluntly that the Court no longer supports its earlier rule that "all government aid that directly aids the educational function of religious schools is invalid."

The minority opinion, written by Justice David Souter, accused the majority of a sleight of hand: It "authorizes direct state aid to religious institutions on an unparalleled scale, in violation of the Establishment Clause's central prohibition against religious subsidies by the government," he said. Those restraints had been "put in place by the Framers of Constitution for good reason. Religions supported by government are compromised just as surely as religious freedom of dissenters is burdened."[19]

Souter represents a strict separationist perspective. But the severe erosion of legal protections against the easy flow of cash from the public to the private sector can be seen in the majority opinion. The strategies and appeals of the Religious Right and its coalitions with establishment ideologues are influential and effective. Further, its agenda is broad, consisting of a number of points at which a concerted effort is made to break down the wall that has made religious liberty in the United States a matter of the envy of the world.

III. A "MADISON" PERSPECTIVE ON CURRENT ISSUES

The agenda of the Religious Right, broadly speaking, can be considered as directly related to questions pertaining to religious liberty. This section will provide a sampling of items from issues in the church-state arena and show certain parallels to controversies faced by Madison. How he dealt with the problems provides guidance for our struggles.

Vouchers and/or Charter Schools

The first issue is the concerted effort to secure public funding for religious and/or private schools. Efforts to obtain "vouchers" for students to attend the schools of their "choice" is a favorite strategy of Christian coalition types. Dick Armey (R–Tex.), Joe Lieberman (D–Conn.), and Dan Coats (R–Ind.) recently announced a $28-million voucher program for Washington, D.C., called the District of Columbia Student Opportunity Scholarship Act. It would authorize vouchers up to $3,200 each to pay tuition for two thousand poor children at religious and other private schools.

Clever rhetoric and misleading labels characterize these efforts to raid the deep pockets of government largesse. The appeal to a "voucher" is less direct than speaking of public funding; "choice" seems to echo the American concern for freedom of choosing from among a variety of alternatives; children in the D.C. area are primarily disadvantaged and

African American. The program thus appeals to the American sense of fairness and egalitarianism.

Vouchers for schoolchildren are supported by all Religious Right groups. In order to get it for themselves, they are willing to let all similar groups have it. Through such efforts, Christian Coalition types have put "a foot in the door" or a "camel's nose under the tent" in order to loosen the restrictions on educational funding. Opponents see the voucher effort as a transparent money-laundering scheme designed to funnel public funds into private and parochial pockets.

Getting private school funding is paired with efforts to privatize the American educational system. The same groups proposing vouchers have also attempted to dismantle the U.S. Department of Education. William Bennett, who was appointed by Ronald Reagan to shut down the Department of Education, has been named one of America's Ten Worst Enemies of public education. Frosty Troy, publisher of the *Oklahoma Observer*, puts him ahead of such notables as former Speaker Newt Gingrich and polemicist Rush Limbaugh. Bennett's job in the Reagan years was to do all he could to cut off federal funding for public schools.[20] Bennett has become something of the point man for the effort by the Religious Right to do away with the public school system.

Critics have noted, for instance, recent support for using "vouchers" from the federal government has been paired with no federal monies for refurbishing public school buildings. Jerry Falwell once hoped out loud that "I hope I live to see the day when, as in the early days of our country, we won't have any public schools. The churches will have taken them over again and Christians will be running them."[21] In Congress, Newt Gingrich was among the enemies of public schools. He harshly criticized the D.C. school system, saying that a voucher program was the only solution to inner-city educational problems. He predicted that vouchers would create "an explosion of Catholic and other private schools overnight. They would be incredibly safer. You'd have the collapse of the worst public schools overnight."[22] In leading the House to vote on vouchers, he said public schools were "dens of illiteracy and dens of ignorance." His high praise for Catholic schools was a study in contrast. He declared that "at one-third the cost they do five times the job." He called public schools "holding pens for children," and said that he supports a system that allows poor children to "go to a school that actually cares."

His accusations were a calumny against public school teachers and the social values provided by a publicly supported system. Gingrich was a stark example of a politician so deeply indebted to the Religious Right that his support for public schools virtually disappeared. Self-interest for the politician was not just financial, it was also a matter of who delivers the votes.

Gingrich has since fallen from his position of public power under a cloud of rumors of private scandal. But his perspectives are still to be found in congress, threatening the constitutional freedoms our representatives are sworn to defend.

The terrible irony is that on the same day that House Republicans proposed vouchers, they also killed a request from retired General Julius W. Becton Jr., who is now head of the D.C. public schools. Twenty-two million dollars had been requested to repair several deteriorating schools that fire-code violations had forced to close during the last year. Rep. Charles Taylor (R–N.C.) unbelievably told the *Washington Times* that "there is sufficient money in the [D.C.] budget, many times over."

Charter schools are the crux of another proposal that attempts both to abandon the public school system and to skirt the problem of public funds for sectarian education. The idea is to allow states to spend the same money as it would on public schools for children to attend a private school not operated by religious groups. Some African Americans see this as an attractive option. They view the public school system as a type of warehousing of children serving only to further segregate blacks from mainstream America.[23]

The problem is that charter schools are often committed to religious indoctrination. The ideology is often New Age or evangelical Christian.[24] Teacher Lilian Cooper, of the San Diego Harriet Tubman Village School, was given responsibility for "the spiritual development" of pupils. "Soul consciousness" was to be emphasized throughout the school curriculum. The school was built upon the philosophy of Rudolph Steiner's "spiritual science" called anthroposophy—a type of cultish religion.

The Religious Right has made great strides in shifting public sentiment in favor of some alternative to the public schools which would receive federal funding. A Phi Delta Kappa/Gallup poll released August 25, 1998, indicated that, for the first time, a majority of Americans favor government subsidization of full or partial tuition for students attending private or parochial schools. According to the poll, 51 percent favor the idea, while 48 percent oppose it. Parents of public school students favor full vouchers by an incredible 56 percent to 40 percent. Only five years ago, 75 percent of respondents opposed public funds for parochial schools. Recently, President Clinton signed into law a bill supporting charter school options that had received overwhelming support in Congress.

State Religious Freedom Restoration Acts

On June 25, 1997, the Supreme Court struck down the congressional Religious Freedom Restoration Act (RFRA), which Congress had passed in 1993. The RFRA was an effort to address issues in the case *City of Boerne v. Flores* (1997), which dealt with whether churches should have liberties protected by the First Amendment not enjoyed by other groups in society. At issue was whether St. Peter the Apostle Catholic Church, a Roman Catholic church in Boerne, Texas, could expand and rebuild its sanctuary in spite of the fact the building was on the national registry of historic places.[25] A compromise between church and city officials allowed remodeling without destroying the historic façade of the church.

Congress had passed the RFRA in 1991, following the *Employment Division of Oregon v. Smith* (1990) decision, which had dismissed the importance of the "compelling interest" standard government must demonstrate before interfering ("least restrictive means") with the free exercise of religion. The High Court tossed the issue to the states. In *Smith*, Justice Scalia wrote that "laws that were generally applicable and neutral" would be considered constitutional, even if their practical effect was to eviscerate a religious practice. States like Connecticut and Rhode Island quickly passed mini-RFRAs. Ohio and Michigan were considering bills before their legislatures.

The argument of supporters of state RFRAs is that religious freedom should be protected for all groups and individuals, including prison inmates. The concern of those who oppose a proliferation of state RFRAs is that a type of social hysteria in reaction to *Smith* and *Flores* may lead to worse results than the decision itself. The need is to consider the ways in which religious liberty does not defend just any eccentric and unreasonable demand. Religious liberty is not a carte blanche for freedoms for churches or other religious groups to do as they please, heedless of the public good.

The Istook Amendment

Rep. Ernest Istook's (R–Olka.) proposed Constitutional Amendment to Protect Religious Freedom (H.J. Res. 78) has been defeated. Given the makeup of Congress and the pressures from the Christian Coalition, similar proposals will be seen in the near future. They will be disguised as legislation designed to assure protections for religious freedoms. Istook promoted his Amendment as a good-faith remedy for the RFRA having been struck down by the Supreme Court. But it amounted to a severe intrusion into limits the Court has set around the Establishment Clause. His Amendment proposed:

> To secure the people's right to acknowledge God according to the dictates of conscience: The people's right to pray and to recognize their religious beliefs, heritage or traditions on public property, including

schools, shall not be infringed. The government shall not require any person to join in prayer or other religious activity, prescribe school prayers, discriminate against religion, or deny equal access to a benefit on account of religion.

On first reading, the Amendment seems innocuous enough. But it is hardly neutral in its impact or supportable in its content, once examined. Church-state watchdogs were quick to point to its numerous problems and called for right-thinking Americans to join in defeating the proposal.

Certain outcomes that could be reasonably expected were hardly the intent of Christian conservatives. One possibility was vividly demonstrated by Rep. Chet Edwards (D–Tex.) in July testimony before the Senate subcommittee. He read a Satanist prayer, making the point that "student initiated prayer" was neither innocent nor innocuous.[26] He pointed out that "history has taught us the best way to ruin religion is to politicize it."

Other problems include the not-very-subtle effort to leverage public funds for religious enterprises. Istook's proposal would "[not] deny equal access to a benefit...." He is talking about public monies. Money is the "benefit" most coveted by theocrats and church-over-staters. Americans United for Separation of Church and State called it a proposal for taxpayer funding of religious institutions. The Istook Amendment would have created the funding mechanism in answer to the Christian Coalition's fondest dream. Little wonder it was a top priority of the Religious Right.

Amendment 4

Amendment 4 is a special concern in Kentucky, but it has relevance to every state tempted or pressured to provide tax subsidies for religions. This amendment to the Kentucky Constitution was hastily proposed and placed on the November ballot in 1990. It amounted to an indirect but massive subsidy to the churches in that all personal and property taxes, real and intangible, were removed from religious organizations.

The interests and loyalties of the leaders were in open evidence. State Senator Karem, from Louisville, was a Presbyterian. The Presbyterian National Headquarters had recently moved to Louisville and would stand to gain enormously from this financial windfall. But they would not be the big gainers. Baptists are the largest single denomination in Kentucky and probably hold as much property (acreage) as any single religious group. Roman Catholics, however, hold by far the greatest amount of financial holdings since they own industries such as distilleries which do big business in Kentucky.

Further, the strategy was well developed. By the time the amendment was announced, the Kentucky Council of Churches and the Catholic Conference were well organized to promote its approval at the polls. Opposition hardly had time to develop. The widespread affection for religion gave the amendment a presumption of support. One essay appeared in opposition[27] and the Kentucky Network aired a discussion of the issue by the chair of the Council of Churches and an opponent. The Council chair argued that certain (unnamed) small churches in Kentucky would have to close if the amendment did not pass. That was simply untrue but it carried enormous emotional leverage. Any "small church" in Kentucky was already protected under the constitutional provision that no property taxes would be paid on three acres in the country and two in the city. By the standards of the day in which the Kentucky Constitution was passed, those were generous allowances. Churches and their affiliate institutions now occupy large acreages and most of that is in urban settings.

A Madison Perspective

James Madison had strong feelings about the accumulation of property by religious groups. He saw great danger in "Religious Congregations with the faculty of acquiring & holding property real as well as personal ... [which] may always be gaining without ever losing, speedily gain more than is useful, and in time more than is safe?" The issue was not the actual monetary value of the property that is held, but the principle at stake which was the concern of the First Amendment.[28] Madison pointed to the European background in which the church owned as much as half the property of the nation. Rebellion against such religious materialism and power from wealth "promoted if not caused" the Reformation.[29]

Madison was faced with a bill that would incorporate the Anglican (Episcopal) Church in the District of Columbia. He saw it as a bill that "enacts into and establishes by law, sundry rules and proceedings" that pertain to the operation of the Episcopal Church. The effect, therefore, "would so far be a religious establishment by law" of this particular institution. The bill also followed the old Virginia pattern of having the church operate as the agency for charity and the education of the poor. Madison saw this as "a precedent for giving to religious societies as such a legal agency in carrying into effect a public and civil duty."[30]

A week later, Madison vetoed a bill that would have provided federal land to a Baptist church in Mississippi Territory. He thought it necessary to avoid any action that "compromises a precedent for the appropriation of funds of the United States for the use and support of religious societies," which quite simply, he thought, violated the First Amendment.

Madison thus felt that "every new & successful example therefore of a perfect separation between ecclesiastical and civil matters, is of importance."[31] His writings in "Detached Memoranda," shortly after he left the presidency, were reflections on questions of public policy. Some of these comments dealt with "ecclesiastical endowments" in which he grouped churches with monopolies and corporations. He noted his vetoes of the Episcopal and Baptist bills, seeing the bills as subtle steps by which the First Amendment was undermined and contradicted, or, as he put it "become a nullity." He feared not enough attention or diligence was given to "the silent accumulations and encroachments by Ecclesiastical Bodies."

Madison thought the states should be especially attentive to "the indefinite accumulation of property from the capacity of holding it in perpetuity." Madison argued that the Western world should have lesson enough from that history and cautioning that it could happen again.

Madison continued by asking whether or not people were "duly awake to the tendency of the precedents they are establishing, in the multiplied incorporations of Religious Congregations with the faculty of acquiring & holding property real as well as personal?" Since most acts of incorporation set no limits of time or amount, he wondered whether it was not necessary to "[c]onsider, therefore: Must not bodies, perpetual in their existence, and which may be always gaining without ever losing, speedily gain more than is useful, and in time more than is safe?" He noted that "the people of the U.S. owe their Independence & their liberty to the wisdom of descrying in the minute tax of 3 pence on tea, the magnitude of the evil comprised in the precedent. Let them exert the same wisdom in watching against every evil lurking under plausible disguises and growing up from small beginnings."[32]

Madison was standing on principle. He had persuaded Virginians to disestablish religion as such—all religions equally. Then he took that case to the states. It mattered little that the tax on tea was a mere three pence a pound; but the principle was profoundly important. It matters little that the land on which a Baptist church stands is worth relatively little. The principle matters enormously, however, that the state is not to subsidize or in any way establish religion.

He noted how seductive the notion of establishment for religion actually is in the minds of people, and how noble the motive seems. How can anyone be against public monies supporting religious institutions for which we are terribly fond and most of us embrace by attendance and financial support. But the issue is the integrity of the Constitution: "Is it not safer to adhere to a right principle, and trust to its consequences, than confide in the reasoning however (alluring) in favor of a bad one?"[33]

Madison's attitude toward the separation of powers between church and state was almost absolutist. It even extended to whether the president should issue a proclamation for a special day for religious purposes. On this topic, Madison was caught between the tide of public opinion and the persuasion of his own mind regarding religious freedom. Making proclamations for religious occasions was something that presidents of the United States simply ought not do, he (and Jefferson) thought, and offered five reasons why he would resist the pressure to hand down religious or quasi-religious pronouncements.

First, such an action would be incongruous. Since it could only have recommendatory or advisory power, it would be contrary to the nature of government. An *advisory* government, he said, is a contradiction in terms.

Second, neither the executive nor the legislative branch can in any sense regard itself as or act as if it were an ecclesiastical council or synod, with authority to address "the faith or the Consciences of the people." The ancient councils and synods called at the behest of Emperors and with the cooperation of popes and clergy belonged to the Holy Roman Empire, not to the United States. In America, "Congress shall make no law respecting an establishment of religion...."

Third, presidential proclamations "imply and nourish the erroneous idea of a *national* religion." He wondered whether the American people were actually ready to take the very idea of disestablishment seriously, pointing out that even if we were all of the same denomination and the same creed, any "universal act of religion ... ought to be effected thro' the intervention of the religious and not the political authorities. But since we are not of the same church, such national action by political leaders is doubly wrong."

Fourth, such proclamations tend to employ the language and theology of the dominant group or groups, with the consequent tendency that a conformity to the religious viewpoints of the majority would be surreptitiously encouraged.

Fifth, such proclamations inescapably bend religious principles to political expediency. Religion became a matter of party politics, he thought, however great the effort to avoid that sad result.[34] The exploitation of religious sentiments for political purposes is a distressing violation of the principle of freedom of conscience. The unscrupulous become masters of manipulation, caring little for God or the people but everything for power and control.

More recently, developments in mass media strategies and the tendency to create political coalitions by appealing to a wide variety of opinions on disparate matters, exacerbate and exaggerate the tendency to exploit religious sentiment for political purposes. One need only notice the efforts by the Christian Coalition to consolidate the votes and political commitments of evangelical Protestant Christians since 1979. The rise of the religious right and the extensive efforts to influence public policy by the National Council of Catholic Bishops (NCCB) are studies in the very specter Madison feared so greatly.

IV. CONCLUSION

There are many items on the church-state agenda. They require thoughtful reflection and sincere resolve if Americans are to preserve the freedoms they enjoy and to which they feel entitled. The Bill of Rights is a solemn reminder of the hard-won victories for the freedom of the mind and the liberties of conscience guaranteed by the Constitution. Contemporary Americans need to maintain what Madison called "a prudent jealousy" that guards and protects beloved liberties.

James Madison can rightly be praised for his lifelong dedication to and pursuit of religious liberty. He met the issue head-on in the Virginia legislature and the Continental Congress, and from the office of president of the United States. He has provided a staunch example as champion of this liberty many envy but few enjoy.

Religious liberty has zealous opponents as well as ardent defenders. Open and determined assaults against the principle of a free church in a free society face Americans in critical ways on the contemporary scene. The issue is alive in topics as varied as public funding for parochial education and tax exemption for property owned by religious groups. Madison, Mullins, and others have provided keen insight into the religious and intellectual grounding for the separation of powers and have set an admirable example of being willing to put the powers of their minds and souls on the line to protect First Amendment guarantees. They must also be terribly chagrined by the ongoing efforts by the enemies of soul liberties that would destroy the hard won gains of past centuries. Madison rightly noted that "it is proper to take alarm at the first experiment on our liberties."

NOTES

1. See H. Leon McBeth, ed., *A Sourcebook for Baptist Heritage* (Nashville: Broadman, 1990), pp. 83–90.
2. Ibid., pp. 70 ff.
3. Edwin S. Gaustad, *Faith of Our Fathers: Religion and the New Nation*

(San Francisco: Harper, 1987), p. 37; see Madison, "Letter to William Bradford," January 24, 1774, in *The Papers of James Madison*, vol. 1, ed. William T. Hutchinson and William M. E. Rachal (Chicago: University of Chicago, 1962), p. 106 (hereafter cited as *Papers*).

4. Madison to Bradford, April 1, 1774, in *Papers*, vol. 1, p. 112.

5. Ibid., pp. 112–13.

6. Thomas E. Buckley, S.J., *Church and State in Revolutionary Virginia, 1776–1787* (Charlottesville: University of Virginia, 1977), pp. 138–39.

7. Madison to Robert Walsh, March 2, 1819, in Saul K. Padover, ed., *The Complete Madison: His Basic Writings* (New York: Macmillan, 1953), pp. 309–10.

8. Madison to Edward Livingston, July 10, 1822, in ibid., p. 309.

9. James Madison, *Memorial and Remonstrance Against Religious Assessments* (1785), @ 4. See full text, Appendix A in Edwin S. Gaustad, *Faith of our Fathers: Religion and the New Nation* (San Francisco: Harper & Row, 1987), pp. 142–49.

10. Cited by Gaustad, *Faith of our Fathers*, p. 43.

11. Madison, *Remonstrance*, @7.

12. Ibid., @8.

13. Ibid., @11.

14. Edgar Young Mullins, *The Axioms of Religion* (Philadelphia: Griffith and Rowland Press, 1908), chap. 11, pp.185–200.

15. Interview with Gary North, "The Firestorm Chats," Dominion Tapes, Fort Worth, Texas, 1986.

16. See William Lee Miller, *The First Liberty: Religion and the American Republic* (New York: Paragon House, 1985).

17. *Church & State* (March 1997): 8 ff.

18. *First Freedom* (summer 1997): 1.

19. *Church & State* (September 1997): 16.

20. Cited by Rob Boston, "The Public School Bashers," *Church & State* (October 1998): 10.

21. Jerry Falwell, *America Can be Saved!* (Nashville: Sword of the Lord, 1979).

22. Interview with *The Washington Post*, February 1995; cited by Boston, "The Public School Bashers," p. 8.

23. Norman A. Lockman, "School Vouchers," *Courier-Journal*, September 16, 1997, Forum.

24. Rob Boston, "Charter for Indoctrination," *Church & State* (April 1996): 4–8.

25. *Church & State* (September 1997): 10.

26. Ibid., p. 13.

27. Paul D. Simmons, "Con: #4 Improper Response to Complex Issue," *Kentucky Journal* (October 1990): p. 17.

28. Quoted in Gaustad, *Faith of our Fathers*, p. 53.

29. Ibid., p. 51.

30. Padover, *Complete Madison*, p. 307.

31. Madison to Edward Livingston, July 10, 1822, in ibid., p. 309.
32. Elizabeth Fleet, ed., "Madison's Detached Memoranda," *William and Mary Quarterly* 3 (October 1946): 557–58.
33. Ibid., pp. 560–61.
34. Ibid.

CHAPTER 5

THE DANGERS OF BEING TOLERANT OF THE INTOLERANT

George H. Shriver

Phyllis McGinley, the Pulitzer Prize winner, in her poem "The Angry Man" spoke of a man bearing a banner labeled "Tolerance" who scowled along life's road championing total liberty and, when questioned about his purpose, answered, "Intolerance being, ma'am, a state/No tolerant man can tolerate."

Interestingly, neofundamentalists in the Southern Baptist Convention (SBC) have turned the intention of this poem 180° in the last twelve or more years, insisting that they have really been the ones not tolerated by an intolerant moderate leadership in their convention. The fact is, however, that they were tolerated and even indulged, and that now they fit the picture intended by McGinley originally, for these neofundamentalists have displayed an amazing and even frightening intolerance of all those who disagree with them on any one item of their major political, doctrinal, and ethical agenda. At the same time, they have pled that they are tolerant of diversity. (Their definition of diversity is a far cry from actual and genuine diversity.)

Especially over the last few years, specific illustrations of this intolerance have been reported on a national as well as an international level. Such a pattern of extreme intolerance has emerged that cannot be denied or explained away by the perpetrators. Just a few examples are in

---

*This article was originally published with the title "New Fundamentalist Intolerance in the SBC," *Free Inquiry* 16, no. 1 (winter 1995): 7–9. Reprinted by permission.

order. Heavy and promised funding for the international Baptist Theological Seminary in Rüschlikon, Switzerland, was taken away from the school due to neofundamentalist leadership on the Foreign Mission Board of the SBC. This leadership suggested that the school was too "liberal" and criticized the school's use of Glenn Hinson from Southern Seminary (Louisville, Kentucky) on its faculty. Hinson's "liberalism" is due obviously to his criticism of the style of intolerance of these people, for theologically he is definitely a pietistic, conservative evangelical. In short, he is a very Christian man who also happens to be an excellent scholar. More lately, Hinson and Molly Marshall, also on the faculty at Southern Seminary, have been warned of dismissal if "someone *interprets* [emphasis mine] them to have expressed [beliefs] in violation of the Seminary's Abstract of Principles." These pathetic remarks are made of two *conservative* scholars, conservative as judged by the bulk of American scholarship. Paul Simmons, professor of ethics on the same faculty, has also been labeled as guilty of "insubordination" because he has defended a "pro-choice" position both in public and academic settings.

Over twenty years ago some of these *same* neofundamentalists brought such pressures on Midwestern Seminary that the conservative scholar Ralph Elliott was fired for "insubordination" when he refused to "freely" remove his own book from publication instead of being requested by the Board of Trustees of that institution. The academic logic of all this escapes the average person's mind. Some of these same neofundamentalists have even suggested (seriously) that if any of these or other similar actions are not acceptable to accrediting agencies that they will simply have to establish their own accrediting agency!

A neofundamentalism has certainly appeared in the last fifteen years which is unlike certain forms of fundamentalism of earlier years. This neofundamentalism, especially witnessed more recently in the SBC, is not only insistent about its belief system, but it is also extremely political and absolutely rejecting of other positions. It has joined hands with the political Right of this country and is also using populism to its own ends, as well as employing whatever means seems necessary to achieve these ends.

Years ago when I taught in one of the SBC seminaries, which at that time took its place among the truly fine institutions of higher religious education in this country, I sensed some storm signals on the horizon.[1] I observed that the so-called conservative factions in the SBC were in actuality kinds of "liberals" who had sold out to culture, especially in regard to race relations—much like the theologically conservative "German Christians" of Hitler's Germany. A year later I wrestled with whether the SBC was a sect or denomination.[2] I concluded that in many ways the SBC was indeed a "sect"—more interested in "separation" than anything else. In the conclusion I suggested that "a conversionist sect may, in search for greater insularity and separation, become a hybrid conversionist-gnostic sect." Unfortunately, twenty years later, this is exactly what is happening.

Paul Pressler and his ideological cohorts have learned well the lessons of secular politics, and have successfully "separated" the SBC in more ways than one. A major part of the SBC which had benefited in earlier years from the tolerant and pluralistic attitudes of mainline, moderate conservative leadership has now taken over the SBC politically and will not tolerate those who had been tolerant of them for decades. Indeed, tolerant people are at a distinct political disadvantage when they are forced to deal with intolerant people. Regardless of the smoke screen of rhetoric released by these neofundamentalists, they are ahistorical, anti-intellectual, and antipluralist. They have either distorted or rejected the essence of Baptist history (for example, the priesthood of every believer and the autonomy of the local church), they have refashioned their intellectual centers into indoctrination centers,[3] and they have now come to reject what made the SBC a truly miraculous denomination, namely, pluralism.

The SBC had been, up to 1990, a microcosm of the macrocosm of American religious history. It was its own little ecumenical movement! Missions and evangelism bound different groups together in majestic common causes, and the glue of the mutually cohering parts was the acceptance of pluralism. This has now been rejected and there is really no "place" for those in the convention who truly value a pluralism of experience and perspective within a unified denominational tradition. Numbers in the SBC will increase, or at least be replaced (if some "moderate" conservatives leave), for news stories have already appeared telling of independent Baptist churches, such as the Frank Norris Church of Fort Worth, expressing desires to enter the SBC. Then, perhaps the last step of a "broken history" will take place.

Since the late 1960s, evangelicalism has prospered from the White House to the southern mill town. Ministering to the desire for wholeness and choice in society and church, evangelicals have intensely adapted themselves to the mechanics of modernity but not to the thought patterns of the modern world. Some of them have offered intense and hot understandings from their infallible and unambiguous Bible—cut-and-dried answers to very hard questions. They gained much of the whole world while *some* of them lost something of their own souls. The bulk of "some of them" were neofundamentalists. They were found in virtually all the denominations, but more recently ever so strongly in the SBC. Wherever they appeared they showed a hostility to any and all kinds of pluralism—

theological, political, and moral—thus, the "neo" part of "neofundamentalism." Like the *political* Right, the neofundamentalists pose a serious threat to that part of the American way of life which has been long treasured, namely, pluralism. These neofundamentalists have actually departed from the traditional understanding of the concept of the separation of church and state and have a vision of their own special kind of Christian America evolving sometime in the near or distant future.

Recently, Lloyd Averill, in his excellent book *Religious Right, Religious Wrong*, has perceptively described this type of fundamentalism as a "faith turned in upon itself and consequently ungenerous and unlovely in its religion, flawed in its understanding of history and dangerous in its politics."

Ethically, the neofundamentalists in the SBC have allowed the ends they sought to justify the means employed, including slurs, innuendos, blurred language, and severe political rhetoric (illustrated most recently in the charges against Hinson, Marshall, and Simmons at Southern Seminary). Their leadership has become aggressive and, in some cases, commonly mean. Yet what they do and say they cloak in the name of morality, God, the Bible, and the country. They have all the right clichés at their velvety tongue's tip, and they speak a populist kind of language par excellence. Martin Marty, in his *Religion and Republic*, is absolutely correct as he describes them as a "force of resentment against 'intellectuals,' 'elites,' 'the media,' and the like."

It is problematical whether the neofundamentalists who have caused so much schism in the largest Protestant denomination in the United States, the SBC, understand fully and inwardly what correct Baptist history and true Baptist practice really are. It is certainly time now for the media and well-placed persons on a large scale to expose exactly what neofundamentalists are doing. And this must be done in populist language so that the rank-and-file American will listen and then understand.

The usually mild-mannered Bill Moyers (whose background is Southern Baptist out of Texas) is to be commended for his honesty on television and in interviews as he has used vivid language to talk about the intolerant little "Caesars" (his word) in the SBC who have pranced about in delight of their political successes. It is certainly time to move beyond the overly nice and scholarly presentations of the Nancy Ammermans and Robison Jameses to crystal clear and populist exposures of these people and their ethical styles. Moyers has been brave enough to take some of these people on in their efforts to control and "make" their own news by firing honest reporters from the Baptist news agency and hiring only those who will report what they want to hear, without any internal criticism.

If some of my language sounds harsh, please be aware that it is based on facts of incidents that have already happened. For those who decry *any* harshness, I would gently remind them of Harry E. Fosdick's remarks about fundamentalists of the 1920s, when he referred to Christ as being crucified afresh in his own time by stupidity! It is a grievous experience to see one's chosen denomination fragmented and one's seminary alma mater (Southeastern) decimated by these neofundamentalists, as I have. And then to see these same persons (such as Paul Pressler of Texas) praised by political figures as high as the White House is depressing. The courting of the extreme Religious Right by Reagan and then Bush is not only frightening but dangerous as well—dangerous for American pluralism.

Pure and simple, neofundamentalism is a real threat to the continued existence of American pluralism. As of now, pluralism in the largest Protestant denomination has been irreparably damaged. In part, this article is intended as a wake-up call to the dangers posed for pluralism in American religious life by neofundamentalism. One must search beyond the fundamentalists' rhetoric to find out who they most truly are. At present, pure and simple, these neofundamentalists are completely intolerant persons. Part of their hypocrisy in the SBC involved their acceptance of the moderate conservative's tolerance for all those years prior to their political takeover; now, when they have their majority vote each year, they refuse to give the same kind of gentle tolerance extended to them for all those years. Their tactic has been that of Roman Catholicism of Vatican I vintage: When in the minority, favor toleration; when in the majority, oppose toleration. By some means and in some way, neofundamentalists must be taught the lesson of tolerance in a pluralistic society—in their own contextual society as well as the larger one. If this be done, then even they will be well served, for they will enter mainstream thinking at least in relation to pluralism and tolerance.

Religion and Republic's last chapter, "Transpositions: A Place for Everyone," suggests that the "major religious event of the decade has been the transposition of forces" and then gives six examples. The more important of Marty's observations is that mainline Protestantism lost out to evangelical moralists (and, I might add, neofundamentalists) by misreading three spiritual energy resources—"a passionate hunger for personal experience, a resort to authority in the face of a relativism and chaos, and the pull toward institutions and movements that provide personal identity and social location." To tap these resources so successfully, however, the evangelical moralists have themselves sold out to materialism and modernity. They have become more world affirming and success minded than those they earlier criticized as such.

What the future will bring for moderates and mainliners is problematical. One most important part of their role, however, is the abiding advocacy of tolerance in a still-pluralistic society. Only they stand between the public's being sold a false bill of goods by neofundamentalists and others. To respect pluralism and to accept creative argument and dialogue is not at the same time to reject values and to support moral anarchy, as some neofundamentalists seem to say. There is no heresy in a dead religion; there is no effective dissent in a totally intolerant state. On the other hand, where there is pluralism and variety of creative positioning, there is democracy and an American culture true to the essence of its history.

Phyllis McGinley has a strikingly appropriate poem entitled "In Praise of Diversity." She observes in the early lines those "Confusing thus from the beginning / Unlikeness with original sinning." Unfortunately, this is the viewpoint of neofundamentalists. To such people, continues McGinley: "There's white, there's black; no tint between. / Truth is a plane that was a prism." "Ah! But let us praise diversity," she urges. "Rejoice that under cloud or star / The planet's more than Maine or Texas. / Bless the delightful fact there are / Twelve months, nine muses, and two sexes; / And infinite in earth's dominions / Arts, climates, wonders, and opinions." Finally, her last stanza captures the essence of that lesson fundamentalists must learn to remain in a pluralistic society and what a pluralistic society must teach them if it is to remain pluralistic:

> Praise what conforms and what is odd,
> Remembering, if the weather worsens
> Along the way, that even God
> Is said to be three separate Persons.
> Then upright or upon the knee,
> Praise Him that by His courtesy,
> For all our prejudice and pains,
> Diverse His Creature still remains.[4]

NOTES

1. George H. Shriver, "When Conservatism is Liberalism," *Christian Century*, August 6, 1969.
2. George H. Shriver, "The SBC: Sect or Denomination?" *Christian Century*, September 16, 1970.
3. See the tragic and poignant story of Southeastern Seminary as reported by AAUP's *Academe* (May–June 1989).
4. "In Praise of Diversity," from *Times Three* by Phyllis McGinley. Copyright © 1938, 1942, 1944, 1945, 1958, 1959 by the Curtis Publishing Co. Used by permission of Viking Penguin, a division of Penguin Putnam, Inc.

CHAPTER 6

BOOTLEG BAPTISTS?
Robert M. Price

We are a Baptist church. At least that's what the signboard outside says! That's what the church bulletin says! But that is not *quite*, not *exactly* the impression that all members of this particular church have! I have heard comments like these: *"This church is Baptist in name only!" "People don't check us out because when they hear the word 'Baptist' they get the wrong idea." "Maybe this church is evolving beyond its Baptist identity."* Do any of these sound familiar to you? Have you perhaps made some of these comments? Are they justified? Perhaps. But I think it would be worthwhile to examine the Baptist identity, in order to see whether we really have gone beyond it, whether or not it still fits. You may be surprised.

There are various possible ways to proceed. It would make sense, for instance, to review the *history* of our denomination, starting with the Englishman John Smyth in the seventeenth century and the separation of Baptists from the Church of England. Or one might examine the *beliefs* most Baptists do in fact hold. But instead I would like to look at the Baptist agenda, the platform on which Baptist doctrines rest. I think that we will find what will seem to some of us a long-hidden treasure. We may discover that being a Baptist is a cause for rejoicing, even if, or even precisely *because* one deems oneself a freethinker in matters of religion.

A RADICAL VOICE

In the eighteenth century, Matthew Tyndal wrote a tract called "Christianity as Old as the Creation." Well, it occurred to me to call this sermon "Baptists Older Than Christianity." The Baptist voice of dissent and affirmation is heard first on the eve of Christianity. In more than a trivial sense, the Baptist movement was alive and well years or decades before the first convert was baptized in the name of Jesus. After all, Jesus himself, we are told, was immersed by John the Baptist, i.e., the Baptizer. And John represented only one segment of a larger movement of Jewish baptizing sects including the Essenes, the Hemerobaptists, the Masbotheans, the Mandaeans, and so on.

What did this "Baptist" movement stand for? What made it a distinctive and controversial voice within Judaism? *It took nothing for granted!* It insisted that the individual cannot take refuge in his parents' religion, the faith of her state or culture, even that of *one's own past!* It reminded the uneasy conscience that it must deal directly with God. You cannot let the Sanhedrin, the temple, the ancestors believe in God *for* you. "Do not say to yourselves, 'We have Abraham for our father.' " In other words, don't kid yourself thinking, "We've got religion all taken care of! Father Abraham and all our forbears in the faith have worked out a deal with God. The whole people tacitly agrees with it. So I won't rock the ark of salvation."

"*No!*" says John the Baptist. If all God wanted was children of Abraham, he could cause stone statues of the patriarchs to come to life. Instead, what he wants is *new* Abrahams who will decide for *themselves* about the God question. He wants to make a *new* covenant with each one, as he made with Abraham. That is why John and the others baptized: Each person who stepped forth to confess sins and be baptized was assuming *individual responsibility* before God. No religious credential mattered. Paul spoke in the tradition of John the Baptist when he said, "If any other man thinks he has reason for confidence in the flesh, I have more: circumcised on the eighth day, of the people of Israel, of the tribe of Benjamin, a Hebrew born of Hebrews, as to the Law a Pharisee . . . as to righteousness under the Law blameless. But whatever gain I had I count as loss for the sake of Christ" (Phil. 3:4b–7). Yes, such a resumé, impressive to others, is nothing before God. It is simply *God and you*, right now. Will you face him? This is the dynamic, uncomfortable message of the Baptist movement.

Now all this could be said and *was* said before Jesus Christ entered the picture. You see, there is a Baptist heritage that is prior to and distinct from the Christian heritage! And this is no purely semantic distinction. There are Christian churches that are *not* Baptistic in the sense I have described, churches in which faith *is* a matter of humbly acquiescing in the tradition and the authority of Mother Church. We are Christians; we are also Baptists. In this light, let us review some implications of the Baptist identity.

THE BAPTIST AGENDA

Baptists have always advocated *separation of church and state*. This belief is almost universally held in America today, not just by Baptists, usually because people in a secular society don't want to be forced to live by the norms of some religion they don't believe in. In the State of Israel and the Islamic Republic of Iran, religious leaders can govern the behavior of secular citizens according to religious laws. Americans don't want that. But Baptists first championed church-state separation for a slightly different reason. We wanted to live by religious values, all right—but the ones we chose! Thus Baptists had to leave England, then Puritan Massachusetts, to escape the Church of England's jurisdiction. The issue for us is freedom of the individual conscience before God. We recognized it is evil equally for a totalitarian state to forbid religious faith and for a "Christian" state to assume responsibility for *your* religious decisions.

Baptists have always *rejected infant baptism* for the same reason: We do recognize the responsibility of parents to educate and to nurture their children religiously, but we do don't think you can infuse faith with mother's milk—*or that it would be right to do it even if you could*! Presumably, you could hypnotize or brainwash someone into having faith, but would such "faith" be worth anything? It wouldn't really be *their* faith. It would be *yours*, having supplanted theirs. And how is indoctrinated faith any different, when you think about it? Instead, we put our young people *on the spot*! We say our faith is one thing you simply cannot inherit. Secondhand "faith" is not good enough for us! You must accept or reject faith for yourself. Don't say to yourselves, "We have Abraham for our father, and that's sufficient." If you do get baptized, it's your decision!

Baptists have a *congregational system of governance*; we reject interference from bureaucracies and hierarchies. We view the local church *not* as the local franchise of a national chain, taking orders from the home office, but as a voluntary association of individuals here and now. We have a representational democracy. We don't take orders. Why? Because to recognize any authority over our consciences outside of God and Christ (whom *we* will interpret, thank you), is again, to abdicate our responsibility. You can't let some bishop (or some Baptist pastor!) decide for you what you are to believe in and do. As Kant said, *you* must try to discern the will of God within and then be solely accountable for your decisions. (This, by the way, is how our congregation can be dually aligned with both the Southern Baptist Convention and the American Baptist Churches: Neither tells us what to do. It's true, as Jesus said, "You cannot serve two masters" at the same time, but whoever said you couldn't have two *servants?*)

For the same reason we *do not have creeds*, that is, *prescriptive* statements of what you *must* believe to be a Baptist in good standing. No! That would preempt your autonomy and responsibility before God. Some Baptists *have* drawn up "confessions of faith," to be sure, but that is a rather different thing. Indeed, the difference is crucial! I think that the Southern Baptist Convention's future hangs in the balance over whether they can keep that difference straight! You see, a confession is a *descriptive* statement, a survey reporting what most or all Baptists in a particular area or organization happen to believe. It comes *after* belief, not *before* it! It reports on faith already freely decided; it does not try to preempt free decision.

Similarly, Baptists uphold *freedom of the individual conscience in interpreting the Bible*. No preacher can tell you to believe that the text means so-and-so. No seminary professor can insist you adopt such-and-such a theology, whether inerrantist or higher-critical. Don't get me wrong: It's not that neither pastors nor professors *do* it! Sadly, *plenty* of them do! It's just that they are not being good Baptists when they pontificate, because we're not supposed to have a pontiff!

NOW! ARE WE BAPTISTS OR NOT?

I believe this congregation, liberal and freethinking since the days of its illustrious pastor, Harry Emerson Fosdick, renewed that spirit by the Reverend Don Morris, stands foursquare in the Baptist tradition as I have described it. We are all for liberty and responsibility of the individual conscience. That is why we encourage, even demand, free thought of our members. That is why we respect the different conclusions drawn by various of our members, whether conservative or liberal, traditional, or radical.

We at First Baptist of Montclair are pluralistic and freethinking. Does that mean, as some suggest, that we are not really Baptists? No! On the contrary, it means we are being very good Baptists indeed! No matter how much a Falwell or Criswell might disapprove of us! They called Harry Emerson Fosdick a "Bootleg Baptist" when he was serving a Presbyterian church. Are we "Bootleg Baptists" in another sense? Do we not perhaps belong in another denomination, maybe the Unitarians? I have made as clear as I can why I think we are not Bootleg Baptists.

But then what about the Falwells and the Criswells, the Paige Pattersons and the Paul Presslers? Are *they* the phonies, the bootlegs? Well, insofar as they are trying to impose a kind of creedalism, I think they are being inconsistent with their proud Baptist heritage, but let me hasten to add that is not their theological fundamentalism per se that makes them unbaptistic. No, they have every right to decide for conservative beliefs. More power to them! Let them frame confessions of their fundamentalistic faith! That is a perfectly good thing to do. But don't insist that I sign it! That *wouldn't* be Baptistic! Falwell and Criswell are good Baptists! Amen! But so was Fosdick! So is Harvey Cox! So is Jesse Jackson! And, my friends, so are you!

PART II

ACADEMIC FREEDOM: CONSCIENCE IN THE CLASSROOM

Academic freedom, as already noted, is rooted in the freedom of conscience or conscientious judgment. The professor's convictions may be based either on philosophical or religious thought and commitments. The problem emerges when the conscientious thought and convictions in the classroom confront contrary convictions and patterns of intolerance toward diversity.

Both secular universities and religious institutions of higher learning are battling over the limits to freedom in the context of scholarly research and publication. The restrictions encountered in religious settings are protected by constitutional guarantees concerning the separation of church and state, as Professor Bullough notes. But denying academic freedom is morally and religiously problematic. Religious liberty takes on a special meaning in the context of Baptist understandings that are neither appreciated nor defended in fundamentalist circles where opposition to critical studies is normative.

Vern Bullough is a university administrator who strongly defends academic freedom but recognizes limitations of both application and protections. He introduces the section with a reminder of free speech guarantees that are paired with religious liberties in the Bill of Rights. His survey of the history of the concept of academic freedom and Court opinions regarding its protections (or lack thereof) add depth and breadth to a discussion that tends to generate considerable passion. He notes that academic freedom is no cover for incompetence; nor is it protected legally in religious circles. Harsh political pressures often place ideals like freedom in the classroom in severe jeopardy.

George Shriver provides an interpretive map for understanding various approaches to academic freedom among religious groups. These range from the "defenders of the faith" to "free" institutions that encourage intellectual curiosity. Where a particular school is placed in this framework may generate some discussion. His thoughtful analysis grows out of painful experience and his life as an observer and historian in the academic setting.

My essay addresses the issue as one who experienced both freedom and then oppression at the Southern Baptist Theological Seminary in Louisville, Kentucky. I treat academic freedom as a powerful myth that is both desirable and deceptive. I also outline the theological and moral grounds for academic freedom from a Christian perspective and deal with some of the dynamics at work and the people involved in the fundamentalist takeover at Southern.

Bernard Farr's insights about the relation of "truth" to "freedom" reveals important factors at work among the defenders of religious orthodoxy and why scholarly or academic freedom is either nonexistent or in jeopardy. He shows keen insight into the fundamentalist aversion to freedom because of a prior belief that questions of truth are already settled. His treatment will bear a careful reading, as will his provocative conclusion that scholarship must proceed with a type of epistemological agnosticism.

Joe Slavin's "Last Lecture" as Justin Bier Distinguished Professor and Chair of the Department of Religion and Humanities at the University of Louisville is a clear call to the convictions and courage that are necessary if academic freedom is to survive. Dean Slavin represents those who associate humanist thought with the wisdom and traditions found in the study of the humanities. As he says, what is at issue is the freedom and encouragement to think. The educated are those who are able to wrestle with the great intellectual questions through the writings of the philosophers and poets, the novelists and dramatists. His moving and inspiring address is both a witness to his own commitments and the challenge for academics today.

CHAPTER 7

ACADEMIC FREEDOM

Vern L. Bullough

Academic freedom is a special interpretation of the Freedom of Speech clause in the Bill of Rights. It is one of the newer arrivals in the ranks of freedom since it did not appear in the English language until 1897 and the first real treatment of it was in the Harvard President Charles W. Eliot's Phi Beta Kappa address of 1907. The first U.S. Supreme Court case to mention academic freedom was *Adler v. Board of Education*, decided in 1952, and it reaffirmed the police powers of the state to protect the schools from pollution of alien or subversive ideas.[1] The case, in spite of its negative findings, is most important because of its dissenting opinion by Justice William O. Douglas, who argued that the First Amendment was designed to protect the pursuit of truth.

This brief background is essential to the understanding of how tenuous the idea and concept of academic freedom is. Thus, although the American Association of University Professors has advocated academic freedom since its founding in the World War I period, it has been a concept which was often more a matter of rhetoric than of reality. Gradually, however, the mainstream of higher education has agreed with various AAUP statements on the importance of academic freedom, and organizations such as Phi Beta Kappa, the American Association of University Women, and numerous specialized professional groups ranging from the American Association for the Advancement of Science to the Medieval Academy of America have come to support the importance and necessity of academic freedom, at least in a college and university setting.

In a sense, the assumption underlying the concept of academic freedom is, in the words of Justice Felix Frankfurter, the belief that teachers are the priests of democracy, and that they must be exemplars of open-mindness and free inquiry.[2] While I regard this as rather extravagant language, the assumption behind it—namely, that the teacher is engaged in a search for truth—is one that I accept. This implies that in the process of the search the teacher has a right to challenge traditional and accepted ideas. In return for this freedom, the teacher, particularly the college and university professor, is supposed to go through a careful selection process by his peers and by the college community for a lengthy period of time. It is not until she or he is given tenure, usually after some six years, that the full guarantees of academic freedom apply. Although academic freedom is supposed to apply in the original selection process, and with the various affirmative action programs this is more likely to apply now than it was in the 1950s and 1960s, the very selection process for an appointment is not always in the best tradition of extending freedom to conflicting ideas. Moreover, in times when there are numerous candidates for every academic vacancy in higher education, gaining tenure implies running a gauntlet where the untenured professor is likely to be very cautious and not particularly outspoken. Those who survive by so doing rarely rise to challenge the system in which they were tenured.

Moreover, the assumption behind academic freedom is that the teacher will be open-minded and not dogmatic, emphasizing the search and not claiming to know the absolute truth. This is perhaps asking more of many of us than we can really do, particularly when the issues reach into the core of our belief or value systems. During my career, as a student, teacher, and administrator, I have known faculty who were avid racists, militant feminists, narrow-minded orthodox believers in Marxism, biblical literalists, and many others who were a far cry from the open-minded seekers after the truth that lies behind the concept of academic freedom. As an administrator, I accepted this for the most part, providing there were at least a variety of dogmatists on the faculty and that no professor punished those students who had the temerity to disagree with them. On the whole, however, most professors did engage in dialogue with their students, and encourage them to think and find their own way. It should be added that, theoretically at least, academic freedom does not protect the incompetent, and that there are procedures for letting go a tenured professor who fails to meet the standards or who managed to slip into tenure without the kind of examination and peer review that should have been done. To bring about the dismissal of such a faculty member, however, is, as it should be, a long and tenuous process, and involves the peers of the professor at every step of the way.

From my own personal experiences in academic settings, I find that the ideal is better observed when there is a shortage of faculty and the need to meet the needs of an ever-growing number of students. It does not work so well when there is an overabundance of tenured professors and a need to meet the changing needs of society. I think the latter describes conditions today. Even under the most desirable conditions, however, there are problems, and as one who has been more or less fired for political activity (in the Democratic Party) by an institution of higher learning in the 1950s, I recognize the fragility of the concept. Even though the administration at the university in which I was then teaching was eventually forced to back down and reinstate me, I left anyway.

There is little a teacher can do by himself or herself if an administration is determined to violate academic freedom. She or he is dependent upon colleagues, the willingness of AAUP to censure an institution, and the courts. Although colleagues rally to support the person involved in an administrative violation of academic freedom, when push comes to shove, few are willing to put their own jobs on the line. The AAUP might investigate and put an institution on its censure list, but the very existence of a large number of censured institutions indicates that many administrators are not bothered by it, and fighting a case in courts requires a lot of money and a willingness to wait for the decision. One of the more notorious cases in the last year or so has been the dismissal of large number of faculty from Bennington College, including twenty-two tenured professors. Nominally the reason was that the administration at Bennington wanted to go in new directions and that many of the current faculty were therefore redundant. As a result of these firings, Bennington has been censured by the AAUP and condemned by the Modern Language Association, among others. Even so, the college won a grant from a major foundation to support its restructuring, and though it lost some students, the past year was a record year for fund-raising. In short, academic freedom is still a goal rather than an actuality.

If this is the case in a "secular" college, the case is even more difficult in a denominational religious setting, particularly in a seminary. Does not a denominational institution have the right to demand that all faculty members adhere to the basic principles of the denomination or church that supports it and the parents who send their children there because it is affiliated with their denomination? In part the answer depends upon whether federal tax money is involved. Those colleges or universities that run without it have few restrictions put upon them.

Denominational seminaries pose special problems, and the AAUP recognizes that. Churches have a right to set the criteria for hiring, for example, membership in good standing and adherence to basic principles of the religion. This, however, traditionally posed few problems for Baptists because the standards have been rather general and the belief pattern of Baptists so varied. The issue came to a fore when the Southern Baptists redefined the standards and demanded a new orthodoxy which the seminaries supported by them were required to meet. As new trustees were appointed in the seminaries, the freedom of expression was further limited, and faculty members working under traditional Baptist principles found themselves at odds with the new standards. They could either keep silent, hoping that the crisis would pass, try to engage in discussion for possible compromises, or maintain that what they had been doing was in the best tradition of Baptists in America. The result has been resignations, dismissals, the turning of one faculty member against another, and tremendous personal suffering. In my opinion, also, it has been a major violation of Baptist principles, since Baptists traditionally have been in the forefront of the fight for academic freedom. Baptists founded many meritorious educational institutions such as the University of Chicago (which I attended), which has been a bastion of academic freedom. Unfortunately, academic freedom still remains somewhat tenuous and those who are on this panel have very personal stories to tell about it. In short, the panelists are on the cutting edge of the battle for academic freedom, and as a humanist who has long been involved in it, I offer them support and consolation, and pledge to work with them to achieve our goal of academic freedom. I must admit, however, that I believe that the cause of academic freedom has a long and difficult road to travel before the end of the journey is reached, not only in seminaries but in secular colleges and universities. Perhaps working together we can make some progress.

NOTES

1. *Adler v. Board of Education*, 342 U.S. 485 (1952).
2. *Wieman v. Updegraff*, 344 U.S. 183 (1952).

CHAPTER 8

THE ANATOMY OF ACADEMIC FREEDOM AND RELIGIOUSLY ORIENTED INSTITUTIONS OF HIGHER LEARNING IN THE UNITED STATES

A Selected Look

George H. Shriver

A colleague at Georgia Southern University, whose specialty is modern German history, recounted the following incident. On November 1, 1837, Ernst August was crowned king in Hanover and immediately dissolved the parliament and abolished the constitution of 1833. Seven well-known professors at the University of Göttingen protested the political coup d' état and were summarily dismissed from their positions. In addition, three of them were expelled from Hanover. Nothing was done to restore the constitution. "Göttingen Societies" appeared in protest in Switzerland, Great Britain, and the United States, but without effect on the king. Ernst Agust brushed aside the incident and reactions with the comment: "Professors, actors and whores one can always get."[1]

Susan Rose opens her essay on "Christian Fundamentalism and Education in the United States," with a more contemporary but no less interesting story: "Baptist church padlocked. Minister arrested along with seven other parishioners." In September 1982, Faith Baptist Church was closed and locked by state order to stop its operation of a Christian school not authorized by the state. Four months later the pastor of the church was released from jail, having completed his sentence for the operation of an unaccredited school in violation of a court order not to do so. On his release, he made the following statement to reporters: "I do ask in the authoritative name of Jesus, the supreme law of the universe, that God bind the officials of the state of Nebraska and Cass County from further interference with the ministry of God at Faith Baptist Church . . . by either converting them or restraining them or removing them or killing them."[2]

Both rather dramatic stories raise explicitly and implicitly most of the important issues involved in the anatomy of academic freedom in our time—from external politics to resurging fundamentalist activities of various types.

My current interest in academic freedom and religiously oriented institutions was spurred by the 1992 presidential address of the American Society of Church History by George Marsden, an address later published in *Church History*.[3] Marsden, an excellent historian of fundamentalism in the United States, addressed himself to "The Ambiguities of Academic Freedom" in a rather strange way. The first half of the essay nicely rehearsed the well-known story of John Mecklin, Ethelbert Warfield, and the Lafayette College incident, which concluded with the resignation of Mecklin. The Lafayette case was one of those directly related to the founding of the American Association of University Professors (AAUP) in 1915 and its founding interest in academic freedom in institutions of higher learning in the United States. The last half of Marsden's essay never rises to the same worthy level of the first half. Though Marsden seems to indicate that he has discovered something relatively unique, namely that academic freedom is a "concept fraught with deep ambiguities," I maintain that the idea is not of recent vintage at all. However, perhaps a reinterpretation of these long-known ambiguities is in order, but not from his rather strange viewpoint, which exhibits a kind of paranoia about whether his and others' scholarship is not considered by outsiders as first class because of his/their religiously based viewpoints. He even unfairly remarks that for the last "several generations the prevailing style expected in the ASCH has been to hide the relationship of one's faith to one's scholarship."[4]

I judge this not only to be incorrect but also a discredit to the memory of such past presidents of that organization as Roland Bainton, Ray C. Petry, and H. Shelton Smith, to name only a few. An interesting footnote to this essay was a session at the January 1994 national meeting of the American Society of Church Historians in San Francisco, which was composed of a panel to discuss the Marsden presidential address. Marsden was challenged on a number of critical matters by Randall Balmer of Barnard College and Amanda Porterfield of Syracuse University. Marsden responded to some points, but in the main said that he had been "misunderstood." If that be the case, a large number of us in the audience had also "misunderstood" him. I rather think we all actually understood him too clearly. I found it extremely revealing that five of the six persons participating, including Marsden himself, are not members of the AAUP and that not one of the panel had experience on the state or national level with the AAUP! For some strange reason I find it difficult to listen to persons talk rather dispassionately about academic freedom who have not been in the trenches and are not even members of the organization which has contributed more to the nurture and fostering of the idea of academic freedom than any other in the world. At least my interest in academic freedom comes in large part from my experience in the trenches. And, though I have been a member of the AAUP, ASCH, AHA, and AAR for over thirty years, I have felt no tension or intimidation in relation to my faith and scholarship.

In the wake of growing fundamentalism and dictated intellectual constraints, the following notation is extremely illustrative of numerous points:

> On April 30, 1987, 25 members of the faculty of Southeastern Baptist Theological Seminary established a chapter of the AAUP.... Southeastern professors, sensing a threat to academic freedom, and the inability of the administration to assure protection much longer in light of trustees' stated intentions and actions, organized the chapter. Officers of the chapter sought legal counsel, met regularly to discuss issues and lay plans, met frequently with the press and made their views public. By the end of the year all members of SEBTS faculty had joined.... The AAUP chapter preserved unity within the faculty, improved morale, and provided a kind of pressure which has had a restraining effect on more radical trustees. Naturally, it provoked the ire of the new leaders in the board who regard it as a "union." Rumors come to SEBTS that administrators at other seminaries do not approve of the SEBTS faculty having a chapter of AAUP and do not want chapters on their campuses.
>
> On June 18, 1988 the national organization awarded the Beatrice G. Konheim Award to the SEBTS chapter ... and its Alexander Meiklejohn Award (very *rarely* given) to W. Randall Lolley [President of SEBTS]. This is the first time such an award ever went to a theological seminary.[5]

In June 1989, the national AAUP placed SEBTS on the list of censured administrations where it still remains, at this writing, along with nearly fifty other administrations, about one-third of which are religiously related institutions. The poignant and vividly descriptive report of the

AAUP campus visitation is found in *Academe*.[6] George Marsden's comments notwithstanding, in this case the AAUP gave unusual attention to a religiously oriented institution and not one of the faculty there seemed to be challenged in relation to scholarship! When the chips have been down, both individuals and larger numbers of faculty have turned to this organization for help, understanding, and sensitivity in relation to academic freedom. However ambiguous anyone's definition of academic freedom is to most of us, such threats as at Southeastern Seminary to academic freedom are unambiguous as well as perilous. I suggest that the acceptance or nonacceptance of one's scholarship as a Christian, Jewish, Muslim, or otherwise scholar pales into insignificance in the presence of these greater threats to academic freedom as well as to religious and academic pluralism.

Let us now turn to the documents of that most contributive organization and to some of the specific issues involved in relation to academic freedom and religiously oriented institutions of higher education.

If time and space permitted, I would like to have presented the entire 1940 AAUP statement on academic freedom.[7] Since that is not possible, allow me to quote the most relevant passages.

> Institutions of higher education are conducted for the common good [which, I urge, involves the religious sphere] and not to further the interest of either the individual teacher or the institution as a whole. The common good depends upon the free search for truth and its free expression.
>
> Academic freedom is essential to these purposes and applies to both teaching and research. Freedom in research is fundamental to the advancement of truth. Academic freedom in its teaching aspect is fundamental for the protection of the rights of the teacher in teaching and of the student to freedom in learning. It carries with it duties correlative with rights. . . .
>
> The teacher is entitled to full freedom in research and in the publication of the results. . . . The teacher is entitled to freedom in the classroom in discussing his subject, but he should be careful not to introduce into his teaching controversial matter which has no relation to his subject. Limitations of academic freedom because of religious or other aims of the institution should be clearly stated in writing at the time of the appointment. . . .
>
> During the probationary period a teacher should have the academic freedom that all other members of the faculty have. . . .

As Metzger observes, "though margins of vagueness remain," the perennial discussion about academic freedom took on a "cogency and clarity" that had not been present earlier.[8] And for all this, the AAUP deserves a great deal of the credit.

In relation to religiously related institutions, the most debated section of the AAUP statement is the "limitations" sentence or clause. William W. May is correct, I believe, when he observes that when the limitations clause was written, "it was intended as *reluctant permission* to limit rather than *encouragement* to limit."[9] By the mid-1960s, however, there was felt the need to clarify the *meaning* of the limitations clause. Some believed that by unreasonable self-restriction some institutions might actually remove themselves from the community of higher education. A 1964 committee report of the AAUP observed: "At some point in the scale of self-imposed restrictions a college or university that comes under them may, of course, cease to be an institution of higher education according to the prevailing conception."[10] Indeed, even before the founding of the AAUP, William Rainey Harper, a religionist and president of the University of Chicago, urged:

> When for any reason, in a university of private foundation or in a university supported by public money, the administration of the institution or the instruction in any one of its departments is changed by an influence from without, when an effort is made to dislodge an officer or a professor because the political sentiment or the religious sentiment of the majority has undergone a change, at that moment the institution has ceased to be a university, and it cannot again take its place in the rank of universities so long as there continues to exist to any appreciable extent the factor of coercion. . . .
>
> Individuals or the state or the church may found schools for propagating certain special kinds of instruction, but such schools are not universities, and may not be so denominated.[11]

Later in the 1960s, a special committee of the AAUP, composed predominantly of members from religiously related institutions, was appointed to study and make more explicit the meaning of the limitations clause. The committee was chaired by W. J. Kilgore of Baylor University. The committee did not construe the clause as an "invitation to impose restrictions, nor does it read into it the implication drawn by some that the adoption of religious purposes necessitates different standards or conditions of freedom."[12] It further urged that "religious privilege not be employed to provide a sanctuary in which to avoid the full responsibilities of higher education."[13]

The committee made it very clear that it did not approve of any practices that restrict academic freedom and included in its official report six specific recommendations geared to the guarantee of academic freedom. Two critical sentences were as follows: (1) "Any limitations on academic freedom should be *essential* [emphasis mine] to the religious aims of the institution . . . ," and (2) "The faculty member should respect the stated aims of the institution to which he accepts an appointment, but academic freedom protects his right to express, clarify, and interpret positions—including those identified as his own—which are divergent from those of the institution and of the church which supports it."[14] It is obvious that these committee members, churchmen all, were at pains to interpret the limitations clause not as a high fence to hide behind in relation to the curtailment of academic freedom.

The limitations clause continued to bother the academic community, however, and in 1970 a number of interpretive comments to the 1940 Statement on Academic Freedom were adopted by the AAUP, including the following comment on the clause: "Most church-related institutions no longer need or desire the departure from the principle of academic freedom implied in the 1940 Statement, and we do not now endorse such a departure."[15] It is critically important to note that the interpretive comments did not rule out the limitation clause—it is neither endorsed nor proscribed. Both the basic statement and the later interpretation affirm academic freedom at the same time that they accept limits on academic freedom based on religion. The interpretation did not resolve the tension but it did observe some differences among religiously oriented institutions, which I will explore later.

In 1988, the AAUP continued the discussion with a subcommittee report on the limitations clause.[16] The report was an interesting study of the problem and interpreted the 1970 de-endorsement statement as a repudiation not of the limitations clause but rather of "the interpretation of an 'acceptable' or 'indulgent' limitation that had grown up by the late 1960s." It urged: "An institution has no 'right' under the 1940 statement simultaneously to invoke the limitations clause and to claim that it is an institution of learning to be classed with institutions that impose no such restrictions. Consequently, it is obligatory that such institutions make clear when they hold themselves out to the public, in seeking public support as well as in dealing with students and faculty, that they are not to be so classed."[17] This observation has genuine merit for use in the courts in relation to the allocation of public funds. Two members of the four-person committee were religionists—Shubert Ogden of Southern Methodist University and David Tracy of the University of Chicago. Critical questions were raised about certain aspects of the report by Leon Pacala and William Van Alstyne, and it remains in a state of limbo at present—perhaps never to be officially adopted by the AAUP.

Jimmy Carter has recently said: "Every nation that violates human rights justifies it by claiming they are acting within their laws." Herein lies the main problem with the limitations clause when the chips are down, namely that every religiously oriented college or university that violates academic freedom justifies it by claiming it is acting within the rights allowed by the limitation clause. The limitations clause remains ambiguous—but let it be understood that the intention was not in the direction of license but of responsibility.

A helpful description of religiously affiliated institutions in relation to academic freedom and the limitations clause is given in the 1965 report of the Danforth Commission on Church Colleges and Universities.[18] At one end of the spectrum is what the commission calls the "non-affirming college." These are the Dukes and Emorys, which may have a general or historical denominational affiliation, and may indeed be committed to moral and spiritual values as a part of their purpose, but in terms of curriculum and teaching and an understanding of academic freedom, they can hardly be distinguished from a secular institution. However, the October 23, 1993 inaugural address of Duke University's president, Dr. Nan O. Keohane, deserves special notice for its serious effort to explore the motto of the school, *Eruditio et Religio*, in its true and contemporary meaning. Urging the discovery of harmony between the two principles, she quoted William Preston Few, president at the founding indenture of the university:

> Here stand side by side science and religion—science and scholarship completely given to the full, untrammeled pursuit of the truth and religion with its burning passion for righteousness in the world—and commit the University in its very inception alike to excellence that dwells high among the rocks and to service that goes out to the lowliest.[19]

Seeing this as a promising point of departure for the contemporary university, President Keohane closed her address by rededicating Duke University to "full untrammeled pursuit of the truth" and to the "burning passion for righteousness in the world." One could hardly damn this vision as a negative secularization of the academy or a loss of the soul of the university.

At the other end of the spectrum are those schools described by the commission as "defender of the faith" colleges. These are the Bob Joneses and Tennessee Temples. While some subjects are taught as they might be in secular institutions, so-called faculty freedom is boxed in by the orthodoxy to which each school is committed. In between these two types, the commission found a third type of school which it termed as the "free Christian or Jewish college." These schools have a definite religious commitment but also strive for a free play of the mind. In general, the faculty shares these religious purposes and many students are recruited on the basis of a religious vitality there. The report describes them:

> The college does not tell its students what they should believe, but it does expect them to grapple with the basic religious and philosophical questions and try to arrive at a position of their own. Much attention is given to the relationship between religion and the intellectual problems of our day. Religions and liberal learning are regarded as mutually supportive. In making appointments to the faculty, the college prefers scholar-teachers who see the relationship of religion to their own disciplines, but it likes to have a few constructive critics of religion to challenge colleagues and students. Once appointed, faculty members have the wide freedom consistent with law and good taste.[20]

These schools strive to further their religious interests as well as allowing intellectual freedom. Granted, there is not always smooth sailing, but that nevertheless is their goal. This group would certainly include the Stetsons, Furmans, and Baylors.

Indeed, this construct is helpful but not conclusive. Which schools are to be placed where would not bring a unanimous vote. And, more recently, other schools are perhaps strung out on a linear construct somewhere *between* two of these three types. On the right, some distinctions can now be made between different types of fundamentalist as well as neoevangelical schools, for example. Most helpful in describing this scene is a recent essay by Quentin Schultze, entitled "The Two Faces of Fundamentalist Higher Education."[21]

Schultze locates the difference in "the two faces" as being the degree of separation. On the extreme right he locates two absolutely separatist schools, Tennessee Temple and Bob Jones, the most successful of the old-line "defenders of the faith" types. In 1967 Bob Jones University students applauded in chapel when it was announced that *McCall's* magazine had tabbed the school as "the most square university." The creed of the university stipulated that it was to combat "all atheistic, agnostic, pagan, and so-called scientific adulterations of the Gospel." Their excelling emphasis on communication skills was not matched in any way by any interest in open intellectual discussion. At BJU academic freedom is really irrelevant, as well as tenure and faculty governance. Control by administrative hierarchy is the order of every day. To join or relate to any academic association is to "sacrifice God's blessing through disobedience" to this hierarchy.

Jerry Falwell's Liberty University and Pat Robertson's Regent University introduce Schultze's second "face." From their founding days, neither of these schools sought separation. From the beginning, for example, they were interested in accreditation. Early on, Falwell announced: "What Notre Dame is to Roman Catholic youth and what Brigham Young is to Mormon young people, Liberty University will become to the Bible-believing fundamentalists and evangelical students of America." Regent never supported separatism, either, and fully 50 percent of its first graduating class was Roman Catholic.

Both schools emphasized their academic excellence as being somewhere between academic separatism and collegiate liberalism. Scholarship was probably more limited by the heavy teaching load than by an absolute lack of academic freedom. Immorality was more likely to have been a reason for dismissal than heresy. Both schools were desperately trying to be many different kinds of things to many different kinds of conservative Christians. Regent even supports tenure as well as faculty governance. Both Falwell and Robertson wanted religious commitment as well as academic status in the larger academic community. They were definitely not separatists. It must be noted, however, that no faculty member at Regent is a member of the AAUP, while at Liberty there is one lonely soul who is a card-carrying member.

Academic professionalization on this right side of the scenario is to be observed in the history and interests of the Christian College Coalition, founded in 1976. By 1989, at least 80 colleges and universities which made up this coalition had rejected separatism in favor of more open intellectual discussion. However, Schultze is correct in his observation that "it was not obvious that academic freedom was especially important in the new approaches to organizing and marketing evangelical higher education."[22]

As a cogent illustration of this, typical coalition member schools and their relationship to AAUP are as follows: Liberty—one member; Regent—no member; Gordon—no member; Wheaton—three members, and, interestingly, Seattle Pacific—a chapter of AAUP is located there. Several future scenarios for some of these schools are possible. If American higher education continues to make an impact on these schools, some of them will move toward the center of "free Christian and Jewish colleges," while others, in reaction, may move back to a separatist stance. The most optimistic scenario for this new evangelical education is that it, having been "transformed by the world it sought to change, may contribute religious and even intellectual vitality to American higher education."[23]

More recent dialogue about academic freedom, as I have earlier pointed out, seems to involve a concern by some, such as no less a scholar than George Marsden, that one's scholarship as a committed religionist is somehow looked down upon or not accepted within the context of some people's interpretation of what academic freedom means. I am afraid in this case that Marsden and others are not only being defensive instead of assertive and participatory in the total university experience (Marsden himself is not a member of AAUP), but they are being somewhat paranoid in fighting "straw persons."

Robert C. Neville's 1992 American Academy of Religion presidential address on "Religious Studies and Theological Studies" is far more correct and perceptive when he notes the pluralism and openness in this case of the American Academy of Religion. He urges from his own experience: "The leadership in all my years of involvement . . . has attempted consciously to guarantee representation from all perspectives. That attempt has been overwhelmingly successful. No one approach to the study of religion dominates the leadership of the Academy, and nearly every approach that can be identified is represented. The result is the robust diversity and intellectual power that characterizes our regional and annual meetings."[24]

Neville then proceeded to post eight theses on his "church door" for debate and discussion in relation to the sense of identity in the academy. Calling for excellence in scholarship and continued acceptance of pluralism, he closed by cogently observing: "Excellence in the study of religion is vulnerability to correction."[25] After over thirty years of membership in the AAR as well as the AAUP, I find all his remarks not only to be correct but also descriptive of what academic freedom involves.

Academic freedom has implications for all three legs of the academic stool—teaching, service, and research. If one leg is missing or if others are cut short by abuse of academic freedom, the stool is very rocky or it totally falls. The institution that gives short shrift to the idea of academic freedom certainly has the legal right to do so, but never let that school claim that it subscribes to the idea and practice of academic freedom or that it deserves to be considered as a legitimate part of the American academic enterprise known as higher learning. However smooth the rhetoric and polished the hypocrisy, such schools eventually expose themselves for what they truly are. Such an attempt was made by the fundamentalists who have taken over Southeastern Seminary, in a recent article in the PR journal known as the *Outlook*. The article was entitled "The Mythical Line Between Indoctrination and Education." Though smoothly written, the article simply revealed the writer's own ignorance of American education and also of a correct understanding of academic freedom.[26] The article proceeded to speak of "student-product" as if all of us involved in education are producing music boxes with the tune to which we are committed. How absurdly asinine!

However, let it be stressed that one leg of the stool has two parts. To mix the metaphor, the teaching desk has two sides and student rights are certainly involved in academic freedom as it applies to teaching. One hears very little these days about certain student rights in relation to academic freedom, but for decades the AAUP has subscribed to and supported a "Statement on Rights and Freedoms of Students."[27] Indeed, "freedom to teach and freedom to learn are inseparable facets of academic freedom," urges the document. The professor is to "encourage free discussion, inquiry, and expression," and the student is to be "free to take reasoned exception to the data or views offered in any course of study." Further, "the student press should be free of censorship." In a later elaboration of this document, the teacher is reminded that it is "improper for an instructor persistently to intrude material which has no relation to his subject, or to fail to present the subject matter of his course as announced to his students...."[28]

These sentences carry some very heavy freight insofar as responsibility, academic freedom, and students are concerned. Let us all be reminded that every day of teaching is new and fresh when it is conducted in an open and community setting. Service and research are equally important legs of the academic stool, though in some religiously connected schools the principle has been one of publish and perish, rather than vice versa, service efforts have been criticized, and pressures have been brought when one does not reflect majority viewpoints or an orthodoxy as interpreted by hierarchical power grabbers. Perhaps the most recent chapter in the violation of academic freedom as it relates to teaching and service is the Cecilia Farr case at Brigham Young University, involving a faithful Mormon scholar who happened to express pro-choice beliefs in service speeches. At this point, Brigham Young codified its understanding of academic freedom to say that the "principles of academic freedom did not protect speech that attacked or contradicted the church, its leaders, and its fundamental doctrines.[29]

Also, within the last few years Glenn Hinson and Molly Marshall of Southern Baptist Theological Seminary were warned of dismissal if someone "*interprets* [emphasis mine] them to have expressed [thoughts] in violation of the Seminary's Abstract of Principles."[30] And Paul Simmons of the same faculty has been labeled as guilty of "insubordination" because he has spoken positively in relation to the pro-choice viewpoint in academic settings. Over twenty years ago in a similar fundamentalist setting, Ralph Elliott of Midwestern Seminary was fired for insubordination because he refused to "freely" remove his own book from publication instead of being requested by Midwestern's Board of Trustees. The moral and academic logic of all this escapes the average person's mind, not to speak of the mind of the general academe!

These violations of the general understanding of academic freedom are so obvious that no further comment or elaboration is necessary. Even though we can probably never arrive at a definition and account of academic freedom such as everyone will be pleased, not to say happy, with its practical outcomes all the time, there are numerous cases such as these which are blatant enough not to merit further discussion.

Thus, academic freedom involves the three legs of the academic stool as well as both sides of the desk. Also, it is warp and woof of the very idea of *universitas*—a *community* of learning. If religiously oriented institutions have anything to bring to the table of discussion about academic freedom at present, they certainly remind us that education takes place best in community—*university*. Academic freedom in this community also affirms collegiality, pluralism of views, "interdisciplinariness," and ecumenicity. A denial or curtailment of academic freedom is at the same time a denial of one or the other of these descriptive principles which are at the heart of any community of learning. Those whose first commitment in education is *control* in one way or another deny these crucial principles. University education begins a continuing process. The denial of academic freedom is at the same time a denial of change and pilgrimage, which are intellectual, moral, and spiritual. Political and hierarchical control prohibits change and aborts pilgrimage. Martin Luther in a university setting found out something about this. Those persons with an agenda of control, those with a formal or informal infallibility complex, have already ruled academic freedom out—whether in a religious or a secular setting. Those who recreate history in order to secure political power in an educational setting are either grossly ignorant or terribly immoral. Harry E. Fosdick once referred to Christ as being crucified afresh in his own day by stupidity. This carries it a bit further than ignorance but is kinder in relation to the question of morality.

There has emerged in the last ten years a neofundamentalism in some circles which has led to numerous painful experiences in some religious educational circles. These fundamentalists obviously have no interest in academic freedom, pluralism, ecumenicity, collegiality, tenure, or faculty governance. Needless to say, they do not even recognize organizations like the AAUP.

That leads me to one of my final points, namely the "sounds of silence." Violations of what you and I would call academic freedom are rarely even heard of in these religious settings because the faculty, students, and administration have such a different idea of what that is than the bulk of academe, both religious and secular. And if any one faculty or student comes to the insight that there has been a violation of some kind in relation to academic freedom, there is no court of appeal; there is no AAUP "witness" to the truth and to the defense of those accused or accosted. These are the "sounds of silence" in academe.

Academic freedom abounds in numerous religiously oriented institutions of several types; academic freedom is violated in a comparatively few religiously oriented institutions. Where it does happen, there is really a denial of what an educational seat of higher learning in the Western world is all about. I trust that most of us can agree about this general statement of principle. As William May has succinctly put it:

> The problem that remains, if we accept the argument about pluralism and the contribution of church-related institutions to our society, is where to draw the line on the limitations to academic freedom.
>
> There is no question that institutions have the right to define themselves as they wish. However, if they want to be identified and accredited as institutions of higher education, they must meet the standard of free inquiry that higher education demands. Clearly that standard, which has evolved in the last fifty years, places the burden on the institutions to justify any limitation on free expression of the results of sound scholarship.[31]

Walter Metzger's really outstanding volume, *Academic Freedom in the Age of the University*, closes with this perceptive reminder:

> No one can follow the history of academic freedom in this country without wondering at the fact that any society, interested in the immediate goals of solidarity and self-preservation, should possess the vision to subsidize free criticism and inquiry, and without feeling that the academic freedom we still possess is one of the remarkable achievements of man. At the same time, one cannot but be appalled at the slender thread by which it hangs, at the wide discrepancies that exist among institutions with respect to its honoring and preservation; and one cannot but be disheartened by the cowardice and self-deception that frail men use who want to be both safe and free. With such conflicting evidence, perhaps individual temperament alone tips the balance toward confidence or despair.[32]

Robert McAfee Brown is right on target when he describes the essence of the spirit of Protestantism as involving a tentativeness of statement and a finality of commitment. As ambiguous as our several definitions of academic freedom are in both secular and strictly religious contexts, this understanding of the spirit of Protestantism becomes a touchstone of confessional truth for religiously oriented institutions of higher learning that are also deeply committed to academic freedom.

NOTES

1. Cited by Holzer H. Herwig, *Hammer or Anvil?* (Lexington: Mass.: D. C. Heath & Co., 1994), p. 87.
2. Susan Rose, "Christian Fundamentalism and Education in the United States," in *Fundamentalisms and Society*, ed. Martin M. Marty and R. Scott Appleby (Chicago: University of Chicago Press, 1993), p. 452.
3. *Church History* (June 1993): 221 ff.
4. *Church History* (June 1993): 235.
5. *Faith and Mission*, Journal of Southeastern Baptist Theological Seminary (fall 1988): 58.
6. *Academe* (May–June 1989). Allow me to refer to two other censured administrations and the revealing reports of the AAUP investigating teams: Concordia Seminary of Missouri, *AAUP Bulletin* (April 1995): 49–59; and Catholic University of America, *Academe* (September–October 1989): 27–40.
7. See the full statement in Walter Metzger, *Academic Freedom in the Age of the University* (New York: Columbia University Press, 1961), pp. 213–15.
8. Ibid., p. 215.
9. Cited in "Report of the Special Committee," *AAUP Bulletin* (December 1967): 369.
10. William W. May, "Academic Freedom in Church-Related Institutions," *Academe* (July–August 1988): 28.
11. Quoted in "The 'Limitations' Clause," *Academe* (September–October 1988): 54.
12. "Report of the Special Committee," p. 369.
13. Ibid.
14. Ibid., pp. 370–71.
15. See May, "Academic Freedom," p. 23.
16. "The 'Limitations' Clause," pp. 52–59.
17. Ibid., p. 55.
18. As described in "The 'Limitations' Clause," p. 53.
19. Nan O. Keohane, inaugural address, Duke University, October 23, 1993.
20. Cited in "The 'Limitations' Clause," p. 53.
21. Quentin Schultze, "The Two Faces of Fundamentalist Higher Education," in *Fundamentalisms and Society*, pp. 490–535.
22. Ibid., p. 522.
23. Ibid., p. 529.
24. Robert C. Neville, "Religious Studies and Theological Studies," *Journal of the American Academy of Religion* (summer 1993): 186.
25. Ibid., p. 200.
26. *Outlook* (spring 1993): 10.
27. See *AAUP Bulletin* (December 1967): 365–68.
28. *AAUP Bulletin* (December 1970): 375.
29. *Change* (September–October 1993): 70.

30. See Robinson B. James, "Molly Marshall," in *Dictionary of Heresy Trials in America*, ed. G. Shriver (Westport, Conn.: Greenwood, 1997), pp. 242–57.
31. May, "Academic Freedom," p. 28.
32. Metzger, *Academic Freedom*, p. 232.

CHAPTER 9

ACADEMIC FREEDOM IN THE SEMINARY
The Myth, the Reality, and the Future
Paul D. Simmons

Mark Twain once said, "It is by the goodness of God that in our country we have those three unspeakably precious things: freedom of speech, freedom of conscience, and the prudence never to practice either of them." Whether Twain was speaking as humorist or as cynic is of more than passing interest in the context of discussions about academic freedom. I will not try to resolve the question as to his intent. My commitment to academic freedom would require a considerable revision of his statement since I regard the topic as of the utmost importance—in part, perhaps, because I lack some of Twain's cynical humor!

My reflections on academic freedom will focus especially on the problem in theological education and more particularly on Southern Baptist Theological Seminary in Louisville. It is in that context that I have spent the great majority of my adult life and where I learned stern lessons from experience with regard to denominational and institutional commitments to academic freedom or the lack thereof.

My thoughts are also shaped by images, stories, and paradigms from history and current events. Macneille Dixon once reminded us that the human mind is a picture gallery, not a debating hall.[1] I have thought often, for instance, of the powerful story of Maeyken Wens, an Anabaptist condemned by the Inquisition for preaching without a license. After the sentence, her tongue was fastened to the roof of her mouth with a wooden screw to prevent her from talking, protesting, or preaching on the way to the pyre where she was to burn to death. That image of the screw in the tongue is a powerful metaphor in the debate regarding academic freedom.

The story of Roger Williams contending for academic freedom in Puritan New England also haunts my mind. His employers regarded truth as settled. A rigid orthodoxy was required of all professors. Williams saw the academy as a context for reflective inquiry as to the truth or intellectual plausibility of certain propositions in theology and morals. Facing arrest for insubordination, if not heresy, and the imprisonment which would surely follow, he fled to the wilderness during a severe winter. He would not submit to the indignities of the administrative fiat against him. Williams' undaunted and courageous quest for freedom has left a legacy for every person—professor, student, or minister—interested in truth and the academic environment in which it might be pursued. He had the courage to endure near starvation and severe cold rather than sacrifice intellectual and spiritual integrity.

There are also images on the "other side" of my concern. I think of John Calvin, who consented to Servetus's death because Servetus dared to question Calvin's notions of double predestination and the trinity. Servetus is the hero. He was magnanimous in his dying. "We will," he said to Calvin as the fires were lit, "continue this debate in heaven."

I think also of Dostoyevski's "Grand Inquisitor" and the Inquisition's four hundred-year battle against intellectual curiosity or integrity in religious matters. Maeyken Wens was only one of its thousands of victims put to death on the premise that it is better to be executed by the righteous than to die in "heresy" and thus be condemned to eternal damnation.

There are also those disturbing stories of women being drowned, hanged, or burned when found to be "witches." What we know now is that behind so much of both the Inquisition and the witch-hunts were men eager to blame women for their own lechery and debauchery. There was also the sordid factor of greed and avarice—the powerful who coveted the property of the condemned; who reaped rich profits from the confiscations they ordered.

Such stories and their intricate weavings of religious belief with the coercive power of government have a contemporary ethical and religious relevance. They are stories about ideas and whether piety requires submissive obedience or open resistance to perceived injustices based on bad faith and corrupt morals. In narrative fashion, they pose the issue of academic freedom.

Who will say "enough?" And who or what will defend those who criticize and/or challenge administrators and religious leaders who have the power to destroy the critic? Are there institutions whose very being should provide the context and opportunity for challenging such obfuscations of truth which parade in the garbs of piety?

FOUNDATIONS OF ACADEMIC FREEDOM

Academic freedom is an important and powerful myth by which the educational community lives. A myth is an influential belief that contributes significantly to human conduct and the interactions of a given socioreligious culture. Myth contains elements of ideals and hopes, as well as fiction and wishful thinking. Idealists tend to emphasize ideals and hopes and thus encourage creativity and innovation, not to mention openness and candor in the discussion of issues in a scholarly context. As myth, academic freedom functions extremely well in times of stability and prosperity. Academics talk openly and celebrate the wonders of an open environment for critical thought and debate. But when the social or political climate changes, academic freedom takes on the appearance of fiction. At best, it is an ideal or a general rule, folkway,[2] or custom that is largely unenforceable if not impotent to protect professors made vulnerable by controversy or who become the object of ideological crusades.

The greatest value of academic freedom is that procedural safeguards are provided for academics who seek and champion the truth based upon the good-faith insights and conclusions gained from scholarly research and intellectual reflection. The faculty's main concern is having a secure enough environment that they will not be placed in vocational jeopardy for seeking and speaking of truth as they understand it and sharing the results of that inquiry with others in scholarly fashion.

Academic Freedom and Human Rights

Academic freedom rests upon powerful philosophical and theological perspectives. For the most part these are rooted in Enlightenment notions of human rationality and Reformation ideas of truth as personal. Philosophically, academic freedom reflects the twin notions that truth can never be reduced to any number of rational statements, and that truth can properly be known and accepted for oneself only by persuasion, not by coercion.

Academic freedom is also related to human rights. There are inalienable rights—fundamental entitlements to freedom of thought, freedom of speech, freedom of conscience, freedom to publish, and freedom to argue one's opinions in a peaceful (even if raucous) assembly.[3] These freedoms are interconnected and interrelated, as the First Amendment recognizes.

There is a liberty right to express one's opinion in the free market of ideas. In the public forum, contrasting ideas and insights compete to persuade the mind and gain the allegiance of the public.

A further element is that every person has an inalienable right to information and/or insights that might be helpful or valuable in the fashioning of one's life plan or the pursuit of personal happiness. Liberties are enhanced by the truth, which expands human understandings of present and future options and alternatives. Ignorance is the archenemy of happiness—one's own and that of one's neighbor. The good, happy, and decent life cannot be fashioned around deception or falsehood. Every person is entitled to whatever insight or nugget of wisdom another might share that makes life easier or enhances one's prospects for happiness or the avoidance of unnecessary pain and frustration. An open and honest exploration of issues having to do with truth is vital to the truth itself. Academic freedom contributes to human happiness by inviting an exploration of all insights and opinions as to what constitutes the right, the good, or the happy.

Academic Freedom and Free Speech

Academic freedom is also related to constitutional guarantees of free speech. But they are not treated the same at law. Freedom of speech is a civil right assured all citizens. Academic freedom is a qualified right—a privilege related to one's academic role in an educational institution. It is conditioned upon one's conformity with certain obligations to the institution and its rules and standards.[4] Academic freedom is not a universal human right. It is an entitlement belonging to those members of the academic profession who happen also to be privileged to have a classroom and/or be employed by an educational institution. An institutional commitment to academic freedom assures that professors are not simply hired hands who may be told what to think or say. It is a way of saying that dissent does not expose one to the Damoclean sword.

But the philosophical rationale behind academic freedom is closely and vitally related to arguments for free speech. Both freedoms are often based on John Stuart Mill's *On Liberty*,[5] for instance. Scholars typically make the connection when arguing protections for engagements outside the classroom or when they become engaged in debates over social issues. The professor is likely to view off-campus engagements as personal time and freedom of speech as a civil right with constitutional guarantees. What is said in such contexts would or should not be of special interest to nor fall under the province of the governing authorities of the academy.

The Politically Correct

Another source of limit to free expression is the perceived harm to persons or groups that have been especially vulnerable from prejudice or oppression. Injury to persons and groups by the vocabulary of hate groups on the campus is presumably the central concern behind the notion of the "politically correct."[6] Most media attention has been given to left-wing concerns—those especially important to women, African Americans, and homosexuals. These groups are the special objects of derisive, hateful language they find not only humiliating but injurious. They thus attempt to limit certain types of speech because it is immoral and thus unacceptable. Such efforts to control injurious speech is also a limitation of "academic freedom" insofar as it extends into the classroom.

More than 150 U.S. campuses have attempted to implement some code to regulate such hateful speech and harassing conduct which was racist, sexist, homophobic, or ethnically demeaning. The rules were based on the recognition that targeted groups are often the victims of discrimination and objects of hateful actions by the bigoted who use such insults. Such restrictions were justified "by the harm suffered."[7]

The AAUP recognized the fragility of civility, but recommended against any rules that ban or punish speech—even that which is full of hate and bigotry. It gave several reasons. First, the distinction between substance and style is thought untenable. Expressive power may be precisely why the offensive style is chosen (citing the Supreme Court). Second, institutions are not capable of protecting all classes of targeted insults. Thus, such distinctions are neither "practicable nor principled." Third, freedom of expression requires toleration of "ideas we hate," as Justice Holmes put it. Free speech is not simply an aspect of the educational enterprise to be weighed against other desirable ends. It is the very precondition of the academic enterprise itself."[8]

Legal challenges have been almost unanimous in overturning such codes on secular campuses. Stanford University had outlawed "gutter epithets and symbols of bigotry." The code was found unconstitutional by the Superior Court of California. A 1992 law said the university could not restrict speech on campus that is protected off campus.[9]

Education and Moral Behavior

One of the beliefs of liberal education is that enlightened minds will be able to discern the difference in right and wrong and act according to the best insights of reason. Without the free and open pursuit of truth, the baser human passions will lead to injustice and violence. Behavior can be motivated as much if not more by fear and hate than by the insights of quiet reason, as every demagogue knows. Goebbels led the propaganda machine of the Third Reich on the premise that he must appeal to the basic instincts of fear and prejudice in people.

People are capable of reason, but what passes as rational may be little more than rationalization. People may give reasons for their actions that are persuasive and convincing to them, but problematic and self-serving from other points of view. Everything from adultery and rape, to embezzlement and forgery, to murder and genocide have had intellectual structures convincing to the perpetrator. Behind every oppression there is an ideology that justifies such actions. We need only think of the anti-Semitism of no less an outstanding theologian than Gerhard Kittel. His *Theological Dictionary of the Bible* is something of a classic in biblical scholarship. The fact that Kittel once produced material used by the Nazis to support pograms against the Jews is anecdotal but ample evidence that even the intelligent or gifted mind is not always clear about the truth. Education should have as one of its primary goals that of helping people avoid the blinders of self-interest that leads to rationalization, victimization, and oppression.

Doing so requires that insight and imagination, as well as experience and historical perspectives, be blended with reasoned discourse. Thomas Jefferson, who was both a holder of slaves and the author of the Declaration of Independence, recognized the moral incongruity in his position. Rather than trying to insulate himself from criticism, he encouraged free and open debate of the issue. That, he said, was in the best social interest.[10]

Sustaining Democratic Institutions

Further, academic freedom is necessary to sustain the institutions of freedom associated with democracy. Freedom of the mind is vital to political and social freedoms. Totalitarian regimes are best prevented rather than defeated. Hitler captured the allegiance of Germans because he was able to control the three institutions most responsible for shaping the public mind—the press, the university, and the church.

Thought is the first object of control by tyrants and dictators. In the totalitarian state, education cannot be open; it must be doctrinaire and dogmatic. The free exchange of ideas is intolerable because thoughtful, reflective inquiry is the deadly enemy of ideology. Tyranny cannot survive where there is an open classroom; truth is its mortal enemy. Hitler could never have succeeded without the complicity of the church and the university. The freedom of the mind is basic to the freedom of the soul and both are basic to a free society.

In his poem "Stations on the Road to Freedom," Bonhoeffer wrote that Christ alone is to be lord of the conscience. Freedom from the forces that bind us is the precious gift of grace made possible only as Christ takes form within us.[11]

Tyranny cannot reign in either religion or politics if the academy is free to explore issues. Democracy cannot survive if academic freedom is destroyed. By definition, democracy requires an open and honest exploration of issues. Academic freedom is indispensable to that process.

RELIGION AND ACADEMIC FREEDOM

In a Christian religious context, academic freedom rests on at least four foundations. The first is the duty or obligation to tell the truth. The biblical commandment to "bear no false witness" (Exod. 20:16) requires that one be sufficiently and accurately informed so as not to engage in misrepresentations, whether from malice or ignorance. Telling the truth is an exercise in integrity—in speaking from the depths of one's being and rightly representing reality. Karen Lebacqz[12] points to the power vested in the spoken word. To speak is to interpret reality for the listener and thus to devise and portray the world. The truth requires both optimum verbal veracity and a regard for accurate correspondence between insight, interpretation, and one's conscientious affirmations about human reality.

The second basis is the theologian's moral obligation to the other, or neighbor love. *Agape* requires that we withhold no good thing necessary to the well-being of the other. Altruism or beneficence includes avoiding harm as well as preventing harm where possible. One of the goods needed for human well-being is the truth. The Christian life cannot be fashioned around deception or falsehoods. We should be able to understand, analyze, and revise the myths and images by which we live—to rightly separate what is good and helpful from what is false, evil, and/or injurious. We severely deprive the neighbor of the good owed by destroying a climate that encourages a quest for the life of the truth in Christ. Academic freedom contributes to that end by making possible an exploration of all insights into revealed truth.

The third basis is the calling of the Christian theologian. The mandate for truth-telling is a conscientious commitment to live under the lordship of Christ. No dogma or statement of propositional truth can substitute for the obligation to live in constant fidelity to the living Christ. Nor can any loyalty or personal interest—whether to institution, economic well-being, or denomination—displace the transcendent fealty one owes to Christ. Socrates put it well when the bargain was proposed that he be allowed to live *on condition that* he cease teaching. He rejected the compromise, saying he could not be silent for his calling was from God.

The fourth ground of academic freedom is the conscientious convictions of the believer. To deny one's grasp of truth is to deny the essence of one's life. One cannot live the life of integrity if one is unable to speak the truth in love. Internal dissonance is the source of unresolvable personal conflicts which contribute to the disintegration of character and alienate the believer from those ground-of-meaning beliefs and commitments by which he is personally and religiously defined.

In the religious context, therefore, there are ultimate grounds for academic freedom, not simply rational or humanistic reasons such as the ability better to live in freedom or speak the truth as one understands the truth. The Christian academy lives under the lordship of Christ and thus under a divine mandate. To deny freedom to speak to those whose lives are committed to a scholarly quest for the truth of God may well be to deny access to insights provided by divine revelation. Jesus and the prophets lived and spoke by the truth that tradition may make void the word of God (Matt. 15:6). Honest debate and careful scrutiny of the traditions that shape Christian beliefs and commitments as well as ecclesiastical structures and loyalties are indispensable to living in the world under the truth of God.

Institutional Power

Ecclesiastical traditions are suspicious of insights that have not been given official certification, however, and religious leaders tend to be jealous of the power and prerogatives that come by positions of influence within the organization. Power is used to maintain stability and to ward off any perceived threats to institutional growth. Academics who challenge the ideas or goals of the institution may be seen as injurious to organizational strength and thus be accused of being oppositional to the "truth."

The moral and theological bases of academic freedom show both its desirability and indispensability in those contexts that hold truth in high regard. But there are special considerations when dealing with academic freedom in the religious context. For one thing, religious institutions are exempt from legal regulations regarding either speech codes or academic freedom as an aspect of the separation of church and state. Public policy is largely ineffectual in ecclesiastical circles, making activities possible in the religious arena that are entirely unacceptable in the secular. The most egregious controls against freedom of speech or academic freedom are to be found in religious settings.[13]

Furthermore, neither accrediting agencies such as ATS nor faculty advocates such as the AAUP question the right of sectarian academic institutions to demand conformity to orthodox or required religious beliefs.[14] Whatever protections there are must come from within the religious tradition itself; they will not be required or imposed by secular authorities.

Confessional Traditions

Protections for academic freedom are thus especially vulnerable in the educational institutions of confessional traditions. How much freedom might a professor have to raise questions about the basic contentions or beliefs of that tradition? The problem is especially acute in those traditions committed to propositional truth or ecclesiastical structures around a centralized authority. A recent series of articles in *The Christian Century* explored the topic among Protestants and evangelicals.[15] *Commonweal* had earlier examined the severe restrictions placed around Catholic higher education by the Vatican, acting through its American bishops.[16]

American Catholic colleges and universities had adopted U.S. standards of academic freedom, which brought them into conflict with the Vatican, an institution which has a long-lived suspicion of academics.[17] The bishops' intervention into the hiring/firing process of the university was in direct conflict with the aims and purposes of academic freedom. A mandate must now be secured from ecclesiastical authorities before a professor can be named to teach theology, and procedures are set in place for settling disputes between academics and matters of church law. Charles Curran, who taught at Catholic University of America, was made an example of the power of the church to intervene in academic matters. And his difficulties in finding another place to teach revealed the pervasiveness of power wielded by central authorities.[18]

Academic freedom seems especially vulnerable in all denominational schools, whether Catholic or Protestant. How can academics pretend an open quest for truth when religious traditions assume that their truth is a settled matter? The Puritans made no pretense about academic freedom. The educational institution was a direct extension of the church's mission to the world. The professor was a propagandist for Puritan dogma in morals and theology. Professors in this tradition are not seekers after truth, but preachers in the classroom. The revolt by Roger Williams was provoked by his conscientious rejection of a propositional approach to truth, the style of coercion and intimidation with which they were perpetuated, and his own conscientious refusal to teach the intellectually and ethically unsupportable.

The Religious Right: The Politics of Coercion

There is a type of piety that is suspicious of and offended by questions raised by the skeptic or the curious. Academic freedom is regarded as a threat to institutional or ecclesiastical prerogatives or a type of subversive activity. The questioner is regarded as undermining the distinctive aspects of the Christian heritage. "The free exercise of intellect," says Mark Schwehn, "does not extend to the dominant religious centers of our culture."[19]

The reasons for academic rigidity are bound to be complex and multifaceted, from the simple identification of "belief" with doctrines the faithful are to accept without question; to the fearful, angry zealotism that believes that piety is somehow threatened by honest questions. But the very concept of freedom with regard to the truth is problematic for evangelical Christians who are increasingly identified with the Religious Right, which has its own set of "politically correct" expectations.

Groups such as the Moral Majority and the Christian Coalition have identified Christian beliefs with what others see as an oppressive sociopolitical agenda. The items on the agenda are held to be the central moral issues of society and basic to orthodox Christian belief. The Religious Right is a reaction to the revolutionary movements of the 1960s—the peace movement, the women's movement, the sexual revolution, and the civil rights movement. The perspectives of politicized fundamentalists differ radically from those of the Left and most often are their exact opposite. Right-wing extremism is identifiably religious; the left-wing has embraced more secular claims, that is, human rights. Right-wing complaints about secular humanism are usually little more than code language to condemn human rights concerns.

As in the radical Left, certain dogmas are set in concrete for the faithful on the radical Right. Any professor who dares to challenge the veracity or intellectual/Christian grounds of such commitments is thought guilty of violating fundamental confessional and denominational norms for employment. The issues are reasonably well known. A strong antiabortion posture is linked to a negative posture toward women's rights in general. Women are not to occupy positions of authority in church, the academy, or the world of business. Adamant opposition is expressed against those who are openly homosexual, claiming they are seeking special rights or privileges in society. Civil rights for African Americans are treated with benign neglect if not open resistance—both of which are ways of remaining aloof from if not hostile to the justice issues at stake.

Social goals associated with gender, race, or sexual orientation are condemned as threats to family, to children, to society, to God, and to God's truth. Efforts to limit academic freedom and basic civil liberties are based on a familiar argument: The truth is settled, ergo, there is no room for discussion. Since there is harm to be prevented—to children, marriages, families, and society—there can be no room for tolerating a dissenting point of view, according to the ultraconservatives. Indeed, toleration itself becomes a matter of moral turpitude.

The paranoid style that pervades fundamentalist Christian politics in our time builds upon the martyr stories of early Christianity. They see themselves as suffering for the faith, when in fact they are being criticized for their rigidity, if not stupidity, in defending the indefensible. Many see the style as well as the goals of New Right religion as a vulgarization and perversion of evangelical Christianity. William Jennings Bryan was a stalwart defender of the faith to those who construe evolutionary theory as the enemy of good faith and morals. But he was a caricature of Christian theology, making both himself and Christianity look ridiculous in the eyes of thoughtful people. But those who feel threatened are also dangerous to those they perceive as enemy.

Christians of the Religious Right are highly coercive in both ecclesiastical and social matters. For them, academic freedom, like reproductive freedom, is the enemy of faith and good morals. These are the people that would screw Thomas's tongue to the roof of his mouth for doubting that Jesus had actually been raised from the dead. They would do so claiming to do God a favor. Many Christians thank God for Thomas. He asked many of our questions for us, making the affirmations of faith more reasonable, even if not more rational. He also set a pattern of honest doubt in the context of faithful piety—a worthy model for the emulation of any Christian educational institution.

Academic Freedom and Reverent Doubt

Those religious educational institutions that embrace academic freedom believe there is a vital place for critical reflection on the affirmations of faith. Confessional circles need the skeptic in their midst. Those who challenge established opinion and shed the light of scholarly investigation are vital to the educational process. Southern Baptists both tolerated and celebrated Dale Moody for four decades as a professor of Christian theology at the Southern Baptist Theological Seminary in Louisville, Kentucky. He was a person of unquestioned integrity and a profound personal piety. He loved the Bible and could quote the New Testament in both Greek and English. But he questioned the meanings and applications, as well as the intent, of the (Baptist) doctrine of the security of the believer.[20] He was a Baptist with strong Wesleyan leanings on this point. Baptists who espoused liberty of conscience and freedom of conscientious thought felt there was ample room for Moody on the faculty of a Baptist seminary. Few, if any, of his students and certainly none of his fellow faculty were persuaded by his arguments. But they were pushed to study the Scriptures more carefully and articulate more clearly the biblical and theological bases for a traditional Baptist article of faith.

Or, where is the intolerable threat in Langdon Gilkey's confession that his life had disintegrated into "meaningless pieces" which left his "mind empty of relevant and credible concepts" as he contemplated a volume on divine providence.[21]

Or, was Carlyle Marney outside the faith when he confessed he found the very idea of resurrection difficult to believe? He believed it about twice a year, he said, once at Easter and again at the death of a friend.

Baptists have a habit of firing or forcing the termination of intellectuals who get too honest—who are too open to opinions not rooted in dogmatism or a false piety. Some beliefs seem supportable only by avoiding the tough questions of biblical religion and the complex issues of faithful action. Those who champion biblical authority will certainly find challenges or tests for certain tenets of the faith. Beliefs about cosmology, geology, and historical events important to religious beliefs are all challenged by scholarly studies in physics, history, archeology, and evolutionary biology. Evangelicals of the Right view the tools of "higher criticism" as the instruments of Satan designed to undermine faith in God.

Enlightenment Christians believe an educational institution without academic freedom is an oxymoron. They view the academy in the tradition of the skeptic of ancient Israel or the Socratic school of Athens. They are dedicated to the honest quest for insights beyond rigid tradition. They seek the truth beyond dogmatism and believe there is wisdom beyond pompous preachments. The task of the Christian university/seminary is construed as "faith seeking understanding" in the tradition of Augustine.

The struggle between dogma and reason is interminable—they are intrinsically oppositional. Any settled position in creed or doctrine is the subject of the intellectual question as to truth. The task of the Christian academy is not the articulation of truth as a set of final, settled propositions or beliefs; it is to nurture sufficient intellectual curiosity as to avoid creating religious robots—able to spew emphatic pronouncements but blind to their own prejudices and lack of insight as to maturity in faith or discernment. Their representation of Christianity has internal dissonance with biblical images of Christ. They make Christianity a poor messenger of the truth of God. Right-wing religion has as many critics who are concerned about the nature of Christian faith as those who oppose any form of religious devotion.

Those who support academic freedom believe that professors should be able to examine any assertion or explore any avenue of investigation into their historical or scientific bases. Whether Exodus or Resurrection, virgin birth or millennial expectations, the scholar is obliged to know what they do and do not mean—to sift the wheat from the chaff, to discover the truth beyond particular formulations. The aim is not to debunk theological beliefs but to clarify the meaning of faith and the nature of divine activity within history.

Truth, Freedom, and Personal Virtue

The university/seminary also has the task of nurturing character and virtue. Christian education is not a matter of dogmatic beliefs but is built upon models of human excellence. The Christian should be able to temper pride of intellect with wisdom and charity. Society longs for people of mature temperament. We need discerning intellects who envision life in holistic fashion; who are tolerant toward those different than themselves; and who exercise empathy toward the less fortunate. Tragically, these are characteristics often missing in contemporary models of religious or theological training.

Education in the tradition of the prophets emphasizes the justice requirements of love and mercy rather than the practices of sacred ritual. Someone needs to remind religious establishments that they tend to pervert Christian faith rather than maintaining its purity and efficacy. Christian piety encourages intellectual integrity as part of the educational task. There can be no maturity in the Christian life that excludes honest questions. Theologians should be seen as scholars who engage in reverent doubt. Every academic should be a "doubting Thomas"—faithful but curious. Questions help assure that faith is not simply a faith in faith or a hoping against hope, or a web of ideas composed of wishful thinking and daydreams. The task is to teach people how to think, not what to think. Both church and society need Christians who can think, and think as Christians.

Academic freedom begins by believing that there is no question we cannot ask, but knowing there are many questions we cannot answer. Believers live with mystery, if the God of Jesus Christ is worthy of worship at all. Divine reality cannot be reduced to simple syllogisms or any number of propositional truths. Many of our basic affirmations are themselves subject to examination. We need not fear asking the great questions, but fear those who are too certain of the answers. Christianity is not comprised of those with empty minds, misguided hearts, and unethical actions. Jesus emphatically called for us to "love God with all your heart, mind, soul and strength . . ." (Matt. 22:39).

Christianity is not a commitment to a belief in doctrines as an end in itself. Education should help save us from the piety that assumes "the more preposterous the belief, the more pious to believe." Those who advocate creationism as a credible scientific theory or biblical infallibility as acceptable on intellectual grounds need the debunking insights of the intellectual community. Such doctrines seem straight out of the world of *Alice in Wonderland*, who was asked to believe three amazing things before breakfast.

Christian education employs both left- and right-brain perceptions. Left lobe logic is necessary, but not sufficient to faith. The right sphere of the brain deals with poetry, images, and stories. Grace always transcends logic. Knowing God is a matter that involves more than logic or rationality. Christians insist that the intellect is insufficient either to discover or to experience God. Knowing God is not like knowing a mathematical formula or memorizing the catechism. Faith is a deep way of knowing. That is why the Bible challenges us to love God with our entire being—mind, strength, spirit, and soul.

ACADEMIC FREEDOM IN SOUTHERN BAPTIST SEMINARIES

The experience of Southern Baptist theological seminaries during the past decade has shown that ideological rigidity in the form of theological dogmatism and narrow moralism is the main threat to the maintenance of anything like academic freedom. The hostile takeover of the Southern Baptist Convention (SBC) by politicized fundamentalists has marked the end of what many regard as a glorious era in progressive theological education.[22]

Fundamentalists in the convention especially targeted seminaries in Wake Forest, North Carolina (Southeastern), Kansas City, Missouri (Midwestern), and Louisville, Kentucky (Southern),[23] and brought about sweeping changes. These seminaries had been deeply influenced by the Social Gospel movement and embraced historical-critical aproaches to biblical studies. They accepted many of the ideas of the Enlightenment, including academic freedom and openness in theological inquiry. It was Baptists nurtured in the tradition of Roger Williams and religious liberty who carefully nourished these seminaries to prominence. They were excellent seminaries when judged by almost any standard of academic excellence. They stood tall, not only among Baptists, but in the world of theological education. But their commitment to theological openness and academic excellence was especially offensive to the fundamentalists, who were determined to impose their own brand of coercive religion on the faculties and students of these schools.

The takeover was politically astute, swift by most measures, and certainly effective. Demonizing the opposition as "liberals" who did not believe the Bible, and claiming the necessity of believing the Bible to be "the infallible word of God," the fundamentalists succeeded beyond their wildest dreams. All Southern Baptist seminaries are now solidly under the leadership of dogmatic fundamentalists.

Threats to Academic Freedom

The greatest institutional enemy of academic freedom among Southern Baptists is an adversarial authority structure sympathetic to a dogmatic ideology. Administrative realities go beyond the president and executive staff of a given school, of course. The presidents of American Catholic universities voted unanimously against the power of the bishops to intervene in faculty appointments. But they lost to the larger realities of power within the Catholic heirarchy.

Southern Baptists have developed a similar extension of administrative power from the convention to its agencies and seminaries. They have ceased being a "sect" and have become a "church," to use the categories of Ernst Troeltsch.[24] Even the mysticism associated with experiential religion and the lordship of Christ has fallen prey to clerical and denominational authoritarianism in moral matters. The SBC increasingly centralizes authority, diminishing the traditional importance given to local church autonomy. Trustees are now appointed by SBC processes with the expectation/mandate that they will micromanage their respective institutions. The shift to ultraconservatism within the convention left seminary presidents like Randall Lolley, Milton Ferguson, and Roy Honeycutt under severe pressure to carry out the odious mandates of an oppositional Board of Trustees. Only ideologically/theologically compatible and fully cooperative administrators now serve the six seminaries.

The impact upon the educational enterprise has been dramatic and far-reaching. Direct interventions into classroom procedures were carried out at Southern, as were unilateral changes in seminary policies and procedures regarding faculty prerogatives and freedoms. Expectations regarding faculty compliance reach far beyond the campus. Faculty is expected either to adopt the social agenda of the Religious Right or cease speaking publicly on the side of the opposition. As indicated above, religious institutions are free to impose speech codes under the protection of separation of church and state. Freedom of conscience and freedom of speech have special protections where the religious life is concerned. For fundamentalists, this allows those in places of power to impose their views of conscientious convictions in theology and morals on all others, including professors. On the social and political scene, the Religious Right champions this strange (to Baptists) interpretation of religious liberty as the freedom of religious groups to impose their sectarian opinions on others. Fundamentalists seem to take a special delight in doing so.

Religious groups are now able to fire professors for reasons that seem good to them, and that without fear of legal intervention.[25] Russell Dilday, president at Southwestern Seminary in Fort Worth, was fired without warning. The announcement was made to him while trustees replaced the locks to his office doors. No reason was given for his sudden dismissal aside from the general accusation of "lack of cooperation." Apparently his refusal to withdraw the invitation to Keith Parks (former executive director of the Foreign Mission Board, SBC) to be the commencement speaker at the May graduation was reason enough. Parks had earlier been forced from his post and had aligned himself with the Cooperative Baptist Fellowship, a splinter group from the SBC.

There is, of course, a veritable arsenal of weapons available to antagonistic administrators to impose their will on faculty. Such procedures may have either the direct intention of or net effect of limiting academic freedom. Examples are not hard to find.

The AAUP's investigation of Bennington College in Vermont, for instance, concluded that the structure of the plan for reducing size of faculty was "merely a device to purge from the faculty individuals who for one reason or another were persona non grata to the administration or the board."[26] Neither presumptive tenure nor length of service appear to have had a role in designating faculty for termination. The manner in which the terminations were carried out was described as "disrespectful, petty, indeed vindictive and inhumane."[27]

All too typically, the system of rewards and penalties within an institution is based on perceived loyalties and lack of opposition to administrative policies. Virtually all those terminated at Bennington had opposed actions of the board or the president at one time or another. Faculty security was premised on submissiveness to administrative policies.

Needless to say, the full and unequivocal support of administration is indispensable to anything like academic freedom in the religious context. Since religious groups operate in their own sphere of academic pursuits and these are dynamically related to the larger sectarian enterprise, education is viewed as integral to the mission of the group. "Teaching," unfortunately, becomes a matter that has unsalutary associations with indoctrination.

The transition at Southern Baptist Seminary can be traced by summarizing the different styles under Presidents McCall and Honeycutt. President Duke K. McCall led the seminary during its zenith as an outstanding theological seminary. He enjoyed the strong support of a sympathetic and liberal Board of Trustees. But not all were friendly to faculty teachings. McCall's policy was to stand between faculty and trustees. His commitment to academic freedom with integrity was unquestioned, though he did not hesitate to raise questions about actions of faculty he thought imprudent. No member of faculty had the Abstract of Principles interpreted to or for him or her. It was not treated as a creed. All faculty were Baptists seeking to remain basically within the parameters of the confessional statement. The president allowed no direct interrogation of faculty persons by members of the board.

President Roy Honeycutt labored under harsh antiseminary attitudes within the convention. He was caught in the riptide of a convention rushing to the Right. He accommodated administrative policy to the new political realities. He attempted to maintain some semblance of institutional stability while everything was coming loose. He adopted an accommodationist strategy, thus facilitating the transition to fundamentalist domination and control. To his credit, he was not simply a hatchet man against the faculty. His efforts were apparently dominated by the desire to effect both his most facilitous retirement and a smooth transition in the midst of harsh realities. Faculty was and is divided on the question of whether his style of "resistance" was heroic enough. He was nonetheless successful in delaying the worst of fundamentalist inroads until his departure in 1993.

Honeycutt had implemented two policies that made faculty more vulnerable to trustee intimidation and intervention. One was to allow direct trustee contact with faculty. Faculty were put on their own to fend off attacks from angry trustees who were not open to scholarly argument. Trustee determination to remove troublesome faculty became an ominous and personal reality. The second policy (though unannounced and unwritten) reflected a politicized approach to dealing with professors who resisted the fundamentalist takeover or who were involved in controversy within the convention.

Dale Moody was the first to be sacrificed on such grounds. He was attracting too much attention to his belief about apostasy, which was contrary to an article in the Abstract of Principles. He conscientiously felt that the article dealing with biblical authority was in direct conflict with that article supporting the notion of the security of the believer. At a minimum, it was a topic worth discussion. But the politics of the convention created an atmosphere that was harshly critical of any professor who seemed out of step with the fundamentalist emphasis on doctrinal conformity. Moody had been raising the issue for four decades on the Louisville faculty. He had been Honeycutt's professor and had served on the search committee that brought Honeycutt to Southern as dean of theology. Moody had suddenly become expendable in the mind of his former student. Tragically, Moody's contract was terminated with the seminary after forty-three years on the faculty. He had become a political liability in the judgment of the seminary president.

Glenn Hinson, who had been critical of anti-Semitism among the fundamentalists, was vehemently and repeatedly attacked, ostensibly for having a low Christology. He avoided the prospect of coerced removal by resigning to join the faculty at Baptist Theological Seminary of Richmond in 1992. His resignation was a protest against the politics of imposed dogma and micromanaged academia.

I was attacked for my refusal to support a harsh antiabortion moral posture or to seek a constitutional ban on abortion. I found neither justifiable on biblical, theological, and moral grounds. The seminary attorney found no fault in my contractual obligations, including classroom performance and consistency with the Abstract. I was pressured by the Honeycutt administration to stop speaking publicly and by trustees to leave the seminary. Trustees argued that I was simply an employee of the SBC who should acquiesce and adopt resolutions on ethical issues such as abortion that had been passed by trustees and/or the convention.

I became the second to fall under the political ax. My fault was refusing to recant my pro-choice stance or to sacrifice my fundamental commitment to freedom of inquiry and speech. I violated no confessional commitment or contractual obligation, as the seminary attorney reminded trustees and administrators on three occasions. To the contrary, I acted consistent with the guidelines of the faculty-staff manual regarding academic freedom.[28] Even so, the options given to me were either to be silent or be "converted," that is, to champion the fundamentalist social causes, which I found intellectually barren and biblically problematic. I refused both options on grounds of conscientious conviction and academic integrity. Since I would not voluntarily remove myself from the faculty or accept the options presented, President Honeycutt agreed with trustees in a February 1992 memo that I should leave the seminary.

The strategy employed as a result of the adversarial line taken by trustees was to intimidate, insult, and publicly ridicule members of the faculty with whom they took exception. Yellow journalism (e.g., *The Southern Baptist Advocate*), the annual Pastor's Conference, and the annual convention were ready-made platforms for the villifying assaults of fundamentalists devoted to their own brand of zealous politics. There was little the administration could do or tried to do to provide a wall of protection between embattled faculty and determined trustees. From the time of the Peace Committee report in 1986 to the present, pressure from zealous trustees against nonconformist faculty has been persistent. That is in spite of numerous agreements along the way that seemed to signal détente.

Agreements between faculty and tustees amounted to little more than successive compromises by moderates who were rapidly conceding ground to aggressive and uncompromising fundamentalists. In 1990, trustees declared they would not revisit the faculty named in the Peace Committee report. But they did—several faculty remained on the hit list—including Hinson and myself. In 1991, a covenant was signed between faculty and trustees, ostensibly agreeing to the end of hostilities. A balance of evangelical/conservative faculty was to be achieved by faculty additions, and new faculty would have to subscribe to biblical infallibility. Old faculty would not be required to make new confessional statements. Nor was mention made about women in ministry, which has since come to be a litmus test for new faculty.

Trustees unhappy with the covenant openly flaunted its agreements. Molly Marshall was forced out in August 1994 in spite of her having passed the inquisitor's questions as to fidelity to the Abstract of Principles. She had the bad fortune of being a woman in the department of theology. Such a position of "authority" occupied by a woman was anathema to fundamentalists.

Faculty and staff at Southern Baptist Seminaries would find terrible irony in the statement by Edward Shils that:

> Boards of trustees have become more refined; they are not as puritanical and self-righteous as they used to be and they are not as arrogant; they no longer regard their trusteeship as a police function or as a moral custodianship of the institution which they must protect from political radicalism or sexual impropriety. Presidents . . . do not watch their academic staff so closely and distrustfully, and if they do, they are very reluctant to do anything which would cause the academics to complain against them.[29]

In other words, the situation at secular universities has gotten better that in Southern Baptist institutions has gotten worse. So much for the "evils" of secular humanism, or the virtue of the true believer!

Religion in the Totalitarian Mode

The problem of maintaining freedom, whether academic or social, is endemic to the totalitarian mindset characteristic of fundamentalist ideology. It is found both in politics and religion. The world has seen horrible examples in Nazism, fascism, and Communism, but such phenomena are not foreign to the democratic experience. Democratic societies allow certain totalitarian systems and ideologies to exist, if not flourish. Religion provides a special protective cover. We need only be reminded of Jonestown and Waco, or be aware of the excesses of fundamentalist religion whether in Christianity, Islam, Judaism, or Hinduism. The *Syllabus of Errors* once declared that error had no rights, thus setting the stage for the four hundred-year Inquisition. Religious wars are an inevitable and tragic outgrowth of either competing tyrannies, or battling against a totalitarianism which tolerates no dissent.

Fundamentalist theological perspectives have now been wed to a sociopolitical agenda which is being imposed upon faculty at all Southern Baptist Seminaries. The aim is to present a united front among all evangelical-controlled agencies in the "cultural war" envisioned by the right. Fundamentalists make no pretense about academic freedom. Coercion is a given; dissent is intolerable. A heavy-handed crusade has permanently altered the Southern Baptist religious landscape. It is an ends-justifies-the-means approach to internal quarrels and political battles. It is a no-holds-barred, winner-take-all ethic that has redefined what it means to be a Southern Baptist. One of the major casualties in this extremist assault has been the loss of commitment to theological excellence in seminary education.

The mentality, strategies, and goals of the Religious Right are identical with the characteristics and directions of Southern Baptist leadership. Those who like what has happened to Southern Baptists in recent years will love what the Christian Coalition has in mind for America.

Student Revisionism

Southern Seminary also has had its "brown shirts," as one Baptist editor called them. They are student vigilantes against professors who resist or challenge the fundamentalist agenda. They surreptitiously record lectures or other statements by professors to share with trustees, administrators, or other convention firebrands. Anonymous hate notes, the circulation of injurious rumors, or misrepresenting faculty perspectives in lectures are other strategies used against moderate faculty. They are also enemies of academic integrity, resisting any challenge to their "evangelical" commitments or assumptions.

Southern Seminary President Albert Mohler Jr., successor to Roy L. Honeycutt, had a group of students who reported to him regularly about things they heard professors say, whether in class or other contexts. Such students have for the past decade contributed to a hostile climate against moderate or targeted professors. They embrace the ethics of the unsigned letter and the anonymous, harassing telephone call. They see themselves as agents of revolutionary change for the good of the kingdom. They are not intellectually curious enough to examine the assumption or its consequences. They are energized—as were Hitler's Brown Shirts—by the triumphant march, the smell of victory. They seem to believe that they must destroy a great seminary in order to save it.

Administrative sanctions against professors who provoked the wrath of these students have had the effect of rewarding unethical behavior. It also had a dampening effect on open discussions or innovative teaching in the classroom. Professors adopted a type of lowest-common-denominator approach to teaching, since it is the academically and ethically challenged student that must be placated. The professor is held responsible for any student complaint or criticism. Such students demonstrate that they are not qualified for Christian ministry. Even so, the administration since 1990 refused to develop any means of holding students accountable for such harmful, unethical actions.

Needless to say, all this has created a negative atmosphere for teaching with integrity. Some topics, such as abortion and homosexuality, are not even discussed—not even in classes in which the topics are germane to the course, as in pastoral care and ethics. Professors tend not to stick their heads above the battlements. Some have even adopted approaches to biblical studies, doctrinal beliefs, and ethical issues they once found theologically problematic, morally repulsive, and intellectually barren. Accommodation is one way to relate to harsh political realities.

I can think of no worse environment in which to attempt to do theological education than what is now the case at Southern Baptist Seminary in Louisville. It has seriously deteriorated even since I left in July 1993. The sheer excitement for theological studies that once pervaded the campus has been replaced by a tangible depression. Professors once discussed their differences openly and heatedly—a debate could break out in the bookstore or the faculty lounge. No more. Direct confrontation by the president designed to intimidate faculty is reported to be a common occurrence. The seminary's rather generous statement of academic freedom is simply empty rhetoric, since it is flagrantly disregarded by administration and trustees. Fear of retaliation suppresses openness in the expression of personal or scholarly perspectives that differ from convention resolutions or administrative expectations. Faculty morale is rock bottom. Professors come to campus for their class and committee assignments and leave as soon as possible. It was once a place of comaraderie, friendliness, and community. It is now fragmented and dysfunctional.

Between 1985 and 1998, there has been a mass exodus (or a total turnover) of faculty of what was once called "the best kept secret in graduate theological education in America." Those who could—or must—have left the seminary. Those who remain do so with severe restrictions around what can be said in the classroom, in the public arena, or in published works. As one cartoon put it painfully, "Poor Carlton, he published and published and still perished!" Anything put in writing will be critically examined for its theological and political correctness.

Professors labor under a newly installed "gag rule"[30] designed to assure compliance even to the most egregious of administrative actions. Part of "the terms and conditions of employment," now includes the obligation "to support and relate constructively to the institution, its policies and administration." The rule is a direct assault on academic freedom. It forbids the use of "class time (or any other forum designated for instructional purposes) for the purpose of undermining or obstructing the policies of this institution."

A procedure has also been implemented giving the president unilateral power to impose sanctions upon faculty. They include demotion of a full rank (as from full to associate professor) with correlative salary reductions. The ultimate sanction remains that of immediate removal, of course. There is no longer any need to go through the expense and negative publicity of hearings.

THE FUTURE OF ACADEMIC FREEDOM

I am not optimistic that academic freedom will ever have much standing or solid support in a confessional tradition. As George Marsden admits, academic due process is often absent from "strongly religious" colleges and seminaries, and "dictatorial rule is particularly common."[31] The myth is too strong that only ultraconservative churches are growing, and the commitment to truth too weak to challenge the assumption.

What is surprising is not that there are objections to raising questions—the fearful, angry, and spiteful we have always with us. What is amazing, however, is that those who prefer ignorance to insight should be able to exercise such power over the educational enterprise. To do so, they must gain the acquiescence and cooperation of administrators who should know better, of faculty who prize income and security more than academic integrity, and of a constituency willing to opt for power rather than truth. What is at work is not the power of truth, but the truth of power.

If there is any hope for academic freedom it will come from professors who are determined not to sacrifice freedom for any mess of pottage—not even security. A significant part of our history and inspiration has been the tenacity of professors who persisted even under threats of arrest or death. There were those who went underground to resist Hitler. They sacrificed themselves for the sake of intellectual integrity in the face of tyranny. Baptists know the story of Roger Williams, who refused to teach the nonsense of orthodox theology and morals at Salem, Massachusetts. He fled to the wilderness, where he nearly died, rather than knuckle under to the clerics and politicians who conspired against both reason and good morals while accusing him of having neither.

Others can take away our freedom only if we allow them to do so. One should think that scholars would know that and be committed fervently to preserving their cherished freedoms, even if it requires learning the strategies of civil disobedience made so effective by Martin Luther King Jr. If we live by the integrity of our teaching, so we perish if freedom is absent.

The truth seems to be that professors have very modest commitments to academic freedom. That may be because they have never had a thought that would sufficiently provoke the anger of the establishment. Who needs freedom if our thoughts are so tame that they serve the interests of the powerful?

Professors in religious institutions are inclined to be submissive in the face of threat. Anything like concerted activity on behalf of a threatened colleague is rare. Indifference is a common reaction, especially when a colleague is sanctioned for views expressed outside the classroom or which are controversial in the political or social arena. The attitude that they are getting what they deserve is commonplace. No allowance is made for the fact that some teach in areas which can avoid controversial issues while others are unavoidably involved by the area of their expertise.

A minority see the issue, of course, and rage at the threats to or loss of academic freedom. They know the colleague is blameless, the victim of misguided trustees or conniving administrators. They recognize the process as blaming the victim. But they are usually too intimidated to complain publicly. Cowardice seems the best policy when the risks are so high. Some colleagues openly disassociate with those who are targeted by the thought police. Anyone causing commotion or attempting to establish a chapter of the AAUP is thought to be a traitor—inviting investigations that might shed an unfavorable light upon the entire enterprise.

By the time the truth that either we all enjoy freedom together or all perish together—or more likely, one by one over a period of several years—finally hits home, it is too late.

Faculty should know the truth embodied in Martin Niemoller's reflection:

They came for the trade unionists, but I was not a trade unionist, so I said nothing; They came for the for the Catholics, but I was not a Catholic, so I said nothing; Then they came for the Communists, and I was not a Communist, so I said nothing. Finally, they came for me, and by that time, there was no one left to speak up for me.

Edward Shils made a devastating indictment of academics in saying that "the academic profession—taken as a whole—... is not especially concerned with academic freedom. Only a small number of persons of high principle... were very concerned with it."[32] He even questions whether many who have invoked academic freedom when their jobs were threatened were deeply concerned about it in principle. Their interest in the topic is provoked by the instinct for self-preservation, he said.

Courage from Jefferson

Even so, I take courage from a recent foray into the writings of Thomas Jefferson, provoked by a vacation visit to Monticello. Jefferson, who was neither a Baptist nor even a Christian in the orthodox meaning of the term, was demonized by clergy for his lack of enthusiasm for metaphysical speculation. The Rev. Cotton Mather Smith of Sharon, Connecticut, accused him of obtaining his property by fraud and robbery, and of taking ten thousand pounds sterling as executor of an estate of a widow and fatherless children.[33] Other ministers accused him of atheism, which Jefferson regarded as calumny. He found it impossible, he said, to contradict all the lies propagated by clergy; while he responds to one, they publish twenty new ones.[34]

Jefferson criticized clergy efforts to use the special leverage of religion in order to gain advantage over all others in a passage that sounds terribly contemporary. Our own hope for the future may be presaged in Jefferson's observation that:

> The returning good sense of our country threatens abortion to their hopes, and they believe that any portion of power confided to me will be exerted in opposition to their schemes. And they believe rightly, for I have sworn upon the altar of God eternal hostility against every form of tyranny over the mind of man. But this is all they have to fear from me: and enough too in their opinion.[35]

The "tyranny over the mind of men" about which Jefferson spoke was religious demagoguery. It had the form of piety but carried the heavy stick of coercion and intolerance. Its preachments claimed the authority of God but attempted to control everyone's life in good Puritan fashion.

Jefferson unmasked the vested interests and narrow ideology of the false piety of his day. He accused it of going "backwards instead of forwards to look for improvement, to believe that government, religious morality, and every other science were in the highest perfection in ages of the darkest ignorance, and that nothing can ever be devised more perfect than what was established by our forefathers."[36]

CONCLUSION

If academic freedom is to be preserved at all it will be by people like Jefferson who take seriously the solemn obligation to pursue truth and expose falsehoods in a context of openness and free inquiry. It requires only a minimal awareness of history to recognize ancient tyrannies in contemporary disguise. Intolerance and heavy-handedness against dissenters is evidence enough to oppose it with all the intellectual and spiritual powers we can muster. Resistance entails significant risks. There is a long line of persons who have fallen or been wounded in the fray among Southern Baptists. But the effort is vital to God's movement that has never been furthered by coercion. God being our helper, academic freedom will not perish from the earth or among religious educational institutions. But it will take a determined courage and a willingness to develop and support structures to replace those lost to this latest wave of religious imperialism.

NOTES

1. W. Macneile Dixon, *The Human Situation* (New York: Oxford University Press, 1958), p. 65.
2. Richard Rorty, "Does Academic Freedom Have Philosophical Presuppositions?" *Academe* (November–December 1994): 52.
3. See Paul McMasters, "Free Speech versus Civil Discourse: Where Do We Go From Here?" *Academe* (January–February 1994): 8–13.
4. Edward Shils, "Do We Still Need Academic Freedom?" *American Scholar* (spring 1993): 189.
5. See John Stuart Mill, *On Liberty and Other Essays* (New York: Macmillan, 1926).
6. See Elizabeth Fox-Genovese, "Debating Political Correctness: A Kafkaesque Trap," *Academe* (May–June 1995): 8–15.
7. *Academe* (July–August 1992): 30.
8. Ibid., p. 31.
9. Ibid., p. 30.

10. Thomas Jefferson, *Jefferson Himself*, ed. Bernard Mayo (Charlottesville: University Press of Virginia, 1942).

11. Eberhard and Renate Bethge, eds., *Last Letters of Resistance*, trans. Dennis Slabaugh. (Philadelphia: Westminster, 1986), pp. 106 f.

12. Karen Lebacqz, *Professional Ethics: Power and Paradox* (Nashville: Abingdon, 1985), pp. 110 f.

13. *Academe* (March–April 1995): 7.

14. Shils, "Do We Still Need Academic Freedom?" p. 193. See also Committee A on Academic Freedom and Tenure, "On Freedom of Expression and Campus Speech Codes," *Academe* (July–August 1992).

15. See Thomas C. Oden and Lewis S. Mudge, "Can we Talk About Heresy?" *Christian Century*, April 12, 1995, pp. 390–403; Roger E. Olson et al., "The Evangelical Mind," *Christian Century*, May 3, 1995; and Mark R. Schwehn, "Christianity and Academic Soul-Searching," *Christian Century*, March 15, 1995, pp. 292–95.

16. Carles E. Curran et al., "'Ex corde ecclesiae' and its Ordinances: Is This Any Way to Run a University or a Church?" *Commonweal*, November 19, 1993, pp. 14 f.

17. Ibid., p. 14.

18. Curran is now Elizabeth Scurlock Professor of Human Values at Southern Methodist University.

19. Mark R. Schwehn, "Christianity and Academic Soul-Searching," *Christian Century*, March 15, 1995, p. 294.

20. See Dale Moody, *The Word of Truth* (Grand Rapids, Mich.: Wm. B. Eerdmans, 1981), pp. 110–20.

21. Langdon Gilkey, *Reaping the Whirlwind* (New York: Seabury Press, 1976), p. vii.

22. See Paul D. Simmons, "The Debusman Firing: The Politics of Silencing the Enemy," *Baptists Today*, May 21, 1998, pp. 18–19; and "Breaking Ranks," *Christian Century*, February 4–11, 1998, pp. 100–101.

23. To a lesser extent, Southwestern Baptist Seminary in Fort Worth, Texas, also came under attack by the fundamentalist extremists.

24. Ernst Troeltsch, *The Social Teachings of the Christian Churches*, vol. 1, trans. Olive Wyon (New York: Harper and Brothers, 1960), pp. 331 ff.

25. See *Joseph P. Lewis; Julia A. Lewis v. Seventh-day Adventists*, U.S. Appeals, 6th Circuit, 1992. The Court concluded that "the First Amendment bars civil courts from reviewing decisions of religious judicatory bodies relating to the employment of clergy. Even when, as here, the plaintiff alleges that the religious tribunal's decision was based on a misapplication of its own procedures and laws, the civil courts may not intervene."

26. *Academe* (March–April 1995): 101.

27. Ibid.

28. See *Faculty-Staff Manual*, The Southern Baptist Theological Seminary, Louisville, Kentucky, sec. E-16. 2. "So long as the professor remains within the accepted charter and confessional basis of this seminary he or she shall be free

to teach, carry on research, and to publish, subject to the adequate performance of academic duties as agreed upon with the school. 3. . . . each professor shall have the freedom in the classroom to discuss the subject in which he or she has competence and may claim to be a specialist without harassment or limitations."

29. Shils, "Do We Still Need Academic Freedom?" p. 196.

30. *Faculty-Staff Manual*, April 1995 Amendment, Sec. E-194.

31. George Marsden, *The Soul of the American University: From Protestant Establishment to Established Non-Belief* (New York: Oxford University Press, 1994); cited in Schwen, "Christian and Academic Soul-Searching," p. 293.

32. Shils, "Do We Still Need Academic Freedom?" p. 206.

33. Jefferson, *Jefferson Himself*, p. 210.

34. Ibid., p. 211.

35. Ibid., p. 210.

36. Ibid., p. 212.

CHAPTER 10

TRUTH AGAINST FREEDOM
Bernard C. Farr

The Bible relates truth to freedom. As Jesus put it, "the truth shall make you free" (John 8:32). The same claim is often taken to underlie the purposes of modern education, Western democracies, scientific method, and personal fulfillment. I examine here the contrary claim that "the pursuit of truth is the main threat to academic freedom." In the course of the discussion, I use the terms "fundamentalism" and "fundamentalist" and am aware that these terms can produce mind-blocking reactions on the part of hearers. Recently, a Muslim academic told me that he enjoyed witnessing the shocked reaction caused in Muslim circles by introducing himself as a fundamentalist. A Christian academic similarly tells me that fundamentalists should be more honest and introduce themselves as extremists or even as bigots. There is, however, a useful place for the term "fundamentalist" in respect of epistemological procedure, and where I use it in this paper it is meant in this epistemological sense, as I hope will become apparent.

THE PURSUIT OF TRUTH: THE TOTALIZING IMPERATIVE OF ALL FUNDAMENTALISMS

The pursuit of truth has been taken by many to be the defining characteristic of academic life. It has been further assumed that a consequence of the pursuit of truth is the liberation of both individuals and societies. Liberal theories of education and critical theories in science, politics, and the arts is liberation through self-fulfillment for the individual and through human fulfillment for societies. Fulfillment for both the individual and the group is attained, it is claimed, through the acquiring of the truth about the nature of the self and the ideal form of society, both being understood in relation to their physical setting in an ordered and truth-giving universe. To be "educated" is to know the truth, to be "scientific" is to discover the truth, to be "political" is to incorporate the truth, and to be "artistic" is to express the truth. And intentionally, through each mode, one is to be free.

"Truth," however, is (as truth) not neutral, is not flexible, is not deniable, is not to be gainsaid. It is, so to speak, not just a theory of everything—everything scientific, everything religious, everything religious, everything human, but the ground of everything. This brings me to raise the issue of fundamentalism in relation to truth and freedom, since fundamentalism in whatever field of human thought is the claim to unique access to the ground of truth, and is thus the endgame of the pursuit of truth.

Fundamentalism, then, is an all-or-nothing matter in relation to truth. One reason for this is that the fundamentalist—whether a religious fundamentalist, or a scientific fundamentalist, or a humanist fundamentalist, or any other kind of fundamentalist—claims to have unique access not only to the grounds for establishing truth but also to the truth which is establishable on those grounds. Having both the grounds of truth and the actual truth in his or her possession, the fundamentalist is able to adopt a singular and consistent approach to life which is designed to remove ambiguity and doubt. This is the case whether the fundamentalist is concerned with the nature and source of authority, the role of reason, the place of the emotions, the grounds of moral action, or the significance of the evidence of the senses. There is an inherent inevitability, therefore, within any particular fundamentalism, since it regards truth as being uniquely and solely accessible within its truth claims and on its truth grounds, for that fundamentalism to totalize its claims to truth. This inevitability I call the "totalizing imperative" of fundamentalism and it has very great significance for the debate about academic freedom.

Fundamentalism, with its totalizing imperative, is a particular temptation for religious people. One reason for this particular temptation may have to do with the psychological profile of any given population, since within any given population there will be a number of people, and sometimes a large number of people, who wish to live their lives free from doubt and ambiguity. Such certitude seekers may well be disproportionately attracted into those religious communities which they perceive as able to remove doubt and ambiguity from their lives, that is, those fundamentalist religious communities and closed religious orders which claim that their truth will make their members free.[1] This situation would be likely to be the case most especially in periods of ideological contestation within a society, since in such periods each individual is called on to make potentially painful choices between the competing belief systems available in that society. This state of affairs is in fact a characteristic of post-Enlightenment Western societies. It is particularly true of the Anglo-Saxon Protestant constituency in the United States and in the British Commonwealth of Nations, where the claims to be in possession of truth guaranteed by divine revelation are particularly strong.[2]

There are features of *all* religious communities, however (not only Protestant and not only Christian), which permit and encourage the development of fundamentalist tendencies within those communities. These features are connected with the peculiar nature of the ontological, epistemological, axiological, and existential claims made by religions as such, even if those religions are not explicitly fundamentalist in a narrower sense. Many religious people are religious, that is to say, because religions by their nature make truth claims which are held to be (a) ultimate, in that they transcend the world of flux and impermanence, (b) universal, in that they are true for all people at all times and in all places, (c) absolute, in that they are based in the will or mind or purposes of the divine and are thus noncontextual and nonrelative, but (d) particular, in that the ultimate, universal, and absolute truth is stateable as a specific set of beliefs, or doctrines.

Fundamentalism within religious communities, when it emerges, does so because believers have collapsed the distinction between knowing (reason) and believing (faith). Belief for the fundamentalist *is* knowledge, so long as it is *true* belief. A belief is known by a fundamentalist to be a true belief because it is revealed knowledge. It is not the case, therefore, as is sometimes suggested, that the Protestant fundamentalist's argument is circular when the claim is made that knowledge lies in the inerrancy of scripture. For example, it is argued by opponents of fundamentalism that the much-quoted 2 Tim. 3:16 ("All scripture is given by God . . .") cannot, as Scripture, validate the inerrancy of Scripture except by circularity of argument. The point is simply that, for the Protestant fundamentalist, since there is no gap between faith and knowledge, there is no possibility of circularity of argument in regard to religious truth claims.[3] The fundamentalist's argument concerning the inerrancy of Scripture, as with all other claims known to be true, serves, therefore, as a good example of the totalizing imperative (the "all-or-nothing" characteristic) of fundamentalism.

This collapse by the fundamentalist of the gap between faith and knowledge raises particular questions about how post-Enlightenment fundamentalists respond to one of the great achievements of European thought in the nineteenth century, namely, historical self-consciousness. The displacement of the ontological question of the pre-Enlightenment, "Where did that come from?" by the question "How did we get this way?" marks the shift from a search for unchanging principles and structures of reality to a search for the underlying processes of change.[4] The difficulty post-Enlightenment Christian fundamentalists have in relating their commitment to absolute truth to post-Enlightenment sensitivity to the philosophical and theological importance of historical processes is reflected in the battlegrounds on which they have chosen to fight their case. These are typically:

- The Bible: Against the relativizing implications of the historical critical method, conservatives in the nineteenth century and fundamentalists in the twentieth continued to claim that the Bible is the revealed word of God and as such is both the ground of absolute truth and the source of actual absolute truths. It transcends all historical contexts. It is suprahistorical. It is the truth once and for all revealed to the saints. It is the authority, therefore, on which basis absolute historical statements can be made.

- Religion: Against the relativizing implications of the "history of religions" school, in which the beliefs of the Bible were claimed to be related to other religions both primitive and modern, conservatives in the nineteenth century and fundamentalists in the twentieth continued to claim that Christianity is unique and uniquely true. One absolute source of religious truth, Christianity, is available.

- Human Nature: Against what they saw as the relativizing implications of the human sciences, especially as represented by the promoters of the theory of evolution, conservatives in the nineteenth century and fundamentalists in the twentieth continued to claim that human nature is fundamentally unique and especially to link this claim to the incarnation (in which human nature was shown in its fullness). There is a qualitative difference for them between the animal and the human kingdoms. The human condition alone is the arena of God's salvific work.

- Jesus Christ: While having a basic interest in the use of archaeology and historical inquiry in relation to the life of Jesus, conservatives in the nineteenth century and fundamentalists in the twentieth continued to claim that neither the quest for the historical Jesus nor the theological response to its failure, which focused on the Christ of faith as alone sufficient for belief, were adequate to the person and work of Jesus Christ. Jesus Christ, as the incarnation and thus the revelation of God, is immediately accessible to the believer either in the Bible or through the work of the Holy Spirit. Neither history nor theology can reduce this immediacy of knowledge of God through Christ. The role of theology is to expound the truth revealed in Jesus Christ, to elucidate its rational grounds and to describe its historical realization.

An excellent illustration of the totalizing characteristic of post-Enlightenment Christian fundamentalism as just described can be found in the four volumes of Carl Henry's *God, Revelation and Authority*. In this massive work he surveys and discusses the claims of science, philosophy, culture, and religion with a view to subordinating them to his understanding of the intelligible divine Christian revelation given in nature and history and recorded in Scripture. Central to his wide-ranging review of intuition, experience, reason, materialism, secularism, existentialism, science, and philosophy lay an all-or-nothing view of theology:

> Theology, we shall insist, sets out not simply with God as a speculative presupposition but with God known in his revelation. But the appeal to God and to revelation cannot stand alone, if it is to be significant; it must embrace also some agreement on rational methods of enquiry, ways of argument and criteria for verification. For the critical question today is not simply, "What are the data of theology?" but "How does one proceed from these data conclusions that commend themselves to rational reflection?" The fundamental issue remains the issue of truth, the truth of theological assertions. No work of theology will be worth its weight if that fundamental issue is obscured. Durable theology must revive and preserve the distinction between true and false religion, a distinction long obscured by neo-Protestant theologians. Either the religion of Jesus Christ is true religion or it is not worth bothering about. . . .[5]

With these claims about the "Truth" in mind (and the implications they have for academic freedom), I now examine the deeper roots of Christian fundamentalism in western European culture.

THE ROOTS OF THE TOTALIZING IMPERATIVE IN FUNDAMENTALISM: POST-ENLIGHTENMENT EUROPEAN THOUGHT

The totalizing imperative of fundamentalism is not, I now argue, restricted to religious communities, but has been an underlying feature of the *general* development of the post-Enlightenment European mind. With the breakdown of the analogical and symbolic Christian apprehension and comprehension of nature, society, history, and metaphysics which held together the pre-Enlightenment worldview, the post-Enlightenment mind sought for new grounds on which to construct a worldview—and did so in areas quite apart from religion.

The resulting shape of thought is often represented in academic circles as critical, liberal, open, and freethinking and as the basis of academic freedom. This is not, however, the case. In the post-Enlightenment search for new and different epistemological grounds for understanding reality, it came about that instead of the "parts" of knowledge being conceived of and gaining their meaning from the "whole" (as had been the case in the pre-Enlightenment world) the post-Enlightenment mind looked for its account of the "whole" in terms of the nature of the "parts." Thus, pre-Enlightenment, the "reason," the "emotions," the "will," the "senses," were, taken together, used as means through which a comprehensive account of the whole could be attained whereas, for post-Enlightenment thought, each was seen as on its own a possible ground for a full account of reality. In this new movement of thought in which the whole is only (and exclusively) comprehensible through the part (a movement of thought now often misleadingly termed "reductionism"), there is embedded the totalizing imperative which is a key characteristic of any fundamentalism. In science, politics, the arts, philosophy, and many other areas of intellectual life there arose as a consequence a positivist stance to the knowledge which was claimed as true, together with a narrowed view of the range of academic freedom to be allowed.[6]

Thus, post-Enlightenment Europe saw the emergence of a wide range of competing epistemologies, each claiming to provide a new and exclusive ground for indubitable apprehension of reality. To survey the emergence of post-Enlightenment Protestant Europe is to see rationalists, empiricists, moralists, historians, scientists, biblical scholars, existentialists, romantics, theologians, and others claiming unique access both to the grounds for establishing truth and also to the truth which is establishable on those grounds, and each presenting his own claims to the exclusion of the legitimacy of the claims of all others.[7]

Some implications of this state of affairs have been pointed out by Leslie Newbigin, who has commented that any attempt to affirm and defend the Christian faith within the modern scientific world view has necessarily to answer the question the Enlightenment put to tradition and the authority of tradition.[8] He notes with approval the point made by Peter Berger[9] that in post-Enlightenment society we are all required to be heretics since we are all called to think for ourselves and to test everything in the light of reason and conscience and to dare to question even the most hallowed traditions. The question for Christians who appeal to the authority of Scripture or of the church, therefore, says Newbigin, is to determine how, in this situation, they can affirm their statements as public, factual, and objective truth. This question is overwhelmingly the question for the fundamentalist Christian since, as has been seen from the view of theology taken by Carl Henry, the modern fundamentalist needs to come to terms with the implications of the whole post-Enlightenment project of thought.

I now argue that the post-Enlightenment project of thought actually shows the essential totalizing imperative of fundamentalism and that, contrary to expectation, there is thus a common ground between post-Enlightenment and fundamentalist epistemological procedures. To make this case, I comment on four post-Enlightenment challenges to pre-Enlightenment patterns of thought, based as the latter were on tradition and authority. These four challenges are:

- the post-Enlightenment challenge to tradition and authority based on "reason";
- the post-Enlightenment challenge to tradition and authority based on the "senses";
- the post-Enlightenment challenge to tradition and authority based on the "feelings"; and
- the post-Enlightenment challenge to tradition and authority based on "moral action."

I find within each of these the same totalizing imperative, the same "quest for certainty" and the same threat to academic freedom which is so characteristic of religious fundamentalism as described above.

Post-Enlightenment Rationalism as a Totalizing Imperative

For most of European history it was thought that all knowledge was necessarily unitary and that reason, experience, feeling, and action were each aspects of this essentially unitary human knowledge. It has been suggested by Hannah Arendt that it was the invention of the telescope that led to the collapse of this unitary view, since its use occasioned an epistemological crisis.[10] Things as they appeared through the telescope were not as they had been supposed to be and this discovery led to a persistent epistemological suspicion which undermined confidence in all aspects of epistemological certainty.

The work of Descartes, Arendt suggests, was a major response to this new and all-embracing epistemological anxiety. He sought, solely within the powers of reason, to show that there are indeed, contrary to the uncertain evidence of the senses, indubitable truths. These trustworthy truths are to be found in the clear and distinct ideas of reason, albeit that the guarantee of their indubitability lay in the veracity of God.

The totalizing imperative of rationalism is thus made clear.[11] It is an all-or-nothing matter. Reason alone is the ground of certainty within human knowledge. This Cartesian claim was, however, developed by Kant in an even more thorough manner when it became apparent, in the thought of John Locke and David Hume, that Cartesian rationalism was also open to a basic skepticism. For Kant, the certainties known to reason are constituted by nothing other than the orderly and rational structure of the mind itself. Thus, neither the phenomenal world, nor guidance for living, nor the nature of ultimate reality have any certainty beyond that certainty which is a requirement of self-understanding. The senses, the emotions, and moral action are thereby brought within the totalizing dominance of the nature of human reason.

Post-Enlightenment Empiricism as a Totalizing Imperative

For the post-Enlightenment empiricist, sense observation is the source of all truth and knowledge.[12] Within this totalizing view of the epistemological role of the senses, reason has a variety of particular functions, one of which is to relate together sense perceptions in an orderly manner. Truth itself, however, does not derive from reason but from experience. Rational deductions relate to experiences available to all people and are based on experimental validation for confirmation. In contradistinction to the fact that sense experience is universal and basic, hypotheses and rational explanations are tentative. There are no indubitable and comprehensive metaphysical truths. Knowledge begins in the senses, cannot outrun the senses, and is essential to the establishment of truth.

The implications of this totalization of the epistemological role of the senses in human knowledge has been differently assessed. David

Hume and Alfred Ayer, for example, both thought that one result was that theological beliefs generally are unsustainable as knowledge since they cannot be shown to be based on perceptual evidence.[13] They are, as Ayer put it, "nonsensical." Furthermore, the totalizing significance of the empiricist case is of particular significance for Christian theology in the distinction the empiricist draws between analytic statements (which are necessarily true but do not have empirical reference) and synthetic statements (which have empirical reference but are always conditional). Specifically, this distinction applies to the very basis of Christian belief since Christians claim that God not only exists but necessarily exists and exists necessarily. The Christian claims are, however, for the empiricist simply confused, since necessity is either practical in nature in a way which the theistic believer does not wish to apply to God or is a characteristic only of certain nonempirical (logical) statements. Thus empiricism, in offering the senses as the ground for epistemology, eliminates the gap between the "method" for knowing and the nature of what is thereby knowable. In one form or another this empiricist analysis has become the basis of modern scientific thought and practice, and it is not uncommon to hear the totalizing imperative of empiricism being expounded in the accounts offered by scientists of the nature and practice of science. For the empiricist, "fact" always has a positivist connotation.

The Feelings as a Totalizing Imperative in the Post-Enlightenment Period

Friedrich Schleiermacher, on the other hand, by widening the definition of empiricism to include the feelings, claimed that the sense of the presence of God in inner spiritual experience is a universal aspect of human experience.[14] It is therefore open to any and every human being to realize the presence of God within himself by correctly comprehending the ultimate significance of the sense of absolute dependence. This version of the totalizing imperative is radical indeed in its claim that piety is neither "a knowing nor a doing" but "a modification of feeling, or of immediate consciousness." Unlike the rationalists and the empiricists, therefore, Schleiermacher brings "metaphysics" within the realm of "physics" through the method of empirical introspection. Not only is this method available to everyone, it is able to attain to knowledge of the infinite and the ultimate by direct acquaintance with the infinite and the ultimate through contemplation. This last comment, however, needs qualification. While there can be no doubt for Schleiermacher about the reality, through the immediate consciousness, of the immediate existence of all finite things in and through the infinite and of all temporal things in and through the eternal, there remains the possibility of ambiguity. The empirical method, whether in the narrower version to be fond in Hume and Ayer or in the wider introspective version as offered by Schleiermacher, is essentially cognitively tentative in character even when existentially certain. Even for Schleiermacher, the concept of God is permanently open to revision in the light of continuing human experience.[15] But it remains the case that for Schleiermacher his empirical/introspective method drives out all other methods. God is known through and only through the inner "senses" experienced as emotions.

A different version of the absolutization of feelings within the development of post-Enlightenment epistemology can be found in the religious empiricism of the emotions presented by Rudolph Otto.[16] Otto in fact represents a boundary case with regard to the possibilities of post-Enlightenment positivisms, and of their attempts to move through numerous narrow doors to a totality of view, since his claim that human beings possess a sixth sense of "divination" marks out the limits of possible epistemological development. The "fear" and the "dread," the "fascination" and the "attraction" which always accompany the sensing of the holy absolutize both the grounds of all knowledge and the content of all that can be known, since Otto's account is not religious per se but claims that the dimension of the religious is always a possible, even if unrealized, factor of all experience.[17] When the "holy" is divined through the mundane and the common, there is no longer any possibility of doubt or ambiguity, the only issue is whether to go forward or to retreat.

Morality as a Totalizing Imperative in the Post-Enlightenment Period

My fourth example of the totalizing imperative in post-Enlightenment thought is the work of Immanuel Kant on the significance for epistemology of the fact and nature of human moral action. His account of practical reason (morality) as characterized by universal unconditionality is clearly a strong example of the totalizing imperative. We are, as human beings, aware of the absolute difference between the demands of the categorical imperative, which constitutes morality, from those of hypothetical imperatives, which are often mistaken for morality. The highest knowledge open to human beings, the knowledge which transcends the world of phenomena (bound as it is within the categorical features of the human mind) concerns the soul, free will, and God. But none of these is knowable in itself; they are, however, together the necessary postulates of human reason. They possess a certainty, therefore, which is of an absolute kind and which is the basis of the categorical imperative, the absolute imperative of the "ought." Not to feel the force of this imperative is not to be human. It is an all-or-nothing feature of being human. It is fundamental.

CHRISTIAN FUNDAMENTALIST RESPONSES TO POST-ENLIGHTENMENT EPISTEMOLOGIES

In the light of the above examples of the fragmentation of the grounds of truth and the associated fragmentation of the contents of knowledge in post-Enlightenment Europe, I now discuss the nature of the three options open to the Christian fundamentalist who wishes to attain certainty and drive out doubt and ambiguity.

In response to the Enlightenment rejection of authority and tradition, the Christian fundamentalist could either (a) seek a further particular ground for truth, (b) accept one or more of the grounds for truth which had emerged in the post-Enlightenment debate, or (c) reject the post-Enlightenment debate and adopt a fideistic approach to religious truth.

In fact, options (a) and (c) have been commonly run together by those who set out to adopt either (a) or (c) exclusively. Thus, those Christian fundamentalists who wished to follow the first option and sought a further ground for truth (for example, knowledge is grounded in acts of God in history) claimed that this ground was inerrant revelation.

However, this choice of option (a) cannot in fact be made on its own since inerrant revelation can only be a matter of belief (faith) and not of experimental knowledge; even if the text were entirely demonstrable as accurate, this could only be in relation to matters of this world. No claim to divine truth, therefore, can be made except as an act and test of faith (fideism), which is the point of option (c). Similarly, those Christian fundamentalists who sought to follow option (c) and rejected all post-Enlightenment grounds as suitable for knowledge of God could not deliver their case without also involving option (a). Since faith must be the sole ground for believing that any claimed knowledge of God comes from God, the Christian fundamentalists were thus in fact offering a further ground for religious truth beyond those offered by post-Enlightenment thinkers; they were also in fact involved in option (a). It turns out to be the case, therefore, that both options (a) and (c) involve the Christian fundamentalist in the "fideistic turn." To this extent, both these options are a reaction to, rather than an acceptance of, the essential nature of the post-Enlightenment project of thought.

For those Christian fundamentalists, then, who were happy with neither option (a) nor option (c), the totalizing imperative in fundamentalism did not lead to accepting any *one* of the post-Enlightenment epistemological grounds but to the incorporation of *all* of them within their religious epistemology. Thus, the post-Enlightenment Anglo-Saxon Protestant fundamentalist will typically coalesce the role of reason, the senses, the emotions, and the moral order into a four-sided unified account of truth. The world perceived by the senses and apprehended by reason, and which is the arena for the experience of human emotions and the achievement of a moral life is, for the Christian fundamentalist, necessarily subject to a single explanatory scheme of thought, since everything comes from the one God. This unitary scheme of thought or totalizing rationality is true insofar, and only insofar, as it accords with the revealed mind of God who alone is the ground and source of all truth. The world that was fragmented by the post-Enlightenment mind is therefore reunited by the Protestant fundamentalist. This reunification is not, however, as in the pre-Enlightenment, on the basis of an analogical and symbolic rationality, but on the basis of the range of epistemologies which emerged in the post-Enlightenment period. To be a Christian fundamentalist is, therefore, to be a comprehensive positivist with regard to the senses, to reason, to the emotions, and to the moral life since truth revealed by the one God cannot be merely relative. To be in possession of the truth, to know the mind of God, is to be in possession of positive facts that the Christian mind knows with regard to these four grounds of truth which had been rent asunder by post-Enlightenment Protestant Europe.

Alternatively, the fundamentalist may hold, fideistically, to a pre-Enlightenment frame of thought based on tradition and authority—though for some fundamentalists the totalizing imperative of the post-Enlightenment experience requires the radicalization of this choice, with the result that authority alone (and not tradition) is the ground of truth and the source of its contents. Whether this authority is the Bible, the Holy Spirit, or a modern leader are but internal variants of the same "all-or-nothing" feature of European Protestant fundamentalism.

Fundamentalist and Modernist Orientations to Truth and Freedom

"Modernity,"[18] the historical period in which we now live, is a form of life characterized by the emergence of new social structures which substantially modify the conditions of human existence. In its *outward* aspect modernity appears as the modern city, the multinational corporation, and the mass media, and results in rapidly changing patterns of social structures such as marriage and the family.[19] Modernity derives both its possibility and its features from major historical movements such as the post-Enlightenment project of thought and the Industrial Revolution, and also from the accumulation of scientific knowledge, the globalization of rapid information exchange, and the emergence of sophisticated technologies.

It is more difficult to identify the *inward* aspects of modernity which underpin the outer aspects just described. John Hull, however, has identified the essential features of modernity as they enter into ideological formation as being "bureaucracy," "rationality," "individualism," "futurity," "liberation," "plurality," and "knowledge."[20] He also argues that these seven features of modernity not only have substantial implications for Christian belief in general but have drawn forth a specific reaction from

> ... those kinds of Christian mentalities which have been invaded so thoroughly by the assumptions of positivistic scientific technology that Christianity itself can only be thought credible if it can compete successfully within the same limitation of knowledge. Christian faith and positivistic science thus become like-minded rivals, competitors within the same terms of reference. So we have a Christian faith in which the irrational, the poetic, the mythic and the imaginative are rejected in favour of a Christianity of solid historical and scientific evidence. This has resulted in an appalling poverty of Christian exploration and creativity in those parts of the world which have been affected by this knowledge bias. A one-dimensional Bible mirrored upon a one-dimensional science becomes the authority for a one-dimensional Christian faith ... the many-sided nature of the Christian faith itself is the most powerful resource for the regeneration of a wider, more complex and more heuristic view of the nature of human knowledge, a view which will contribute increasingly towards the liberation not only of faith but of science itself.

The links Hull makes between this form of Christian positivist mentality and positivist modernism parallel the links I hade above between Christian fundamentalism and post-Enlightenment thought.[21] The reason, I suggest, for the parallelism of this analysis is that modernism is the persistent application through economic, social, and cultural dimensions of existence of the "totalizing imperative" I have identified as a key characteristic of post-Enlightenment thought. In the light of that analysis, it is not surprising, therefore, that when fundamentalist Christians in the West embrace the "modernist" approach to ordering their affairs they also exhibit the same "modernist" features in their approach to religious practice. Consider as an example the biblical fundamentalists' approach to "mission." Mass evangelism through crusades, televangelism, and other forms of mass communication (which are so characteristic of current mission practice by Western fundamentalists) and the use of computers for databases to facilitate direct mailing of the Christian "product" to the religious marketplace, are the end products of the same modernist, positivist ideological commitment by fundamentalists which characterizes secular mass-marketing and mass-communication by the business and cultural sectors of modern society. The technological and information revolutions are embraced as much by the religious fundamentalist as by the most materialist modernist because they have both embraced the view of society as being the theatre of applied reason (technology)—as that applies not just to biblical fundamentalists, but to many other variants also, as American TV viewers will know.

But the analysis of modernity by John Hull typifies only one kind of response to "modernity," namely, that of "modernism," that is to say, that modernism that embraces and rejoices in the possibilities offered by modernity and regards its ideological features of bureaucracy, rationality, individualism, futurity, liberation, plurality, and knowledge as the hallmarks of "humankind-come-of-age." There is a polar opposite response, however, to modernity which would apply negative descriptions to it and which has attracted the collective description of "postmodernism." To the postmodernist, the economic, social, and cultural condition of modern Western peoples is seen as (among other negative epithets) materialist, consumerist, populist, collectivist, and inauthentic. The first matter of importance, says the postmodernist, is to understand the true nature of the postmodern condition; the second matter of importance is to decide how to respond to the modern condition in ways that fully represent the authenticity of the "stand-alone" human being.

The question of postmodernism is, then, prima facie a very different issue for the religious fundamentalist than is the issue of modernism. The current problem for the Christian fundamentalist, specifically, is whether to join with the modernist in embracing the modern condition as a sign of progress or, alternatively, to side with the postmodernist in seeing the modernist understanding of the human condition as being fundamentally flawed. For the fundamentalist to make the former response is to opt for the power of human reason to control all aspects of modern life, but to adopt the latter response is to reject the power of reason and seek some other ground for understanding the human condition, and what that other ground is I address in the next section. Either way, there are substantial implications for academic freedom.

Postmodernist Orientations to Truth and Freedom

"Postmodernism"[22] was a term first applied to discussions of poetry and architecture in the 1940s and 1950s, but was quickly extended to other art forms which shared a common criticism of modernism. Modernism was criticized by postmodernists for (a) emphasising the role of transcendent reason in aesthetics and (b) for its separation of art from history and mass culture. In contrast, postmodernists encouraged an eclectic, antielitist emphasis on sensuous immediacy and performance. This they saw as arising through either (a) existential spontaneity, with an associated ontological pluralization through a focus on the processes or art or (b) narrative disruption, with a radical epistemology based on indeterminacy and multiperspectivism.

By the 1970s, however, the term "postmodernism" had also come to represent a comprehensive sociocultural paradigm evident in Western societies where the combination of mass consumption, electronic reproduction, eclecticism of taste, and informational and discursive proliferation had led to the realization that there was no longer any possibility of a "grand narrative" through which truth was told or by which meaning could be agreed and universalised. The postmodernists, therefore, appeal to the same outward aspects of modern society as do the modernists, but draw a quite different conclusion. For the postmodernist, the conclusion is that insofar as meaning is possible, it is the constructive work of each human participant as one participates in the life process. There is no pole star, no fixed route, no single map, no given destination available by which life can be commonly agreed to be intelligible. There is, that is to say, no "Truth."

J. F. Lyotard[23] brought together the artistic reference of postmodernism with the sociocultural analysis of postmodernism by showing that in contemporary narration the postmodern person constructs views of reality and does so in the light of the interests of a particular social order. Narrative is therefore a mode of sociocultural construction and self-representation and not, as for the modernist, based in a traditional master narrative that projects an orderly and coherent universe. The postmodern person opts for narrative openness over closure, fiction over truth, fragmentation over unity and coherence.[24] Whatever truth is, it is a consequence of human freedom and not vice versa.

It is against this background that the account of self-identity offered by Giddens is comprehensible and instructive. The self, says Giddens,[25] is a "reflexive project," a "trajectory" from the past into an organized future where coherence derives from cognitive awareness of the phases of the life-span, not from external events or institutions. The self is therefore essentially a narrative in which self-interrogation and self-observation provide a continuous and all-pervasive reflexivity of consciousness. Self-actualization implies the control of time through awareness of the personal time zones and is a balance of opportunity and risk in a world which offers potential for being and for acting. To be self-actualizing is to be moral, to be authentic to oneself, and to achieve fulfillment by becoming free of dependencies. The only thread to life is this trajectory of the self in its quest of personal integrity. This personal integrity is the achievement of the authentic self through the integration of life experiences (which are the self's narrative). Belief is created in the autobiographical passage through life where the requirement is to give first loyalty to oneself.

Spelled out in this way, it can be seen that any postmodernist project of thought which sees the self as a mode of sociocultural construction and self-representation is, at the level of factual belief content, strongly at odds with the traditional Christian fundamentalist view of the self as being essentially defined by God and for whom there is most certainly available a pole star, a fixed route, a single map, a given destination by which life can be commonly agreed to be intelligible and which is the source of common meaning because it is given in a noncultural revelation by God in Christ and in revealed word of scripture. Indeed, Gidden's description of the postmodern self could be read by the fundamentalist as an exact definition of the sinful self which is opposed to simple obedience to the will of God and insistent on following its own light.

But at another level, both modern fundamentalism and postmodernism are on the same ground in that they are alternative responses to the *same* dilemma. The dilemma is this: How is it possible for human beings to attain meaning in life when the positive grounds of meaning offered by post-Enlightenment thought have proved to be mutually incommensurate and in any case unsustainable? Neither the appeal to reason, nor to the senses, nor to the feelings, nor to moral action has been able to deliver the sure ground for human rationality that the post-Enlightenment project sought. The solution, therefore, is either, with the postmodernist, to seek meaning through self-determined expressive response to the world, or to make some other move which will allow at one and the same time for the essential correctness of the postmodern critique of society and for the fundamentalist to retain his or her essential commitment to the singularity of revelation retaining the fideistic (fundamentalist) move of claiming that truth and meaning come from without this world and are available through revelation alone, through faith alone.[26]

The rise of charismatic Christian fundamentalism, for example, can be understood precisely in this way. The unique reception of the "spirit" by the individual Christian, the specific and new revelations through words of prophecy mediated through the individual Christian, the interpretation of tongues by an individual Christian for an individual Christian, the emphasis on existential spontaneity and the processes of religious experience, the experimentation with liturgical disruption in many charismatic liturgies, the focus on indeterminacy of liturgical form, and the emphasis on charismatic phenomena making old cognitive boundaries and solidarities irrelevant (thus the cross-denominational nature of the charismatic movement); these are all ways in which charismatic Christian fundamentalism retains the "totalizing imperative" of all epistemological fundamentalists while responding to the dilemma of postmodern society in ways which the postmodernist would recognize.

Reprise

The essential character of fundamentalisms in Europe in the 1990s (political, scientific, artistic, and religious) can best be understood as intrinsically related to the ontological and epistemological underpinnings of thought which characterize academic disciplines at any particular time and place. Despite the totalizing belief claims which are made by Protestant fundamentalists within the Christian tradition, and which are claimed to possess noncultural truth (revelation) and to provide thereby the sure basis for the meaning of human existence, the character of the ontological and epistemological claims on which Christian fundamentalism builds variously match those of the post-Enlightenment, modernist, and postmodernist frameworks of thought.

It would be proper, therefore, to refer to "post-Enlightenment fundamentalism," "modernist fundamentalism," and "postmodernist fundamentalism" according to which features of the modern mind that particular form of fundamentalism responds. Rationalistic, fideistic, and charismatic forms of Christian fundamentalism may, therefore, after all, show that it is not possible to escape from the relativities of cultural location even when exhibiting the "totalizing imperative." It would not be possible, of course, to be a fundamentalist in any modern sense prior to the Enlightenment. But in the post-Enlightenment period in Europe, fundamentalism is a feature in European thought which is common, through the epistemological "totalizing imperative," to both the religious and the secular mind.

There are good reasons, therefore, for being very cautious about the arguments concerning academic freedom which proceed on the common fundamentalist basis which underlies modern Western thought in the European tradition, both religious and secular.

Essential Agnosticism: Freedom for Truth

I take it to be a self-evident truth that all fundamentalisms, whether religious, scientific, educational, political, or cultural, are a threat to, indeed a denial of, academic freedom. But what we have now seen is that fundamentalism is not confined to religious communities but penetrates the core of Western intellectual activity since the enlightenment and is to be found centrally in scientific, political, and cultural realms. Academic freedom is therefore threatened from within rather than from without in Western democracies. What I now propose is that academic freedom can only be built on that freedom which derives from epistemological agnosticism, since it is only epistemological agnosticism which requires that the truth claims of others must (logically) be accorded parity of esteem.

In concluding this paper, therefore, I argue that all human freedoms derive from that essential agnosticism which is intrinsic to the human condition and that for the Christian theologian this essential agnosticism is a corollary of the Christian doctrine of God. My argument is that in Christian doctrine, the only defensible relationship of human beings to God is that of freely offered love, and that such freely offered love is only possible in the absence of that coercive knowledge which is "Truth." To develop this argument I use and build upon John Hick's theological analysis of the logical and actual conditions of human freedom.[27]

It seems, says Hick, in developing a theological response to Anthony Flew's compatibilism, that there would be no point in the creation by God of finite persons unless such finite persons could be endowed with a degree of genuine freedom and independence over and against their maker, since only in freedom and independence could they be capable of authentic personal relationship with him. But how is such creaturely freedom to be defined, he asks, since on the one hand as finite beings they remain dependent on the will of God? The answer is to define human freedom as limited creativity. Such freedom will involve an element of unpredictability; for, while accepting Flew's argument that the action proceeds from the nature of the agent, the nature from which it proceeds is that of "the actual self above in the moment of decision."[28] Thus, while a free action arises out of the agent's character it does not arise in a fully determined and predictable way. It is largely but not fully prefigured in the previous state of the agent whose character is itself only partially formed and sometimes partially reformed in the very moment of free decision.

Some such concept of freedom as limited creativity both Hick and I take to be the necessary postulate for a defensible Christian view of the relation between finite persons (human beings) and God.[29] The primary point at which this limited creativity is required is that at which humans in their freedom are willing or unwilling to become aware of God. For it is *cognitive* freedom in relation to the creator that must be insisted upon, says Hick. And the concept of freedom as creativity would make it possible to speak of God as endowing his creatures with a genuine, though limited, autonomy. We could think of him as forming human persons through the long evolutionary process and leaving them free to respond or fail to respond to himself in uncompelled faith.

This account of the epistemological conditions presupposed by the status of human persons as free and responsible agents in relation to their creator is thus, as Hick points out, in full harmony with the natural history of *Homo sapiens* as now understood. For human freedom requires, and evolutionary theory provides, an initial separateness and consequent degree of independence on human persons vis-à-vis God—that, is a certain relative autonomy over and against God's self.

Thus for a finite creature to possess any significant autonomy while being dependent upon the infinite creator for its very existence and nature, there must be the possibility of that creature being at a distance from God from which to be able, voluntarily, to come to God. But how can anything, Hick asks, be set at a distance from a God who is infinite and omnipresent? Clearly it is not "spatial" distance that could make room for a degree of human autonomy. However, "epistemic" distance could. In other words, the reality and presence of God must not be borne in upon the finite person in a coercive way since this would contravene the freedom of the person and particularly freely given love. It follows that God must in terms of the created order be a hidden deity, veiled by his creation, and that the world must be experienced *etsi deus non daretur*, "as if there were no God." The creator must be knowable, but only by a mode of knowledge that involves a free personal response on each person's part, this response consisting in an uncompelled interpretive activity whereby the world is experienced as mediating the divine presence. Such an epistemic distance between creator and creature will secure for humankind the only kind of freedom that is possible in relation to God, namely cognitive freedom. This cognitive freedom carries with it, of course, the possibility of human beings being either aware or unaware of the creator since it is possible for the mind to rest in the world itself without passing beyond it to the creator. Thus the world, as the environment of human life, is *essentially religiously ambiguous*, both veiling God and revealing God—veiling him to ensure human freedom and revealing him to each person who exercises that freedom. The humanistic and the theistic options are therefore equally valid and equally guaranteed by the essential agnosticism which derives that necessary epistemic distance.

CONCLUSION

Academic freedom also finds its validity and guarantee, pace all fundamentalists whether religious or secular, in this essential agnosticism which necessarily characterizes the human condition. On this, both humanists and Christians should agree, and should be content with the realization that for Christians this freedom is derivable from their doctrine of God, their "Truth." On this common ground, academic freedom is not only possible, it is required.

NOTES

1. It is sometimes suggested, for example, that there is a link between fundamentalism and authoritarianism. If this is the case, then the "totalizing imperative" would also be an aspect of that fact.
2. It would take an article in itself to assess the similarities and differences between the roots of fundamentalism in the United States and in the British Commonwealth, since the immigration patterns of each are very different with regard to the number of immigrants from continental Europe as distinct from the United Kingdom. An important aspect of such an account would be the relative impact of possible Catholic roots of fundamentalism in the United States as against the Commonwealth.
3. This is not the same equation between faith and knowledge made by John Hick in *Faith and Knowledge*, 2d ed. (London: Fontana, 1974), though the conservative evangelical period in Hick's experience may well be reflected in his desire to close the gap between faith and reason. He does this by making "faith-as-experiencing-as" itself a form of knowing.
4. I am drawing loosely here and in the four points below on arguments made by J. C. Cooper in *The Roots of Radical Theology* (London: Hodder and Stoughton, 1968), especially chapter 2.
5. C. F. H. Henry, *God, Revelation and Authority*, vol. 1 (Waco, Tex.: Word Books, 1976), p. 14.
6. I here use the word "positivist" in an epistemologically enlarged sense compared with its singular specificity as used by logical positivists.
7. I like Paul Kurtz's loose definition of "Enlightenment" in "Toward a New Enlightenment," *Challenges to the Enlightenment: In Defense of Reason and Science* (Amherst, N.Y.: Prometheus Books, 1994), pp. 13–14. He identifies it with certain intellectual trends in the seventeenth and especially the eighteenth centuries in Western society through which writers exuded great optimism about the potential of science and reason to unlock the secrets of nature and to understand human nature and the desire by these writers to apply these insights for the betterment of the human condition. For reading on European thought since the Enlightenment, see Colin Gunton, *The One, the Tree and the Many: God,*

Creation, and the Culture of Modernity (Cambridge: CUP, 1993) and his earlier *Enlightenment and Alienation* (Grand Rapids, Mich.: Eerdmans, 1985). For the purposes of this paper I am more interested in those features which are common within post-Enlightenment thought rather than those features which mark out its different strands.

8. L. Newbigin, *The Gospel in a Pluralist Society* (London: SPCK, 1989), p. 39.

9. P. Berger, *The Heretical Imperative, Contemporary Possibilities of Religious Affirmations* (London: Collins, 1980).

10. I take this point from Newbigin, *Gospel in a Pluralist Society*, pp. 17, 28, who cites Arendt's *The Human Condition*.

11. I am not interested here to develop the well-known problems of Cartesian rationalism such as the radical dualism of *res cogitans* and *res extensa*. I do not think they exist for Descartes himself since he believed that his ontological argument eliminated any radical separation of the self, the world, and God—or as he would have ordered these items, the self, God, and the world.

12. Pre-Enlightenment empiricism derived from Aristotle, for whom it meant perceptual induction from which it is possible to elicit clear truths. Thomist philosophy is empirical in this Aristotelian sense.

13. D. Hume, *Dialogues concerning Natural Religion*, reprinted in *Hume on Religion*, ed. R. Willheim, (London: Fontana, 1963); A. J. Ayer, *Language, Truth and Logic*, 2d ed. (London: Gollancz, 1946).

14. F. Schleiermacher, *On Religion: Speeches to Its Cultured Despisers* (New York: Harper Torchbooks, 1958).

15. This point is taken further in F. Schleiermacher's, *The Christian Faith* (Edinburgh: T. & T. Clark, 1928), where he argues that even when God is experienced in feeling, this is always a mediated knowledge of God and not direct cognition. God is disclosed in inner experience, not experienced directly or inferred from experience. I. T. Ramsey in his *On Being Sure of Religion* (Oxford: SCM Press, 1963) also argues for absolute certainty of the reality of God as being entirely compatible with permanent uncertainty as to the nature of God.

16. R. Otto, *The Idea of the Holy*, 2d ed. (New York: Oxford University Press, 1958).

17. This is also the case, but in a different way, with the argument of Martin Buber that all subject/object knowledge can be transcended by subject/subject knowledge. See his *I and Thou*, 2d ed., trans. Ronald Gregor Smith (New York: Scribner, 1958).

18. Kurtz, "Toward a New Enlightnement," p. 14 again provides an accessible delineation: "The term *modernity* refers to the fact that there was confidence in the ability of men and women to control their destiny. They believed that human beings were free, autonomous, and rational agents, and were responsible for some measure for their future. The were convinced that, by means of science, objective knowledge was possible about nature and our place within it. By enlightened understanding and action, they thought that we could improve human life and create a more just and beneficent society."

19. See, for example, John Hull, *What Prevents Christian Adults from Learning?* (Philadelphia: Trinity Press International, 1991), chap. 1.

20. Ibid., pp. 4–36.

21. Compare also Karen Armstrong in her review article "Fundamentalist Fervour" in the *Sunday Times*, January 9, 1994, section 6.4 (review of Gilles Kerpel, *The Revenge of God: The Resurgence of Islam, Christianity and Judaism in the Modern World* [Cambridge: Polity Press, 1993]). Armstrong claims that while Jewish, Christian, and Muslim fundamentalists all reject the secular ethos of modernity which separates religion from politics and makes it one option among many, because they all regard the Enlightenment as the source of this evil which culminated in the atheist ideologies of Nazi and Stalinist totalitarianism, they do not reject the whole of modern experience since the young radicals who have studied electronics and engineering see no conflict between religion and science.

22. See Kurtz, "Toward a New Enlightenment," pp. 16–17: "They not only reject the Enlightenment project but explicitly deny any number of humanist premises: that human beings are capable of free and autonomous choice; that they can be rational and responsible; that universal ethical norms can be discovered; that meta-narratives of emancipation can or should be achieved; that the ideals of liberal democracy and of human rights have genuine authenticity." He continues, "they deplore the grown to technology. They maintain that language is a veil masking Being, that every text should be deconstructed and that objective scientific knowledge is a myth." For further reading see: Z. Bauman, *Intimations of Postmodernity* (London: Routledge, 1992); C. Norris, *The Truth About Postmodernism* (Oxford: Blackwell, 1993); E. Best and D. Kellner, *Postmodern Theory: Critical Interrogations* (London: Macmillan, 1991); and T. Docherty, *Postmodernism: A Reader* (New York: Harvester Wheatsheaf, 1993).

23. J. F. Lyotard, *The Postmodern Condition: A Report on Knowledge* (Manchester: Manchester University Press, 1979, tr. 1984).

24. The jury is out at the present time on whether postmodern awareness can in fact incorporate narrative which is capable of providing a social framework for meaning—and thus be capable of sustaining the universal horizon of the Enlightenment and of historic Christianity. How to accommodate plurality of epistemological and ontological commitments within modern society is the major issue facing political and religious theorists today.

25. A. Giddens, *Modernity and Self-Identity: Self and Society in the Late Modern. Age* (Cambridge: Polity Press, 1991).

26. This is a radical simplification of Paul Ricoeur's suggestion in *The Symbolism of Evil* (Boston: Beacon Press, 1969) that there are six possible forms of response to the ultimate questions of good and evil. Ricoeur lists these as: (1) Religious Optimism (God will take care of everything); (2) Secular Optimism (everything will somehow turn out for the best); (3) Grateful Acceptance (one is grateful for good things, despite the bad); (4) Anger (suffering is unjust, unfair); (5) Resignation (what will be, will be); and (6) Hopefulness (the last word has not yet been said).

27. I follow closely here the version of Hick's thesis concerning epistemic distance as set out in *Evil and the God of Love*, 2d ed. (London: Macmillan, 1977), pp. 275–86.

28. Hick cites Charles Hartshorne, *The Logic of Perfection* (Lasalle, Ill.: Open Court, 1962), p. 20, and C. A. Campbell, *Selfhood and Godhood* (London: George Allen and Unwin Ltd., 1957), chap. 9, as the sources of this idea. He regards the latter as the fullest and most adequate exposition and defense of this conception of freedom.

29. Hick, *Evil and the God of Love*, pp. 275–86.

CHAPTER 11

THE LIBERAL ARTS, TIME, AND TRUTH
The Last Lecture
Arthur J. Slavin

When I was a graduate student at Chapel Hill, I heard the historian George Taylor give his "Last Lecture." The memory of it is still green. The choice fell on him as a retiring member of the university community esteemed as a teaching scholar. When I came here as dean in 1974, one of my first acts for the college was to establish the Distinguished Faculty Lectureship on the same basis of significant contributions to the intellectual life of the college. My successor as dean discontinued the lecture.

I believed then, as I do now, that such rituals are essential parts of the foundational myth of a college dedicated to the life of the mind in a large and increasingly noncollegial university. Perhaps today's events will imbue another new dean with a resolve to make a tradition of the "Last Lecture."

Having pleaded that case, my subject today is the liberal arts, truth, and time. In recent American political life no word seems more abused than the word "liberal," and no element of our national heritage more sullied than a pledge of allegiance as part of our public civic speech. Hence my purpose is to raise again a tattered flag, through a concern for the true meanings of words in an age of invective and abuse of those words. I provide one local example only. On March 4, David Hawpe mentioned that famous bookman Wallace Wilkinson, remarking parenthetically: "And remember, Wilkinson is no simpering liberal. He is a hard-nosed businessman-politician. He got right up into Gex Williams's face...."

Our university is now in the midst of its bicentennial celebrations. It came into being on the basis of Jefferson's concern for liberty in the broadest sense. When Louisville was chartered as a city he had already in mind the necessity of public higher education for the health of a democratic polity. He later signed a charter providing for a seminary here, out of which our university eventually matured.

Seminarium signifies a seed bed. Jefferson laid down the principle of intense human cultivation, from which he thought the new American people ought never to deviate. His charter called on Americans to pay taxes in a liberal spirit and thus provide "the means to enlighten the people generally." If we give allegiance to this as a free people, he said, "then oppression of mind and body will in time vanish."

What he called a seminary, what became a university, Jefferson intended to be a place "where the illimitable freedom of the human mind" might reach beyond the limits of the timid, the conventional, and "a merely supine delight in things as they are."

Jefferson was a classical republican, with a strong education in the *artes liberales*, especially addicted to Roman history, rhetoric, and literature. In speaking of the enlightenment of people, the relief from oppression, and the illimitable freedom secured by a proper education, the liberal arts were to him the fundament, a foundational myth of origins.

I must speak today about the liberal arts, but I shall not weary you with any minuscule examination of current debates about curriculums and canons, however. Enough of that is being done by professors who strike me as profoundly illiberal. I do not want to add one jot or tittle to their cacophony. What I propose instead is to consider closely the Latin origins of our word "liberal," as a way into the promise of my title, in which I joined the word "liberal" to other words: "time," "truth," and "allegiance."

To the early Romans, *liber* signified several things: free-born; to be free from a social point of view, in contrast with those who were slaves; the quality of openness we associate with speaking frankly and without intent to harm by dissembling. None of these is the earliest meaning of the root, however. In the earliest texts and inscriptions *liber* signified the rind or bark of a tree. In time it came to mean a scraped surface prepared from bark, upon which something could be inscribed—for example a text. Hence in the course of long usage *liber* came to denote paper, parchment, rolls made of scraped bark and written upon, in the form of some treatise, literary work, or other text—the whole range of significations we now denominate by our word "book."

It is in this sense that we catch Cicero writing *dixi in eo libro quem de rebus liberalibus*: "In that book I said something about liberal things." By Cicero's time the link between *liber* as a material and the text inscribed on it, also the tie to the idea of something having the quality of being "liberal" had been fixed. For *liberalis* meant that which belonged to a free human being, denoting the condition of being free-born, noble-minded, honest, and tolerant. Again, Cicero is my guide: *liberalia studia accipimus*. "We adhere to the liberal studies." Why? Because to Cicero adhering to liberal studies was the necessary condition of *libertas*, the state or condition of enjoying freedom, as if by birthright.

There is an inescapable relationship between the simple tree bark, its treatment, writing upon it, those studies edifying a free human being, our support for them, and the general enjoyment of liberty, upon which this nation rests as upon a first principle.

Any good dictionary teaches the essential lesson. In the *Random House Dictionary* it is not until we reach the twelfth usage in a list of fourteen examples that we first meet a definition which narrows our vision to party labels and partisan politics. Above that twelfth example "liberal" comes to us in these forms: favorable to progress or reform; the measures necessary to representative self-government against those on which aristocracies and monarchies stand; that which accords with the maximum freedom of action in respect of personal belief and expression; the condition of being free from prejudice and bigotry; open-minded and tolerant; endowed with a spirit of generosity; free in the sense of that which pertains to and is beneficial to a free man and a free woman.

I think we are already somewhat fallen from the height of our heritage, from Jefferson's great admonition, when he called on us to support education in a liberal spirit, to throw off oppression and provide for the enlargement of our selves through an illimitable freedom of the mind. This seems evident in an age like ours, when officials and candidates, from university presidents to national presidential candidates, and journalists and harpers on local issues debase and usurp the word "liberal," with its ties back to tree bark, books, studies that make us free, our enjoyment of freedom, employing the language of commerce while transforming our precious word into a sneer in the language of their political underworld.

What pledge of allegiance to our republic and to the liberty for which it stands shall we long be free to make, if we convict ourselves of amnesia about the centrality of the word "liberal" to our struggle to remain the last best hope for freedom at home and of unfree peoples abroad?

Nothing seems to me of more urgency than a university dialogue about the relationship between the free order of our nation in a time of travail and the debasement of political language and political culture. We are daily assaulted by stories in the newspapers and on television testifying to a lapse from the vision of the founders, by a confusion about the exercise of a public trust and its conversion to private profit. Public distrust in institutions of government and education is growing, threatening the good work of construction done more than two centuries ago and reconstructed in Lincoln's great address at Gettysburg.

Nothing is more central to liberty than its foundation in books and the pursuit of the liberal arts. When our dictionaries tell us that the primary meaning of liberal is that which is favorable to reform, and the second meaning is that which secures the fruits of representative government, a government fitting for a free people, we are invited to think hard about the relationships, to bring them out into the open from the pressures of large books that enclose them, and the like pressures on language from current practice that threatens to invert the meanings of words in ways inimical to democracy itself.

But to give such hard thought to the meanings of words as a way into the notion of the right order of public life is often not only a sobering thing to do but also a dangerous thing to do. Few matters seem to excite greater passion than a consideration of "the right ordering of things." This is especially true in a democracy, where the dictionary again reminds us that it is integral to the idea that there be freedom of action, that there be freedom of expression, giving as an example "of a government following a liberal policy towards literature and the liberal arts to secure the illimitable freedom of the human spirit."

This example has everything to do with the idea that in a free society there be no official teaching on any subject, no banned books, even no issue of subpoenas into the purchase of books by citizens, no party line to tell us what to think in matters touching inquiry and conscience. University teachers and their students in particular must embody these ideas and the sentiments attaching to them by virtue of their commitment to the life of the mind.

But in the ebb and flow of great events, and in our public and political discourse about them, there is ample evidence that the ideals informing processes of education are often at odds with the conduct of government, for example in the recent flap concerning the McConnell Scholars locally, and the ever-expanding idea of secrecy in our national government—which often reaches into the university in the form of restraints on the publication of research results, or even in the injunction that in expressing an opinion on an urgent matter of policy in the commonwealth we must not signal to the public that we are writing letters to editors in our capacity as faculty members.

This last injunction seems founded on a wrong notion about the origins of universities, especially about such great ones as Paris, Bologna, and Oxford. Far from having a merely cloistered and monastic character, the great medieval schools were vitally involved in the great public debates of their time. The idyll of detachment and bucolic seclusion projected on to them is a fantasy and ought to be resisted vigorously. No university worthy of the name can renounce participation in the controversial aspects of the life of its community.

I am not denying what is manifest practice—that we take in students for a variety of reasons, beyond the hope of stretching their minds toward Jefferson's illimitable freedom. Admissions officers judge the intake by thinking of the kind of alumni and alumnae they think we desire to have, the role in community life they think the university should play, the fact that graduates will be engineers, doctors, lawyers, and information managers. But all such goals define graduates in a way that separates them from their role as citizens addicted to the free play of mind on issues. Universities inescapably make judgments about the kind of society its officers think it good to have, even as they deny they are doing this.

Once we introduce the notion of some social good, we return to the idea of the university not as a series of service connections, but as the preeminent place providing a space for the nourishment of our selves—that thing implicated in the word liberal. We must be about providing that place, that space where students take the measure of their own spirit, if for no other reason that our graduates must have an informed perspective on the public responsibilities they will assume and share.

This desire to provide such a place and its spiritual space where students can engage traditions of learning and raise challenges to them reveals its full significance whenever we think about our hopes for the future. Again, I come back to the meaning of the word liberal as that which is favorable to reform. The time spent in thought is time spent in preparation for action, for action that reforms, renovates, renews society and the polity. What we think and believe is dead without enlivening action.

This notion, which seems self-evident to me from my consideration of *liber*, *liberalis*, and *libertas*, has for some decades now been challenged by many politicians, some educators, and even more citizens. Sensibilities have been inflamed by pictures of campus demonstrations, ranging in time from the great antiwar protests and civil rights movements of the 1960s to the struggle for women's rights in their own bodies and equality under the law in matters of sexual preference. Pundits and politicians have often joined in blasting "liberal excess" while urging on the university a reclusive attitude, even a kind of asceticism, as if we were not, teachers and students, citizens at liberty to know and care about how the world turns and to influence it in its gyrations.

Now quiet and contemplation, as I have said, belong to what is liberal in university life, but not as an end, only as a means. The goal of wisdom is not passivity about public policy. But we are told that were we to be too active in the great issues of the day in our capacity within the university we risk alienating taxpayers and legislators. We are all too often asked to leave the complex questions of government to professional politicians, in the name of the liberal arts themselves.

You may think I exaggerate. But at a recent conference I heard a distinguished scholar say "only a fool would prefer debate over public issues to the pleasures of literature and philosophy." I took comfort in recalling Jefferson, teaching us that a university is a seed bed from which shall spring the men and women whose business it must be to renew liberty and defeat every oppression of mind and body.

This means we must refuse the false counsel of some who were themselves distinguished in the academy. I recall George Kennan, from his lofty perch in Princeton's Institute for Advanced Studies, admonishing students to be wary of the idealistic pursuit of public causes. Also the late Jacques Barzan, then dean of the faculty at Columbia, who in testimony before a House Committee of Education blamed the Columbia faculty and students for a falling-off in endowment and extended his comments to say they endangered academic freedom by "indulging is the mistaken notion that they should seek to enlarge the role of the university in public discourse." Barzun went further, saying only he and Hutchins of Chicago had held true to the purpose of the university: "to learn and to teach. Any subject can be taught if it can be reduced to principles which can then form the basis of training."

This, I submit, is the road to subservience and not the way to freedom. The happy embrace of the narrow ideal of training must give us pause. The notion of technical virtuosity is a trap for education in a democracy. A public speech by President Nixon in 1970 shows us why. He broadly indicted universities, saying research and teaching were out of balance, technical training was not being kept current, and curriculums were irrelevant. He ducked the real issue: To what is education supposed to be relevant? He simply assumed the answer in citing the growth of the gross national product. The education president of his time proposed a $100,000,000 fund for what he called career education, "technical training of a kind better suited to the interests of our young people. Too many have fallen prey to the myth that a liberal arts education is essential to a full, free, and meaningful life."

Unknowingly, this would-be mentor had entered into a dialogue of the living with the dead, arraying himself against Jefferson and his quite contrary notions—a president who died as if by some act of Providence on the fiftieth anniversary of the Declaration of Independence.

He also had unwittingly entered into a dialogue with an English educator then working with Africans in the townships suffering under apartheid, who in 1970 published a piece in the BBC *Listener*:

> I think it is very important for the future of Africa that we should hold fast to the idea that the purpose of education is to take young men and women and develop them as human beings to the very highest possibility they have: to educate them to make the best use of their gifts. There are still people who say of the Blacks agriculture is so important to them—and I agree all technologies are vitally important to their futures—that in future universities should aim to train good agriculturalists. I cannot agree. It is not the good we aim at to teach people to know their proper stations in life and to stay put in them. We reject that idea, and for very good reasons. If we are short in miners, we do not ask the universities to train them. We ask the Coal Board to develop new technical opportunities.

I do not deny the importance of equipping our students and ourselves with the means toward making a decent living. I do mean to set my sights on those who argue that what is liberal in a liberal education is a seductive myth, and to reassert here the centrality of the liberal tradition in education against its detractors.

Educating people for fruitful work itself embodies more than training. Vocational training in itself is a species of functional rationalism; it tells people how to get a job done. It is in itself value neutral at best, tending to answer questions about efficiency without posing questions about effects of getting work done. It fits people to jobs, systems, and whatever the values governing a job or system might be and masks thinking about ends rather than means—even when work in a system promotes ecological disaster or, on the historical record, genocide.

The liberal arts and the liberal idea of education are not value-neutral. They seek to develop in people social and ethical principles of action, not by dogmatic inculcation but by exposure to questions of value and the activities of valuing. They are philosophical in the best sense. They are humanistic in the best sense. They are never merely a response to technique. They ask not can we do something but whether we ought to do it. They have at their core the great question put by Erasmus of Rotterdam: *quam sit humaniter vivendum?* How might life be lived in a manner fitting for human beings, in a way that enhances human dignity rather than debasing it?

To put the Erasmian question is at once to leave behind two vast misconceptions of the life of a university: the first, that we build curriculums to find out where students are rather than to help them toward places they might venture; the second, that any university worthy of the name should embrace a technical mission and philosophy rather than adhere to what Jefferson called a liberal one, whose final good was the civic good.

Learning is not a private good, a personal property only, but is rather the basis of an obligation to take an active part in our city, our commonwealth, our nation: *sapiens numquam privatus est*.

The debate on this notion reaches at least as far back in time as Plato's *Protagoras* and the vigorous argument between the Sophist and Socrates whether virtue is a *techne politike*, a kind of political technique, which once instilled in young men gives them the ability to correctly calculate what is necessary to achieve the public good. Socrates argued that virtue is not a practice in which one can be trained but is instead the *telos* of an education grounded in a love of truth. The contest is one between the appearance of things, with manipulation on the surface of affairs by those versed in persuasive rhetoric, and the more arduous pursuit of philosophy whose end is wisdom rather than a timely prudence.

What Socrates and Protagoras agreed on was that no commonwealth could long prosper in which educated persons preferred the life of ease and withdrawal from civic life. Marx had hit this same nail on the head, in criticizing merely speculative thought addressing no public act: "Every real step of movement is worth more than a dozen programs." Or on another occasion: "Philosophers study the world not to admire its workings but to change it."

Several centuries earlier the English Aristotelian Thomas Starkey had written a little treatise, "What is Political Philosophy after the Sentence of Aristotle," intended for the perusal of Henry VIII's chief minister, Thomas Cromwell. And in his little treatise, Starkey made the large claim that a true commonwealth was a conspiracy of multitudes of people who wished to find principles upon which to base a public life aspiring to harmony, justice, and ultimate care for the full humanity of every man and women. "A multitude conspiring in virtue, which is no private thing."

Plato became a royal councillor; St. Augustine died in harness as the spiritual superintendent of a provincial African diocese, embattled by Vandals, but keeping his faith in daily pastoral acts while in his little spare time writing his *Little Catechism* for the children of barbarians. Thomas More, having considered life in the quiet of the Charterhouse of London, decided upon a public career, in time rising from the office of undersheriff of London to become lord chancellor of England, while the struggle over reformation was at white heat, a struggle in which he ventured his life and suffered martyrdom. And Jefferson was by any reckoning an old man when he left Monticello in 1801 to shoulder the burdens of the presidency.

And there were women upholding the highest ideals of public service: Queen Elizabeth I, who in her speech at Tilbury rallied her people against the Armada; Mary Wollstonecraft, who in her *Vindication of the Rights of Women* protested the denial to women everywhere a liberal education and place in public life; Golda Meir, who turned from the quiet of farming on a kibbutz in Palestine in 1921 to politics in Israel, where she ended her public service as prime minister. *Otium* overcome by *Negotium*.

These men and women found no pleasure in either alienation from public life or complaisant service. Each in their own way regarded a free and liberal education as the foundation of any true commonwealth.

I find special significance in their common joining of education and public life, embodied in the Renaissance in a letter from Thomas Starkey, fresh from Padua, that Aristotelian seminary, to Thomas Cromwell, Henry VIII's principal secretary of state:

> First here in Oxford a great part of my youth I busied myself in both Tongues Latin and Greek and also Philosophy and so passed over into Italy where I much delighted in contemplation.... Many times I purposed to spend my whole life therein. At the last, moved by Charity, I applied myself to Scriptures and judged all secret and private knowledge not applied to the common use a vanity, and set myself the study of Law, where I might find a more sure and stable judgment of the right order to be put in use among my countrymen to edify a very commonwealth.

Here is liberal and humanist adherence to the idea of striving for the rule of law, the preference for the public over the private good, grounded in a vision of the university as the place where, through the liberal arts, young people prepare for the urgent tasks of human liberation, through the power of ideas in action. It was precisely his immersion in the *studia humaniora*, the more humane studies, that turned Starkey of necessity from the life of contemplative ease to the hurly-burly of public service.

In so choosing, he was under no illusions. He referred to the lines in Terence: "Slights and fights and spirits vexed/War today and peace the next." He also marked a place in Augustine, where the saint condemned the life of withdrawal, reminding his reader that Jesus had chosen a public life and suffered death for his choice. "We Christians like better the teaching that the life of virtue must be a social life."

It was in this spirit that Jefferson said "the boisterous sea of liberty is never without a wave," and "the politics of liberty are not a hobby to be pursued in passing, but a passion, a vocation, a habit for life bred into citizens as the condition of their freedom." The Sage of Monticello also noted "Calm, the sure haven, is not simply an illusion in a democratic polity, but even the hope of it is illiberal and a life worse than civic death."

The common thread in these remarks, I think, is the foundational myth of a free and liberal society that a liberal education is the resource necessary to secure order within one's self and within the commonweal.

Hence my return to Jefferson's commitment to the liberal arts and their necessity for civic well-being. In our universities there is no shortage of homage to training. It is the humanistic and liberal discourse about values at the center of the humanities and the liberal arts that seems at risk, just those studies that Jefferson said were in his time and remain in an age like our own indispensable to a decent politics in a democracy.

This precious cluster of studies invites reflection on the question "What does it mean to be fully human, in this time and in this place?" No discipline has a patent on an answer. None of us who teach within the cluster is more than a temporary tenant inhabiting the many traditions which offer provisional answers only. But in our tenancy we have an obligation to promote the liberal and liberating civic discourse Jefferson prized so much. It helps us to remember that the whole struggle for liberty against power is the struggle of remembering against forgetting.

It is to this fundamental myth that I pledge my allegiance and invite your pledge. The processes of freedom will be less threatened and young people less inclined to withdraw in disgust from politics if we pay heed to one of the great cries of the young. I mean their demand for intellectual honesty, personal honesty, public honesty. Their cry is to strip away sham, to puncture illusion, to get down to the nub of truth. Unless we find a way to speak plainly and freely and truly about public things, we may find it impossible to maintain our grip on liberty. Our nation's values are as lasting as the ability to afford in each generation the education that maintains them. We produce abundantly, but our values turn not on what we have but on what we believe, what we know, who we are.

In making my own pledge I have had in mind a hitherto unspecified trinity: believing, behaving, and belonging. What we believe as academics does help shape how we behave and what sense of belonging to a community we carry about within ourselves. Belonging by itself can be an empty attachment. Behaving seems necessary to inform a sense of belonging. And how we behave seems to answer to the set of beliefs, the belief system, we harbor within. I am not certain to which I would assign primacy, and whether behavior forms a community of believers or the other way round.

This is something about which one ought not be dogmatic. But I do think that unless we know with some precision what we believe, what we do stand for, then there is the risk of uninformed behavior and the loss of the sense of community resting on shared values. The danger of loss seems great when we are in periods in which there is some ideological mewing up of the setting of our work as teaching scholars. Lovejoy, Dewey, and others felt this danger when, in 1915, they acted to set out a statement of beliefs essential to academic freedom and the undergirding institution of tenure. They knew they were at a turning point in academic life in America.

I think we are faced with a similar kind of closure in the open space of discourse about what is liberal and what is free in our society and in our universities, because of the encroachment of corporatism. This encroachment has been traumatic, which is why I think it so important today to invite you as colleagues to look afresh at our founding myth and defend it in new and compelling ways.

Aggressive government and aggressive corporatism threaten to swallow whole the very idea of a liberal arts education and the beliefs and behaviors engendered by such an idea. Our traditions are no longer self-validating, if indeed they ever were. We must rethink them, reformulate them, and stretch ourselves in so doing. If we do, we will remain recognizably a liberal arts faculty.

In closing, I return to what I earlier called our foundational myth. All such myths order experience, making manifest shapes, forms, and patterns in our lives. The foundational myth of the liberal arts constructs for us an ideal, a lively and living image, of the academic and wider civic world in which liberty flowers. It is not a fiction, though it is itself a human construction. We cannot well stand outside it and remain a community of scholars. Our myth is intrinsic to our community, the key to its creation and in continuing to provide for us an understanding of our raison d'être in the college.

The myth we trace back to the humble bark of a tree animates our community only as long as we believe in it and act in its defense. It is nothing less than our master narrative, the story in which each of us recognizes her or his own story. It reminds us of our origins and our goals.

In pledging allegiance to it today, while yet a full member of our college community, I affirm it, and I affirm also our unrepayable debt to students and colleagues everywhere, in remote times as well as recent times, who have shed their life's blood for our freedom to gladly learn and gladly teach.

PART III
REASON, REVELATION, AND RELIGION

The Enlightenment has had profound influence on biblical and theological studies by stressing the place of reason or rational reflection as a companion to insight provided by revelation. The critical tools of investigation and interpretation available to contemporary scholars in biblical and historical studies are the legacy of the Enlightenment, what Will and Ariel Durant called "The Age of Reason."[1]

Baptist contributions to the Enlightenment and its emphases on the use of reason and universal human rights is a story that has not been adequately explored or fully appreciated. Baptists advocated human rights for all people before the philosophers became champions of such rights.[2] Baptists took their clue from Scripture as filtered through the bitter experience of persecution for dissent. Enlightenment humanists, the philosophers, and scholars of letters stress the indispensability of reason while Baptists will want to add revelation. Even so, Baptists and humanists have a great sympathy for and commitment to essential features of the Renaissance and Reformation.

Dan Via demonstrates the importance of "critical" thought in biblical studies and the indebtedness contemporary scholars have to the social and scientific revolutions identified with the era of the Enlightenment. Much as some would prefer to get back into the Middle Ages, where heat seemed more important than light, the power and place of reason in biblical studies is now a given. Via also shows the connection between various disciples that employ critical method as those of history, literature, and biblical interpretation. He points out that what passes so often as "historical" criticism is more accurately "literary criticism."

Robert Price helpfully explores the meanings behind (religious) notions of "inerrancy" as he examines certain critical problems with the Chicago statements. He rightly contends that "inerrancy" is problematic to large numbers of Baptists because of their historic emphasis on biblical authority. Inerrancy statements survive among thinking people only with a thousand qualifications. Dishonesty vies with other perhaps more honorable motives to keep the notion alive as orthodox belief.

Glenn Hinson's essay makes a strong case for a Christian humanism. Orthodox theology requires attention to the human with its declaration that Jesus was truly man. Whatever Christians perceive in terms of Jesus' connection to God should not compromise Jesus' true humanity. Affirming Jesus as human, however, does not disqualify him in any way as the primary vehicle of God's self-revelation. Hinson challenges secular humanism to come to terms with a number of its claims about the human he regards as terribly problematic, such as its rejection of spiritual dimensions of human existence. A Christian anthropology insists that spiritual realities are as basic as the capacity for rational thought. Thus, it is not only realistic but is informed by common sense reason.

Molly Marshall develops the notion of spiritual formation as "unfinished presence." Personhood is an eschatological concept—life in the spirit is a lifelong transformation moving toward God's future and personal completion. The spirit works within us to create us as the icons of God. That fulfillment is relational and communal, however, not individual. Human personhood within community finds its ground and being in God's being as trinitarian communion. Marshall combines wit and wisdom in this perceptive treatment that helps to focus the meanings of Christian spirituality for everyday living.

NOTES

1. See Will and Ariel Durant, *The Story of Civilization*, vols. 7–10 (New York: Simon and Schuster, 1961).
2. Thomas Helwys, *A Short Declaration of the Mistery of Iniquity* (1612); Leonard Busher, *Religion's Peace: A Plea for Liberty of Conscience* (1614); and Richard Overton, numerous writings, including *The Arraignment of Mr. Persecution* (1642), *A Sacred Decretal* (1645), and *A Remonstrance of Many Thousand Citizens* (1645).

CHAPTER 12

THE BELIEVING BIBLICAL SCHOLAR AND ENLIGHTENMENT HUMANISM

Dan O. Via

Biblical scholarship should be grateful to the Enlightenment and the humanistic tradition for stressing the importance of reason in understanding and for introducing the impetus to look questioningly beneath the surface of texts and reality and to search for sources and origins. That reason *alone*, however, is the only avenue to truth, or that only one particular kind of reasoning is, and that reason gives reliable, objective knowledge, are assumptions that need to be severely questioned.

The Enlightenment search for sources and origins generated in biblical studies the quest for the sources of biblical documents, especially of the books traditionally attributed to Moses and the synoptic Gospels. It also produced the effort to identify the original meanings of Biblical texts by interpreting them in the light of the historical situations in which they were written. Thus was born the critical approach to the Bible in the late eighteenth century. From its beginnings until relatively recently, biblical critics have called the search for sources "literary criticism." But as biblical scholars have learned from literary critics in the last few decades what is actually involved in this field, they recognized that the search for sources is a type of historical, not literary, criticism. Biblical criticism works with a diachronic model, as do other forms of historical criticism, and not with a synchronic model, as do most types of literary criticism.

The rational quest for methodological acuity that grew so strongly during the 1960s produced the historical criticism of the Bible, and, during the past three decades, a multiplicity of critical methods have emerged. Critical questions also emerged about the hegemony of historical criticism as practiced during the nineteenth (and much of the twentieth) century, and about the naive faith in reason itself. The result is the need to rethink what it means to be "critical."

To be truly critical about the Bible today means to employ a *multiplicity* of critical methods, and not just one. How are we to relate critical analysis to the fact that most Christians—including liberal ones—will want to affirm that the Bible is the word of God or revelatory *in some sense*? But in what sense?

Paul Ricoeur's distinction between hermeneutics as the recovery of meaning and hermeneutics as an exercise of suspicion is helpful. As a believing biblical scholar, the final goal of my interpretive work is to recover the meaning of the Bible as a word than can still engage us meaningfully today. But that positive recovery must be on the other side of a multifaceted exercise of suspicion. The very nature of biblical texts calls for a plurality of methods, and interpreters come to the text from a variety of social locations and with diverse preunderstandings. The use of every critical method is an exercise of suspicion vis-à-vis the Christian claim that in some significant sense the Bible is word of God. The critical method says "but." It wants to dispel the illusions contained in naive claims about the Bible's revelatory capacity.

Let me imagine an interior dialogue that I carry on with myself. The first voice represents my believing self and the second, my critical self. The first voice affirms: The Bible is the word of God. The second voice makes a number of suspicious, illusion-dispelling responses, each of which represents a critical method. The following are illustrative but not exhaustive. First voice: The Bible is the word of God. Second voice: But—

(1) historical criticism has shown that its content is shaped by the events and ideas in the context in which it emerged;

(2) literary criticism has demonstrated that biblical writers employ forms and devices used by secular literature and other religions;

(3) existential interpretation has argued that the Bible's understanding of existence is paralleled in certain philosophies of existence;

(4) sociological interpretation has shown that the Bible reflects the social structures and dynamics of the surrounding culture;

(5) psychological interpretation has pointed to how the message is affected by the dynamics of the human psyche; and

(6) feminist and other liberationist approaches have argued that the biblical message is influenced by the need or desire for power or the absence of free and equal access to God and the goods of the created order.

The meaning and thus the authority of the Bible reside in part in the methodological angle of vision and social location of the interpreter. The meaning is not simply "there" in the Bible to be found. The Bible's authority, then, is hidden in its capacity to speak to the needs and interests of a multiplicity of human concerns and approaches. The authority or revelatory power of the Bible is not one clearly identifiable thing.

I have suggested that interpretation is always from some intellectual, cultural, and social location and that there is a multiplicity of legitimate locations. These conclusions have implications for at least three different audiences.

- *The church*. The message to the church is that the meaning of the Bible as a whole or of any particular text is not one determinate sense that is there to be discovered. A biblical text's meaning, and also its authority, is its potentiality to mean a number of different things. Thus no one ever has the Bible as it is in itself. One only has the Bible from some vantage point that is always limited but possibly also fruitful. I have heard in recent years Southern Baptist moderates with doctorates in theology complain that fundamentalists have forced a creed on the Bible while claiming that they—the moderates—have the Bible in its true sense, as it really is. Nothing could be further from the truth. Some hermeneutical angles of vision are better than others, but no one has the Bible except from some limited vantage point.
- *The Guild of Biblical Scholars*. To this audience the message is that all biblical texts are multidimensional and polyvalent and, therefore, no one critical method can claim to be adequate or exhaustive in itself alone. Many historical critics still think that historical criticism by itself affords adequate interpretation. But any interpretation that is adequate to the text requires a plurality of methods. To employ historical criticism alone is to be uncritical.
- *The Inclusive Guild of Humanistic Scholarship*. To this audience the message is that all reflection is from some limited location and from some interested standpoint. Therefore, reason never operates free of bias or presuppositions. It does not give objective or certain knowledge. It is useful and should not be abandoned, but it is only relatively adequate and should not be trusted implicitly. Therefore, in this postmodern age the only way to be truly critical is to be critical of your criticism and of the ratio-

nality that drives it. All our methods and paradigms are entangled in the ethos, institutions, worldview, and power struggles of a particular time and place.[1]

Finally, I want to enlarge a bit on my critique of historical criticism, not just the historical criticism of the Bible but critical historiography in whatever context it is practiced.

First, I simply want to give three quotations from distinguished scholars who have no theological position to defend but who reflect a postmodern point of view.

- Hayden White has said: "Literary discourse ... and historical discourse are more similar than different in virtue of the fact that both operate language in such a way that any clear distinction between their discursive form and their interpretive content remains impossible.... Historical discourse is less a *matching* of an image or a model with some extrinsic 'reality' than a *making* of a verbal image, a discursive 'thing,' which interferes with our perception of its putative referent even while fixing our attention on and illuminating it."[2]

- Hans Kellner has argued: "Getting the story crooked, then, is a way of *reading*.... It is a way of looking honestly at the *other* sources of history, found not in archives or computer databases, but in discourse and rhetoric."[3] Further, "Crooked readings of historical writing ... unfocus the texts they examine in order to put into the foreground the constructed, rhetorical nature of our knowledge of the past, and to bring out the purposes, often hidden and unrecognized, of our retrospective creations."[4] And, "The assumptions [about the continuity and unity of history] do not come from the documentary sources, from existing historical texts, or from our own lives.... Continuity is embodied in the mythic path of narrative."[5]

- Mark Cousins makes the point strongly that: "Historical investigation cannot simply be used to bypass the theoretical problems which necessarily define the human sciences. Moreover, historical investigation is itself subject to theoretical problems. ... Such investigation has to hang with other forms of investigation in a tissue of uncertainty."[6]

Second, having offered some judgments about history writing by historians and philosophers of history, let me suggest some of the reasoning that would support such judgments. I shall have in mind as a concrete example the historical investigation of the Gospels.

Let us consider the nature of the text. Historical critics of the New Testament regularly assume that the texts are transparencies onto the contexts, that the meaning of the text is to be determined by its relationship to his historical context, and that they have in fact discovered the context and interpreted the text in relation to it. But the nature of the Gospel texts does not justify such assumptions. The historical critics assume that the Gospels are referring to the real world of Jesus and/or the real world of the Gospel writer. That is, they assume that the *referential* function of the language is operating in an unproblematic way and that the text is thus transparent to its real-world context. But such factors in the Gospel narratives as plot, irony, repetition, and metaphorical relationships mean that the language is functioning strongly in a *poetic* way. The poetic function of language is its capacity to refer to itself rather than to an external world. The poetic functioning does not destroy external reference it qualifies and obscures it.[7]

Given the poetic function of the Gospel language, the primary referent of the narrative is the imaginative narrative world, and not the real world. But historical critics regularly believe, mistakenly, that they have identified the real historical world when what they have actually described is the imaginative narrative world. They have really been doing literary criticism when they thought they were doing historical criticism. Historical criticism begins after the delineation of the narrative world. Once we have some grasp of the latter, we can then ask about its relationship to the real contextual world. But we cannot establish exact connections between the narrative world and the real world if we do not have information about the latter from sources *outside* of the Gospels. And since we have general, but not precise, knowledge from sources outside the Gospels, we will never know exactly what the historical settings of the Gospels were. Thus our historical knowledge of the Gospels, knowledge that comes from the contextual relationship, is never any better than possible to probable.

I conclude by trying to make explicit some implications of the foregoing discussion.

- The text is more accessible than the context and thus, however puzzling it may be, is less problematic than the context.
- The context has to be constructed from relatively inaccessible materials and thus is subject to all the imaginative, rhetorical, and ideological forces that impinge upon historical construction.
- The context is likely to be heterogeneous rather than homogeneous, and that complicates assessing how the text is related to its context.[8]
- All of this means that to make historical-critical interpretation, the necessary beginning point of interpretation or the whole of interpretation is as strange as it is weak. It amounts to

interpreting the more accessible by means of the less accessible, the relatively clear by the relatively obscure.

Having said all this, I still believe that a relativized historical criticism is indispensable for proper understanding, and I make regular use of it.

NOTES

1. See Edward Farley, "The Passion of Knowledge and the Sphere of Faith: A Study in Objectivity," *Theological Education* 25, no. 2 (spring 1989): 13–15.

2. Hayden White, "'Figuring the Nature of the Times Deceased': Literary Theory and Historical Writing," in *The Future of Literary Theory*, ed. Ralph Cohen (New York: Routledge, 1989), p. 24.

3. Hans Kellner, *Language and Historical Representation* (Madison: University of Wisconsin Press, 1989), p. viii.

4. Ibid., p. 7.

5. Ibid., p. 1.

6. Mark Cousins, "The Practice of Historical Investigation," in *Post-Structuralism and the Question of History*, ed. Derek Attridge, Geoff Bennington, and Robert Young (Cambridge: Cambridge University Press, 1989), pp. 127–28.

7. See Roman Jacobson, "Linguistics and Poetics," in *Structuralists from Marx to Levi-Strauss*, ed. R. T. DeGeorge and F. M. DeGeorge (Garden City, N.Y.: Doubleday, Anchor Books, 1972), pp. 93, 112.

8. On this and the above, see A. Leigh De Neef, "Of Dialogues and Historicisms," *South Atlanta Quarterly* 86 no. 4 (fall 1987): 501–502, 507.

CHAPTER 13

INERRANCY: THE NEW CATHOLICISM?
Biblical Authority vs. Creedal Authority
Robert M. Price

The current struggle among Southern Baptists over the inerrancy of the Bible is only the latest episode of a controversy that began to rage among American evangelicals a decade ago. Then the opening salvo was the publication of the gossipy bombshell *The Battle for the Bible* by Harold Lindsell.[1] Though Lindsell was himself a Southern Baptist, he aimed his guns at other bastions of evangelicalism like Fuller Theological Seminary, with which he had also had some connection. At the time Lindsell complained that some scholarly evangelicals were a bit too friendly toward trends in modern(ist) biblical study and that their resultant rejection of rigid inerrancy was simply a continuation of the modernism of the past led by Charles Augustus Briggs, Harry Emerson Fosdick, and others. Thus his polemic was quite intentionally opening a new battle in the long and never-concluded fundamentalist-modernist controversy. Our current denominational crisis over this issue is yet another engagement in this continuing conflict.

One tactic of the inerrantist camp in the phase of the struggle immediately preceding our own was the founding in 1977 of the International Council on Biblical Inerrancy (ICBI) which seeks to coordinate a ten-year program to promote belief in inerrancy. The most visible accomplishment of the ICBI is the promulgation of two "Chicago Statements"

This article first appeared in *SBC Today* (now *Baptists Today*), August 1986. Copyright © 1986 Robert M. Price. Reprinted by permission.

(in 1978 and 1982) on inerrancy itself and on the proper hermeneutics (or rules of interpreting the Bible) entailed by inerrancy. I want to examine some features of the first two, because I believe they indicate the direction of the inerrancy movement as a whole. The statements themselves are symptomatic of a trend. For one thing, both the Melodyland School of Theology and the Lutheran Church, Missouri Synod, produced similar statements of what one must believe about the Bible and how one is to interpret it, and it would not surprise me to see the fundamentalists who now control our church issue something similar. And beyond this, the statements crystallize inerrancy thinking as a whole, even where it is not so directly distilled.

The Chicago Statement on Biblical Inerrancy (1978) was sometimes unclear on details, perhaps because it was a conference document. Such texts are likely to be compromise documents containing, at some points, a little of this view and a little of that. Even among inerrantists, it seems, there are conservatives and moderates! But the general drift is certainly clear: "We deny that Biblical infallibility and inerrancy are limited to spiritual, religious, or redemptive themes, exclusive of assertions in the fields of history and science" (article 12). Why is the scope of inerrancy so far-reaching? Simply because, we often hear, what scripture says, God says. There is a one-to-one identification. We are not left to guess at this; the statement affirms that "the very words of the original were given by inspiration" (article 6). Perhaps it is finally time for inerrantists to come clean and admit that they do after all believe in the medieval dictation idea of inspiration. If the words just quoted from article 6 do not equal a definition of dictation, what can language mean? It is superfluous for the drafters to say "The mode of divine inspiration remains largely a mystery to us" (article 7). If we are to take article 6 seriously, the mode of inspiration is no mystery at all to the inerrantists. In fact, *this is the whole point of the controversy.* If we really did not know how inspiration "worked" (some of us admit we do not), we could not be sure whether scripture could contain incidental inaccuracies or not. It is only because God is supposed to have said *directly and exactly* "what scripture says" that inerrancy is thought necessary.

Article 8 suggests that the drafters were indeed uncomfortably aware of how close they were to the dictation model. Here they repeat the standard indignant repudiation of the dictation theory. The article denies that divine inspiration "overrode [the biblical writers'] personalities." In other words, as J. I. Packer put it in his *"Fundamentalism" and the Word of God*,[2] verbal inspiration doesn't imply "that the mental activity of the writers was simply suspended." But this is all just a smokescreen. The psychology of divine dictation is not the relevant point ("Were Paul and

Isaiah in a trance?"). If you believe in *any* version of inspiration that forces you to say God caused Paul to write, word-for-word, "I baptized none of you except Crispus and Gaius . . . (I *did* baptize also the household of Stephanas. Beyond that, I do not know whether I baptized anyone else)" (1 Cor. 1:14, 16), my friend, you believe in dictation. Pardon me if I do not.

Another interesting example of using rhetoric and euphemism to cover the embarrassments of one's position is the Chicago Statement's words on "progressive revelation." Though the signers claim to believe in it, "they deny that later revelation . . . ever contradicts [earlier revelation]" (article 5). Now what is going on here? It is obvious to any sane reader that Deut. 24:1 and Mark 10:2–12, to take but one example, simply do not say the same thing about the legitimacy of divorce. Do the Chicago inerrantists actually intend to commit themselves to harmonizing this "apparent contradiction" by some mind-torturing rationalization? Or do they simply mean to avoid the nasty-sounding word "contradiction"?

I do not believe I am merely carping here, because this is what so much of fundamentalist harmonizing results in. The inerrantist says there can be no real contradictions in the Bible, yet he or she freely admits that there *are* plenty of "apparent contradictions." (Gleason Archer has written a bulky "encyclopedia" of such "biblical difficulties.") The fundamentalists' job is to show how some barely possible interpretation of "problem passage" A would square better with the plain sense of passage B, which A "apparently contradicts." Do you see what is almost being admitted here? An "apparent contradiction" between A and B means that we cannot believe and obey the "apparent, or plain, sense" of both A and B, so we must resort to an admittedly strained exegesis of one or the other. For instance, I have often heard it admitted that Phil. 2:12, "Work out your own salvation with fear and trembling," does not sound very much like Paul's doctrine that attaining salvation has nothing to do with works (Eph. 2:8–9), even if you throw in the synergistic-sounding v. 13, so we had better assume (pretend?) that Paul *really* meant, despite what it looks like, "work your already-secure salvation *outward from within*, so everyone can see the fruits of it."

Besides swallowing your better judgment, what is the problem with such harmonizing? Basically, though it is intended to save the doctrine of biblical authority, it does just the opposite. Why? Because Protestants, including, explicitly, the Chicago inerrantists (see article 17 of the 1978 statement, article 15 of the 1982 statement), believe that it is *the plain, literal, apparent sense of the biblical text that is authoritative*, not some alleged esoteric meaning beneath the surface. To a model of biblical authority based on the apparent sense of the text, "apparent contradictions" are the most fatal kind!

To hide behind euphemisms like "biblical difficulties" and to hope piously that once we get to heaven God will explain them all like puzzle solutions in a kind of celestial ICBI seminar changes nothing. Suppose I need to know whether I may or may not seek a divorce, or whether my salvation is purely a gift or somehow needs to be "worked out" by me. The hope of finding out the right answer someday in heaven is not going to do me much good now. If a denial of inerrancy would rob the believer of the comforting certitudes of biblicistic proof-texting, then dropping the problems into the convenient bin of "apparent difficulties" should have the same effect. Either way, the troublesome passages are effectively useless as proof-texts.

The problem of contradictions between biblical teachings finally drives the Chicago inerrantists to a complete abdication of critical reason. In the explanatory section "Infallibility, Inerrancy, Interpretation," the signers affirm that one day all "seeming discrepancies" which stubbornly resist the best ingenuity of harmonists on this side of the hilltop, will in the light of eternity "be seen to have been illusions." Thus inerrantists render their opinions forever immune from disproof: "My mind's made up; don't confuse me with the facts." The Christian Science sect is also adept at this kind of sleight-of-hand; they insist that sickness and evil are just illusions, too.

The 1978 Chicago Statement leaves generalities aside long enough to focus its guns on a particular aspect of modern biblical studies: form-criticism, the attempt to trace original, simpler units which have been elaborated, reinterpreted, and embellished in their present canonical form. A good example of such critical study would be Joachim Jeremias's *The Parables of Jesus*.[3] Jeremias tries to show how we can sometimes reconstruct an earlier form of this or that parable and show how Jesus would have meant something a bit different by it than Matthew or Mark did when they reinterpreted or updated it for use in their gospels.

The Chicago signers do not like such attempts to go back behind the canonical form of the text: "We deny the legitimacy of any treatment of the text or quest for sources lying behind it that leads to relativizing [it] . . ." (article 17). At least they *think* or *say* they do not like this kind of thing, but the fact is that they have always loved it. Harold Lindsell and company are doing precisely this when they harmonize the contradictions between the various accounts of Peter's denial by suggesting that Peter denied Jesus *six* times. This hypothetical "original version" of the story (which is only imperfectly reflected by the surviving canonical versions, they say) rivals anything put forward by "modernist" form-critics.

What are the constant appeals to an unavailable "inerrant autograph," but a desperate retreat to a lost and *purely hypothetical* "original version," superior to the text we have today?

Both Chicago Statements try to give the impression that inerrantists are really as interested in serious biblical scholarship as anyone else. The drafters of the 1978 statement affirm that the Bible student must be ready to "take into account [Scripture's] literary forms and devices" (article 18). The 1982 statement similarly affirms "that awareness of the literary categories, formal and stylistic, of the various parts of Scripture is essential for proper exegesis, and hence we value genre criticism as one of the many disciplines of biblical study" (article 18). But not so fast! Chicago 1978 pulls the reins at genres which might "reject . . . [a biblical book's] claims to authorship" (article 13), while Chicago 1982 rules out "generic categories which negate historicity [in] biblical narratives which present themselves as factual" (article 13). In other words, we may recognize the biblical use of proverbs, acrostic poems, parables, allegories, genealogies, court chronicles, and so on, but we cannot admit the possible presence of midrash (edifying editorial expansion or creation of stories) or pseudonymous authorship.

Both of these allegedly ungodly genres were quite common and unobjectionable in ancient times, so why are they excluded from the Bible, like unicorns from Noah's ark? Simply because they do not conform to the prior dogma of absolute inerrancy held by the Chicago divines. A good example of a text taken as an inspired piece of midrashic fiction by virtually all mainstream biblical scholars is the episode of Peter's walking on the water (Matt. 14:28–31). The spiritual meaning of this text (which appears only in Matthew) has been plain to every preacher, fundamentalist, or modernist: As long as we fix our eyes on Jesus, we will not sink amid our troubles. The story teaches this point incomparably well. But if it were *literally* true as *historical fact*, it is just inexplicable why Mark and Luke (or their sources) could have failed to mention it. The inerrantist, instead of drawing the obvious conclusion, will wait till he or she gets to heaven to find some other, more acceptable explanation, because according to the dogma of inerrantism, the midrash explanations sound like "sibboleth" (Judg. 12:5–6).

What is the problem with deeming Mat. 14:28–31 a piece of edifying midrash? It involves no denial of miracles per se. It involves no "disbelieving the Bible," because a midrash is not asking to be (mis)taken for historical reportage. Midrash only *poses* as history in precisely the same way as parables do. I once had an eccentric student who insisted that all the parables *actually happened*: There was, *literally*, a prodigal son, a *particular* dishonest steward, and so on. Inerrantists for the most part do not insist that parables are nonfiction, but for some reason they *do* so insist when it comes to evident myth (e.g., talking snakes) and midrash. Are these the same individuals who "deny that Scripture should be required to fit alien preunderstandings" (1982, article 15), who "deny that it is proper to evaluate Scripture according to standards of truth and error that are alien to its usage or purpose" (1978, article 13)?

All of the above observations lead to the most important criticism of the Chicago Statements. They are essentially Catholicizing documents. This, of course, is not fault if one is a Catholic, but our drafters affirm instead that "the Scriptures are the supreme written norm by which God binds the conscience, and that the authority of the Church is subordinate to that of Scripture" (1978, article 2). But in practice, the Chicago Statements subordinate exegesis to prior doctrine; indeed, this is their express purpose: Why else draft a statement of how the Bible may and may not be construed, what it may and may not be heard to say?

At the beginning of the Protestant Reformation, the lines were clearly drawn on issues that were no less clear. On the one side was medieval Catholicism. It had determined that the Bible might only be interpreted so as to support church dogma. The only way to ensure this was to see that traditional dogma governed the interpretation of scripture. To that end the church fostered the allegorical method whereby the troublesome literal meaning of texts might be cast aside in favor of a subtle "meaning" that *would* accord with Catholic dogma. If such a course were not followed, Catholics feared, every Bible reader would become his own pope and the monolith of Catholic theology would be replaced by a thousand competing "heresies."

On the other side were the Reformers who proposed to peel away the layers of dogma and at last see what the biblical writers had intended to say, let the chips fall where they might. Scripture alone (*Sola Scriptura*) must be the only court of appeal. To avoid the church ventriloquism of allegorizing exegesis, the Reformers proposed the "grammatico-historical" method of exegesis: in other words, interpret the Bible as you would Ovid, Livy, or Tacitus. If God did not dictate the words of Scripture, there is no other way to understand it than to understand it *as* human literature. There could be no "sacred hermeneutics," only the sacred *authority* of a text interpreted in a "secular" way.

But then, as now, some people could tolerate only so much diversity, perhaps because their own faith was not secure unless it could depend on a majority consensus, and Protestants began to try to impose uniformity by enacting creeds of their own. "We believe in the bible, *and the essence of that belief is thus and so.*" So the cycle began again, and new nonconformist "sects" and "heresies" arose, using *Sola Scriptura* or "Back to the

Bible" as their cry. The dynamics of this ever-repeating process are probably more psychological than theological.

At any rate, I think that in the evangelical "battle for the Bible," no less in our own Southern Baptist imbroglio, we are again lining up in the same old roles. Conservatives have determined that the "old-time religion" must be maintained and that any contrary interpretation of scripture must be disallowed. The heresies that threaten the inherited "orthodoxy" today (Christian Feminism, Theistic Evolution, Liberation Theology, and so on, some explicitly named in the 1982 statement) seem to depend on modern biblical criticism, just as Protestantism itself was made possible by the grammatico-historical method. So biblical criticism must be ruled out by a set of theologically determined rules of interpretation. This statement of the inerrantists' intention and goal is not a distorted caricature. In the June 1986 ICBI newsletter, chairman James Montgomery Boice rejoices that "our two sets of 'Affirmations and Denials' have achieved almost creedal importance in many places."[4]

At the dawn of the Reformation, the position of each side was at least self-consistent. Catholics were candid about their elevation of ecclesiastical tradition and creeds over the Bible. But today candor has given way to slippery logic and double-speak. The tragic irony of our evangelical battle is that these "Catholics" think they are Protestants! It is the authority of the *Bible* they think they are defending! Yet what kind of "biblical authority" is carefully filtered through a hermeneutical grid constructed by church dogma?

I believe that to believe in and to adhere to the authority of scripture alone may upset our scholastic systems, our cherished assumptions, or our comfortable certainties. Those not willing to take that risk may be "zealous for the law" (Acts 21:20) but they are unwitting opponents of biblical authority.

NOTES

1. Harold Lindsell, *The Battle for the Bible* (Grand Rapids, Mich.: Zondervan Publishing, 1976).

2. J. I. Packer, *"Fundamentalism" and the Word of God* (Grand Rapids, Mich.: Wm. B. Eerdmans, 1958), p. 78.

3. Joachim Jeremias, *The Parables of Jesus*, rev. ed., trans. S. H. Hooke (New York: Charles Scribner's Sons, 1963).

4. ICBI Newsletter (June 1986): 1.

CHAPTER 1 4

MUST HUMANISM BE SECULAR?

E. Glenn Hinson

The question I would like to pose in this article is whether humanism must be secular. If we accept the four presuppositions attached to humanism by British humanist H. J. Blackham, we will have to say yes. (1) We are on our own. (2) This life is all. (3) We are responsible for our own lives. (4) We are responsible for the life of humankind.[1] As a Christian, I can agree with two of those points: We are responsible for our own lives. We are responsible for the life of humankind. I can see no way to reconcile Christian presuppositions to the other two, that we are on our own and that this life is all. Fundamental to Christianity is belief in an Other, a transcendent reality beyond this life. Only if such an Other exists do we finite mortals have reason to hope or make sense out of life.

In addition, I would not place myself among those who want to exclude religion altogether from our society, as Marxists have attempted in several countries and secular humanists seem to favor in the United States. If the collapse of Marxism in the Soviet bloc attests anything, it attests, as the French Marxist Roger Garaudy pointed out in the Christian-Marxist dialogue of the sixties, that human beings cannot live by bread alone. They need a transcendent purpose which provides meaning for life. The Soviet Union did not die because the West outspent it in the arms race, however much those expenditures dented the treasuries of both powers and put their economies in precarious positions, but because it had no room for transcendence.[2] Garaudy was excommunicated from the French Communist party for saying that and has since become a Muslim.

No, I would argue both against secular humanists and against religious fundamentalists who do not know that "secular" and "humanism" are two words. Not only is there a Christian humanism, but a God-conscious humanism is desperately needed today. In defining humanism I would have to revise the *Encyclopedia Britannica*'s definition just slightly. It calls humanism "the attitude of mind which attaches *prime* importance to man and human values, often regarded as the central theme of Renaissance civilization."[3] If we leave the definition a bit more open by substituting *substantial* for *prime*, we will find what Jacques Maritain calls a "true humanism"[4] at the heart of the Judaeo-Christian tradition.

The word *humanista*, as a matter of fact, referred in the sixteenth century to the study of the humanities. The first humanists were teachers and secretaries, successors of the *dictatores* of medieval Italy. They imitated classical style in writing letters. Study of the classics gradually brought a revival of Greek philosophy with its high confidence in the rational capacities of humankind, accent on education, heightened historical consciousness, individualism, naturalism, cosmopolitanism, and encouragement of toleration.[5] Virtually all Renaissance humanists thought they were Christians, nevertheless, and sought to reconcile classical learning and outlook with faith presuppositions.

This interest in classical learning, however, did not have its birth in the Renaissance of the fourteenth century. The first great mission field of Christianity was the Roman Empire, and reaching people in that empire required the first Christians to address not only the religions but also the prevailing philosophies—Stoicism and Platonism. Although some early Christian theologians posited a conflict between Christianity and their culture, some of the leading ones in the East, such as Clement of Alexandria and Origen, did a pretty good job of accommodating Christian faith to Platonism. Even in the West the contentious Tertullian, his "What has Athens to do with Jerusalem?" notwithstanding, used Stoic philosophy and his culture pretty adeptly.[6] As Christianity became the dominant religion following the conversion of Constantine, the "Great Cappadocians"—Basil of Neocaesarea, Gregory of Nyssa, and Gregory of Nazianzus—worked out a synthesis of Christian faith and Greek *paideia* (culture) which could appropriately be called Christian humanism.

In talking about Christian humanism, of course, we must be quite clear about our basic presuppositions. Christianity is realistic about human nature and capabilities. It affirms that though humankind has vast potential for good, in our present situation we human beings do not live up to our potential. What is especially perplexing and disturbing about our present state is that we find the good of which we are quite capable turned to evil and destructive purposes. Our scientific achievements furnish the clearest testimony of this fact. Though science has *humanized* with its remarkable discoveries, it has also *dehumanized* at the same time. Technology, which has eased human toil in countless ways and raised human potential to unimagined plateaus, has stood the human plan on its head. Thomas Merton observed perceptively and with a touch of humor:

> If technology really represented the rule of reason, there would be much less to regret about our present situation. Actually, technology represents the rule of *quantity*, not the rule of reason. . . . It is by means of technology that man the person, the subject of qualified and perfectible freedom, becomes *quantified*, that is, becomes part of a mass—mass man—whose only function is to enter anonymously into the process of production and consumption. He becomes on one side an implement, a "hand," or better, a "bio-physical link" between machines: on the other side he is a mouth, a digestive system and an anus, something through which pass the products of his technological world, leaving a transient and meaningless sense of enjoyment. . . .
>
> If technology remained in the service of what is higher than itself—reason, man, God—it might indeed fulfill some of the functions that are now mythically attributed to it. But becoming autonomous, existing only for itself, it imposes upon man its own irrational demands, and threatens to destroy him. Let us hope it is not too late for man to regain control.[7]

Christianity, however, does not leave humankind despairing in this situation. In its belief that a God of infinite and unconditional love has become involved in the human struggle in Jesus Christ, it holds forth to humankind a ray of hope. The incarnation says, God is on your side, having enlisted in your struggle to be human. Death is not the end of life—life is! Though momentarily life may seem swallowed up in meaningless futility, you have every reason to hope. With the apostle Paul you can cry out triumphantly, "For I am sure that neither death, nor life, nor angels, nor principalities, nor things present, nor things to come, nor powers, nor height, nor depth, nor anything else in all creation, will be able to separate us from the love of God in Christ Jesus our Lord" (Rom. 8:38–39).

The Christian doctrine of incarnation implies the highest possible view of humankind. Alfred Delp, a Jesuit priest and a martyr to the Nazis in 1945, summed up exactly what we must see in the Christian message today:

If the whole message of the coming of God, of the day of salvation, of approaching redemption, is to seem more than a divinely inspired legend or a bit of poetic fiction two things must be accepted unreservedly.

First, that life is both powerless and futile in so far as by itself it has neither purpose nor fulfillment. It is powerless and futile within its own range of existence and also as a consequence of sin. To this must be added the rider that life clearly demands both purpose and fulfillment.

Secondly, it must be recognized that it is God's alliance with [humankind], [God's] being on our side, ranging [God]self with us, that corrects this state of meaningless futility. It is necessary to be conscious of God's decision to enlarge the boundaries of [God's] own supreme existence by condescending to share ours for the overcoming of sin.[8]

God's self-giving in Jesus of Nazareth is the bright ray of hope shining through dark, forbidding clouds. It is precisely what Isaiah had yearned for as he awaited the birth of a new king, namely, that "the people who walked in darkness have seen a great light; those who dwelt in a land of deep darkness, on them has light shined" (Isa. 9:2). On the basis of this, we can proclaim "good news."

Christianity dreams a dream for humankind, and humankind needs that. It is a dream of a new creation, a new humanity, and new human beings. This is not a mere fantasy, an overly optimistic view of humankind, for we do not believe this dream ever realizable in the here and now. Rather, it is *becoming*, always becoming. God, this humanism supposes, is at work bringing to completion the work which God began ages ago. Old things are passing away; all things are becoming new! One who represents the Alpha and the Omega of all existence is bringing our dream to completion.

THE OLD CREATION AND THE NEW

This dream involves first the completion of the creation. If we accept Paul's view of things, the "whole creation" is being redeemed by God, "set free from its bondage to decay to obtain the glorious liberty of the children of God" (Rom. 8:21). This view accords well with the modern scientific theory of the evolution of the universe, which entails progressive enlargement and development. Fitting this scientific understanding into a theological framework, we must assume an incompleteness in the created order. This incompleteness is reflected in natural catastrophes—earthquakes, floods, landslides, volcanic eruptions, and other disasters. It is reflected also in the continuous expansion and rearrangement within the vastly complicated solar systems of a hundred fifty plus billion galaxies which make up our universe.

What we must theorize concerning this, given the Christian belief in a personal God who is the source and end of all things, is that God continues God's creative activity. What has come into being is not the completion and perfection of God's plan; it is only the beginning. The creator is continuously at work, bringing this creation toward completion. Therefore, nothing that is now going on is futile, though its place within the whole scheme of things may not seem clear to us. God alone knows how even wars or tragic accidents within the cosmic order may fit into the whole. But our hope lies in the confidence that God does undergird all things with some kind of purpose and, as it were, pulls all things forward toward Godself. As Teilhard de Chardin has avowed,

> The skeptics, agnostics and false positivists are wrong. Within all this shift of civilizations, the world is neither moving at random nor marking time; beneath the universal turmoil of living beings, something is being made, something heavenly, no doubt, but first something temporal. Nothing here below is lost to [humankind], nothing of [their] toil. As I am convinced that the only real science is that which discloses the growth of the universe, I have been distressed to find nothing in my travels but the traces of a vanished world. But why this distress? Surely the wake left behind by [hu]mankind's forward march reveals its movement just as clearly as the spray thrown up elsewhere by the prow. . . .[9]

In an age of unceasing shifting and change, of continuous enlargement of scientific knowledge about the universe, we must find solid ground in such an understanding of the world to which we belong. Faith in a God who brings order and meaning out of seeming futility has sustained the Christian Church from the first. This is the Seer's dream in the Revelation, when, Roman savagery notwithstanding, he caught a powerful vision of a new heaven and a new earth (Rev. 21). It is not enough to posit a "better day" tomorrow, when people will cease their battling momentarily; such faith will not sustain us against the threat of nuclear annihilation or metropolitan anonymity. The only faith which will suffice is the conviction that there is an "Alpha and Omega, the beginning and the end" (Rev. 21:6), and that God makes all things new.

THE OLD HUMANITY AND THE NEW

This dream of a new heaven and earth prepares the seedbed for another—that of a new humanity. What we see as a humanity now is not what can be. God created humankind out of love in order that the latter might share God's own creative and purposeful existence. From the human point of view, this means that God created humankind to respond in love to God's love. God desired a unity of the whole human race in God's own life.

What we *actually* see is a broken and fragmented humanity. Instead of mutual love and community, there is conflict and brokenness. Human stands pitted against human, nation against nation. There are some encouraging signs of human cooperation, to be sure—the United Nations providing a forum to address world tensions, sixteen nations pooling resources to build a new space platform, the International Monetary Fund doling out advice and emergency aid to financially strapped countries. Alongside those, however, stand devastating conflicts within and between nations, starvation of millions in sub-Saharan Africa, ethnic genocide even in European countries.

According to Christian understanding, this situation has resulted from humankind's estrangement from God. Willingly and with clear intent, we human beings have put ourselves in the place of God. Instead of subordinating everything to a higher purpose, we have pushed God out to the periphery of life. Our alienation has created hostility toward our fellow human beings and resulted in our enslavement to the creation. In short, it has cost us our humanity, our true humanity. Even our reason, which should guide us in using the world and things in it, has become a hindrance rather than a help. For the good things that we plan somehow go awry. While striving to humanize ourselves and to help us realize our potential as human beings, our science procures our dehumanization—our reduction to the animal or even the inanimate level. We who were destined to be "lords" of all have become the "slaves" of all.

Our hope, the scriptures everywhere declare, lies in what God has done and is doing. Out of the old humanity God labors unceasingly to create a new. Jesus of Nazareth—dead, buried, and risen from the dead—is the beginning of the new humanity, just as Adam was the beginning of the old. Whereas Adam typified human estrangement from God, however, Christ typifies our union and communion with God. In Christ's obedience to and trust in God, God did for humankind what we could not do for ourselves; God created a new relationship with humanity and thus launched a new phase in humankind's story.

This new humanity is by no means complete. No, it too is becoming. It is manifest to the whole world in those who openly acknowledge their obedience to and trust in God even as did Jesus Christ; at least in part, it is manifest in the Christian Church, but not only so. God's Kingdom, God's mysterious presence within the whole created order, appears visibly in diverse places. Here, in fact, God's own life pulsates through the members of Christ's body, which is not just the Church but the whole universe. In Paul's words, this means that "we are to grow up in every way into him who is the head, into Christ, from whom the whole body, joined and knit together by every joint with which it is supplied, when each part is working properly, makes bodily growth and upbuilds itself in love" (Eph. 4:15–16).

What creates the new humanity is the spirit of God. Working within those who acknowledge God's mysterious presence in Christ, the spirit transforms them into instruments of the divine purpose. The spirit actually fashions a new breed of people whose lives are characterized by "love, joy, peace, patience, kindness, goodness, faithfulness, gentleness, self-control" (Gal. 5:22–23).

In a sense it would be quite correct to regard all scientific and other advances which contribute to our humanization as God's creation of the new humanity. Where we see persons use the creation wisely, we do see God's purpose for humankind fulfilled. Insofar as metropolis has satisfied this divine intention, therefore, we must applaud it. But we cannot be so blind as not to see what is wrong with metropolis and all human scientific achievements as well. Where they lead to our dehumanization—to our becoming less than we should be—there God's purpose for us is not achieved, and there the new humanity visibly represented in its diverse forms has a job.

The task of the new humanity is to pour out its life toward humankind's attainment of true humanity. This, I believe without apology, occurs only when people acknowledge the sovereignty in their lives of the transcendent One who is the source of all that is. God alone can give completeness to our lives by welding us into one humanity. The new humanity's task is to persuade people overtly to find in God who they are and what life is.

But the new humanity itself stands confronted with a major problem. Before it can serve as the means of transmission for the life of God in the world, it must experience that life itself. Hence, its first imperative is to be attentive to God.

Many who called for radical secularization of the church in the sixties and seventies were mistaken. While chiding the churches to give up their "churchiness" and get out into the world where the Kingdom of God is, they abandoned the concern Christians have always held foremost, that is, attentiveness to God. I agree fully with Thomas Merton. The "religionless religion" people, he said, "seem to me to lack a real sense of God, the living and indwelling God, and to end up in a rather pitiable infatuation with everything that is superficial, mendacious, and cheap in technological culture."[10] To be the new humanity, we must have not *less* but *more* effective attention to God, both public and private. At every point we must deepen our sense of awareness of the transcendent personal, our dependence upon the One creating the new humanity. Otherwise, what will we have to offer the world that the world doesn't already have more of than it needs?

OLD HUMAN BEINGS AND NEW: THE RECOVERY OF SELF

The new humanity has a reason for being, to assist in the fulfillment of God's purpose in the process of creation. As it is itself built up, therefore, as the new humanity manifest in the world, it seeks to implement God's creative process in two directions—in the direction of individual human beings, on the one hand, and in the direction of humankind, on the other.

With reference to individuals, the new humanity must aid in the recovery of self. Human beings suffer particularly from division of their personalities, loss of identity, and fear of death or nonbeing. Our scientific achievements have not solved these problems; if anything, they have added to them. Indeed, they have pointed up sharply the fact that we cannot live by our wisdom alone. Rather, as incredibly complex beings, we require means by which we may achieve wholeness.

The way by which modern persons may achieve wholeness is the "good news" of God's infinite and unconditional love. Even a Marxist conceded that "the new dimensions and the meaning that Christianity has given to love constitute the most fruitful contribution ever made to [humankind's] continuing creation of [itself]."[11] This "good news" may come to different persons in different ways, for all have varied needs. To one it may be cleansing of leprosy, to another receiving of sight, to another healing of lameness, to another forgiveness of sins. Yet to all it must come as the *good* news of an aid from beyond ourselves.

Unfortunately, in the past Christians have often made the "good news" bad. We have held before people the awful terrors of judgment and hidden from them God's love. We have berated them for their sins and shortcomings and kept secret from them God's immeasurable forgiveness. We have chided them for their sickness and infirmity and withheld from them God's healing. We have outdone the Scribes and Pharisees in censoriousness and self-righteousness and forgotten that Jesus Christ came to announce God's infinite care for sinners and outcasts.

We should not continue to do this in our day. Modern persons have too low an estimate of themselves already. They suffer from an awesome sense of inadequacy and unworthiness. Various and sundry voices hound them with cries of insufficiency and sin. If the new humanity would help human beings to find themselves, it must come with an announcement of *good* news. To those who suffer from divided selves, it must say, "God heals and restores your oneness within." To those who plead for acceptance, it must declare, "God has identified Godself with you and given you a new identity in Jesus Christ." To those who quake at death and nonbeing, it must affirm, "In Jesus Christ God is triumphing over these enemies. As he lives, so also shall you live in him."

As the New Humanity, therefore, we play the role of priests—literally. This priesthood involves more than getting someone to make an oral confession and join the church. It involves ministering to persons throughout their lives so that they may become whole, knowing the fullness of personhood as it is found in Jesus Christ.

The church has a challenging opportunity to help men and women to find identity. It represents one of few institutions in our society which should be able to transcend all barriers. It is one of few which, by its very nature, should give a sense of worth to each of its members. It cannot do this, of course, unless it comprehends fully its own nature. *Agape*-love furnishes the cord which would bind all into one, creating and heightening the sensitivity of each member to every other member. Within the new humanity none must be depersonalized or dehumanized.

So also must the church offer assurance concerning the present and the future. The greatest danger facing the church today is that it will lose its nerve in affirming the Christian hope. However challenging the task, it must continue to point to God's enlarging the boundaries of God's own existence to participate in human life in the life, death, and resurrection of Jesus Christ.

THE NEW HUMANITY AND THE OLD: THE RECOVERY OF HUMANITY

Hope should also be the keynote of the church's ministry to the world, for despair and disillusionment cloud the horizon and shut out bright rays of sunlight above. The presence of despair is evidenced strongly in nations which have suffered from the destructiveness of two world wars in quick succession. A spirit of pessimism, nihilism even, grips much of the world in a time of turbulence and economic uncertainty. Nobel Prize–winning playwright Jean-Paul Sartre featured the absurdity and meaninglessness of life in plays such as *End Game* and *No Exit*. Many, having already given up hope, seek relief in drugs, alcohol, trivial pursuits, and even suicide. They view life as one mass of futility.

The new humanity has an awesome task of proclamation, inspiration, and restoration in such settings as this. Somehow it must channel the "good news" to a disheartened generation in such a way that humankind may begin to recover their humanity. This channeling naturally entails the denunciation of humanity and all forms of dehumanization. By virtue of what the incarnation implies, the new humanity will not put its seal of approval on those features of modern culture which dehumanize, depersonalize, and degrade—materialism, sexism, racism, violence, and all the monstrous inventions which reduce human beings to subhuman levels. It will proclaim, rather, that the divine involvement in the human struggle symbolizes God's judgment against such things.

Yet the "good news" comes as more than a declamation against dehumanization. Rather, as we see in Jesus' own ministry, it results also in the new humanity playing the role of the servant of God, pouring out its life in and for the world. Like its head, it will call attention to God's mysterious presence in the world as it heals the sick, feeds the hungry, builds houses for the homeless, provides homes for orphans, clothes the shivering, and meets human need wherever or in whatever form it finds it. Through these activities the new humanity calls attention to God's restoration and completion of humanity in the new humanity itself.

But the new humanity must always be realistic regarding its resources. It is not another social agency. Its task is not simply to do whatever needs doing. On the contrary, through what it does, it calls attention to God's activity in establishing God's mysterious presence, Kingdom, in the world. This, in turn, signals the birth of the new humanity, for the new humanity becomes reality only insofar as people recognize God's presence and power and have their hopes aroused in that knowledge.

The number of things that the new humanity can do to manifest God's creative and recreative activity in the world is unlimited. Despite all human scientific and technological advances of the past half-century, human needs remain overwhelming. Nothing is more important for the future of humankind than hope springing eternal which can enable human beings to rise up out of the ashes of war, to rebuild the core of dying cities, to feed and clothe and house starving children, to minister to the sick and dying, to negotiate peace, to sustain life in meaningful ways and at meaningful levels. To discharge the servant role, the new humanity must always be prepared to abandon old institutions and to design new ones. Let us not forget that Christianity has been the most institution-creating of the world's religions, affirming once more its true humanism. Divine love should give Christian humanists a sensitivity to human need which secular humanists do not possess. Their realistic view of the human plight should enable them to understand humanity's real needs and to discover proper remedies for them.

My own study of Christian humanism has convinced me that it makes a great deal of difference what approach we make to human problems. Though Greek and Roman humanism in its best form contributed a *method*, Christian humanism produced the soul for the humanization of humankind through scientific progress. The method has been refined and science moved on apace since Bacon and Descartes, but Christianity must still keep alive the concern for humankind which has sparked science's greatest advances. If it works together with its children who work in the sciences, it can keep humankind from losing their humanity through irresponsible inventions which have too little regard for humankind's ultimate end as God's creatures. It can sustain humanity's faith in itself as grounded in human faith in God.

In his touching biography of Michelangelo, *The Agony and the Ecstasy*, Irving Stone tells how Michelangelo sculpted one of his most famous works. Many noted sculptors were invited to compete in a certain contest. The stone with which they were to work was a giant marble column, seventeen feet high. When the great artists of Europe passed by the column one by one, they shook their heads in dismay. Nicks and chips and gouges marred the column in the very center. But Michelangelo, greatest of all the great sculptors, paused longer than the others. Looking at the whole column and not merely its defects, he saw something the others did not see. In his mind's eye he envisioned a human form taking shape, and from that column he carved his statue of David.

Human life, humanity, is like that marble column. It is not unblemished, but marred by nicks and chips and gouges. As Christian humanists, we have to help human beings catch the artistic vision of life which Michelangelo had. We have to help them see more than the blemishes. They must see in their mind's eye the fashion of humankind which God intended and now is working within the whole created order to achieve. Indeed, we have to see God drawing a design for the new creation, the new humanity, and new human beings. What Paul said still applies, "We have this treasure in clay pots in order that the transcendent power may be of God and not of us" (2 Cor. 4:7). In that vision there is hope for humankind in our day.

NOTES

1. H. J. Blackham, *Humanism* (London: Penguin, 1968), quoted in *Expository Times* 80 (December 1968): 66.

2. Roger Garaudy, "Christian-Marxist Dialogue," *Journal of Ecumenical Studies* 4 (1967): 207–22.

3. "Humanism," *The New Encyclopedia Britannica*, 15th ed. (Chicago: Encyclopedia Britannica, Inc., 1974–1994), 6:137. Emphasis mine.

4. Jacques Maritain, *Integral Humanism*, trans. Joseph W. Evans (New York: Scribner's, 1969).

5. R. Kreider, "Anabaptism and Humanism," *Mennonite Quarterly Review* 26 (1952): 124.

6. See the recent biography of Tertullian by Eric Oxborn, *Tertullian: First Theologian of the West* (Cambridge: University Press, 1997), pp. 27–47.

7. Thomas Merton, *Conjectures of a Guilty Bystander* (Garden City, N.Y.: Doubleday Image Books, 1968), pp. 76–77.

8. Alfred Delp, *The Prison Meditations of Father Alfred Delp* (New York: The Macmillan Co., 1963), p. 24.

9. Teilhard de Chardin, *Letters from a Traveller* (New York: Harper & Brothers Publishers, 1962), pp. 102 f.

10. Merton, *Conjectures of a Guilty Bystander*, pp. 320–21.

11. Garaudy, "Christian-Marxist Dialogue," p. 214.

CHAPTER 15

SPIRITUAL FORMATION
Humanity As Unfinished Presence
Molly T. Marshall

B aptist Christians and humanists have strong disagreements about the relation of the human to the spiritual. Humanists have difficulty believing in God or accepting theistic explanations for the origins of nature or humanity. Christians begin with affirmations of each, that God not only is, but is creator and redeemer, the source of all that is and the power of the future. Christian affirmations of faith are more often the central questions of humanist philosophy.

The purpose of this essay is to outline a Christian interpretation of humanity that affirms the power of God's spirit to shape our being as persons. Thus it addresses the human as an issue of personal eschatology. Our humanness is unfinished. Who or what we are is open to the future. The question becomes one of how the person might be open to the work of the spirit in becoming most fully personal. More specifically, the focus of this essay is on the role of the spirit in forming us into living icons of God. The place to begin is with a discussion of spiritual formation.

SPIRITUAL FORMATION AND THE FUTURE

What is spiritual formation? Perhaps I should begin by saying what it is not: It is not a separable part of life, a sort of disembodied denial of the

---
This essay was given as part of the Ingram Lectures at Memphis Theological Seminary.

full range of human experience. One does not have to "flee the world" (Rahner) or deny one's humanity in order to embark on our life's project of spiritual formation. This world and all our relationships in it are potential sculptors of God's formative work in our lives. Yet, Christian leaders have not always known this!

In the eleventh century C.E., the Byzantine emperor Constantine IX, judging females too great a threat to spiritual life, signed a charter barring them from crossing the boundaries of Mount Athos, an enclave dotted with twenty monasteries. Even the donkeys that serve as the only mode of transport on the steep, rocky slopes of this Aegean peninsula must be males. Thus, no woman has ever seen Mount Athos' priceless treasures.... But all that is about to change. Rather than letting the women come to the monasteries, the fabled riches will be allowed to leave. Their destination is the new Byzantine Museum of nearby Thessaloniki; the exhibit opened June 21, 1998. For the first time, women will be able to see 621 unique objects of church art. The decision is being hailed as a sign of the elders' new self-confidence. The outside world no longer seems so menacing.[1] This amusing and interesting turn of events suggests that even Greek monasteries are growing in their willingness to "go public" with their spirituality. And so should we!

Until about a decade ago, most persons in the free church tradition knew very little about spiritual formation. (Some perhaps thought it was early morning exercise at camp to ensure "firm believers" or that it was walking in a straight line to required chapel at the Christian college.) "Formation" was thought to be an exclusively Catholic term, a regimented preparation for those with a vocation for the priesthood. It entailed adopting a "rule," a careful, methodical approach to spiritual disciplines which shaped the whole life of the seminarian. Attending to one's spiritual formation was deemed in this context as important as learning biblical exegesis, homiletical skills, theological and liturgical history, and pastoral care.

Further, the Protestant Reformation's insistence on *sola fide* ("faith alone") has, unfortunately, fostered a deep suspicion about the efficacy of any human effort in matters of salvation. "Only believe" became the watchword of those shaped by a tradition which accented the justifying action of God to the neglect of "growing in grace," the transforming movement of sanctification.[2] In addition, hyper-Calvinist strands within the Reformed and Baptist traditions have treated the biblical idea of perseverance as a logical corollary of God's unilateral election; therefore, "working out one's salvation with fear and trembling" has not been viewed as the essential expression of personal redemption. Our soteriology has been characterized by one Baptist historian as: "Jesus did it, come and get it."[3]

Alongside this theological legacy is our acquisitive culture's preoccupation with achievement, programmed outcomes, and easily won certitude. Give us the formula, the opinion of the expert, or the right software, and we are certain we can solve the problem. Thus the acute spiritual longing of contemporary persons—what Mark Burrows has called "soul hunger"[4]—is vulnerable to purveyors of spiritual lives of many, even among those who claim Christian identity. The idea of a patient, receptive, collaborative process with the divine spirit in which one's true spiritual identity is forged over time seems strangely out of sync with today's instant communication, instant credit, and instant gratification.

Attentiveness to the interior life (one's spirituality), long the staple of monastic life, is gaining ground among Protestant ecclesial communions. Retreat houses are full; spiritual directors are in demand. Academies of spiritual formation are flourishing. Even seminaries like ours are seeking to design curricula that will prompt new emphasis upon what students are becoming—not just what they are learning. The spiritual geography of a theological education is now shaped by a more reflective look at the contours of the whole life of persons being formed for ministry. The cynical refrain, "Keep it in the cloister; it won't work in the demands of real life," is being replaced by a new appreciation for ancient forms of spiritual disciplines and community through which contemporary Christians are experiencing a new sense of transcendence and divine companionship in their daily living. Indeed, the divide between intellectual inquiry and the devotional life which Thomas Aquinas fostered is finally being bridged in our day.[5]

Closer than our very breath is the spirit; more knowledgeable of our unique identities than we are ourselves is our divine companion. How does God's work of transformation occur in our lives? I want us to consider the theology of spiritual formation as "unfinished presence." As John's first epistle puts it, "it does not yet appear what we shall be . . ." (1 John 3:2), but we have traces, inchoate longings, the welling up of hope, all of which are crafting our grace-full participation in the ways of God. What is the goal of human living as Christians and how are we to move toward this God-beckoned destiny? How will we become most fully God's and most fully ourselves? Colin Gunton argues that the spirit "far from abolishing, rather strengthens and maintains particularity. It is not a Spirit of merging or assimilation—of homogenization—but of relation in otherness, relation which does not subvert but establishes the other in true reality."[6]

Venturing with the spirit into lifelong transformation is a daunting task in many respects, for, as Margaret Miles observes, "in the entertainment culture of contemporary North America, there are few cultural inducements to understand one's life as an integrated project."[7] But that is precisely our calling if we are Christians: to view the whole of our lives through the paschal rhythms of salvation, that we might "make our own that for which Christ has made us his own" in the words of the apostle (Phil. 3:12).

The idea of "unfinished presence" can be developed around four movements: (1) unveiling our faces; (2) transfiguring divine presence; (3) changing from glory into glory; and (4) seeing face to face. Real presence comes about through an abiding communion of persons, divine and human. Yet, Christian spirituality bears the marks of unfinished presence throughout our pilgrimage toward what the spiritual teachers have called the "beatific vision," when we shall see the Christ "as he is" by the power of the abiding spirit. (Necessarily our pneumatological reflection will now be more directly related to Christology; however, the spirit will not be subordinated as if she is only an agent of Christ—it is a much more reciprocal, perichoretic relationship.)

Unveiling Our Faces

We were meant for closer relationship to God than has been evident throughout human history. Our forebears turned away from the One who desired to walk and talk in the cool of the day, Genesis' description of the original divine-human intimacy. Not content to be those in whom God delighted, they had a burning desire to be as God—"knowing good and evil" (Gen. 3:5c). Certainly God wanted this too, but as gift, not something to be grasped.[8] They gazed longingly at what was forbidden, just out of reach, rather than toward the One whom they were created to image in the creation. They sought to establish their own presence independent of the One who formed them.

Presence is a relational concept. We know our personhood through relating to others, even though "otherness" remains a difficult challenge for humans who tend to be *incurvatum in se* ("curved in upon themselves").[9] Created to love God and to reflect the divine presence, humans early on exercised a propensity to love the creation more than the creator. Long ago St. Augustine wrote: "If you want to know whether a person is good, do not ask what he believes or what he hopes, but what he loves."[10]

Our love, like that of our ancestors, is too often misdirected. We tend to confuse means and ends. Some things are to be used and others are to be enjoyed. Our problem as humans is that we tend to use God for some greater good when, in fact, only God is to be enjoyed, according to St. Augustine. Our human forebears are described as "falling short of the glory of God." Their story is our story, too. As a child I used to ponder this text; of course, I reasoned, we all fall short of God's glory because we are not God. Only later in theological study did I learn that to fall short is to refuse to encounter the presence, that is, glory of God, and that the primary way that Scripture speaks of glory is, the human representation of the divine. We are the glory of God! Thus, falling short of God's glory is our refusal to turn toward the divine; not only do we fail to image the holy, we also refuse to claim our true identity. St. Irenaeus (125–202 C.E.) perhaps said it best: "The glory of God is humanity fully alive."

Perhaps it is the mysterious and graphic contrast of the mode of God's presence that makes it difficult for humans to see clearly. Blaise Pascal understood the paradox of presence in absence which permeates the entire Bible, when he wrote: "A religion which does not affirm that God is hidden is not true."[11] God comes in the grandeur of the heights of Sinai and the disfigured suffering servant, from whom we hide our faces (Isa. 53:3). The elusive reconfiguring of divinity throughout Scripture[12] makes human encounter with the Holy One a horizon of risk. (Yet the spirit is the "go-between-God," in the words of John Taylor.)

Humanity's fear of the divine presence leaves the face veiled, and thus the divine image is often unrecognizable or nearly effaced. You recall the incident: Moses went up the mountain to receive the law from the Holy One. The encounter transformed his visage so that his face shone with the reflected glory of God. Although fading, the radiance of his face was apparent to everyone: He had been in the presence of the Living God. Yet even this was too much to behold for those fearful of the stunning expression of God's splendor. In the 2 Corinthians reading Paul recontextualizes this understanding when he speaks of the permanent transformation which comes to those who unveil fear and suspicion of God's trustworthiness and look steadily toward the glory of the Lord.

How is this fearless beholding made possible? Can one look upon God and live?[13] Are we prepared for what might occur when we encounter the Holy One in our likeness? In the words of Stephanie Paulsell, "there is an intimate connection between sacredness and vulnerability."[14] God's transfiguration into the form of humanity, conceived by the spirit, beckons the reconfiguring of our lives, too.

Transfiguration of God: Presence in Human Form

Hebrew Scripture is quite forthright in its proscription of graven images to represent God; further, humans could not presume to encounter the divine visage. Indeed, Moses could only see God's back after requesting to "see God." This phenomenon prompted Martin Luther to comment at length on the "hind parts of God."[15] (How's that for a sermon series?! Some occasions just seem to call for Luther's earthy exegesis!) Annie Dillard, perturbed with God's hiddenness, writes of this biblical episode: "Just a glimpse, Moses: a cleft in the rock here, a mountaintop there, and the rest is denial and longing. You have to stalk everything."[16] Surely this is often our experience, "stalking God," longing for a glimpse. Yet, found in the same chapter, Exodus 33, is the account of a more intimate encounter, Moses and God converse as "friend to friend." God's definitive befriending of humanity, however, awaits the coming of Christ.

The spirit of God, in humility and grace, offers a human face in Jesus.[17] In him God enters the turmoil and promise of the human fabric and draws it beyond itself toward the possibility of union with God's own life. This union will not diminish individuality, Christianity maintains, but ultimately enhance it. Once the individual is decidedly joined to the depth of God through baptism and the transforming work of the Holy Spirit, that person begins to become a self, is freed to shake off masks and false identities, and to become authentic, like Jesus.

This is a sense of C. S. Lewis's 1956 novel, *Till We Have Faces*. Throughout the novel Psyche puzzles over the silence of God and agonizes that God does not clean up the world's chaos and make truth plain. She despairs of an answer at first and suspects God—if a God there be—of cruelty. But in the end she realizes that God intends to draw the meaning of self precisely from self, a painful birth process, to guarantee that one's life with God is still truly one's own. The life task is, then, to find and develop the true face, the unveiled face, with which to meet the face of God. It is an ongoing process whereby we clothe ourselves "with the new self, which is being renewed in knowledge according to the image of its creator" in the lyrical words of Col. 3:10 (NRSV).

Changed from Glory into Glory

In 2 Corinthians we hear Paul's sense of a deepening and clarifying vision of divinity. In the verses here, increased understanding also takes the form of personal transformation: The faithful, by steady contemplation of the "splendor of the Lord," come to share in that splendor. Simone Weil's perception is instructive: "One of the principal truths of Christianity, a truth that goes almost unrecognized today, is that *looking* is what saves us."[18] We become what we behold. Joseph Sittler speaks of the ability not simply to *see* but to *behold*. To behold something is to see in and through it the mystery of God.[19]

The Orthodox Christian world has long known the power of holy images. In the icon the devout worshiper sees not a mere devotional picture or a visual representation of some significant event or person but a divine archetype. The New Testament speaks of Christ as the true icon of God; the one through whom the iconic presence of God is revealed. Once in the form of God by the power of the spirit, the eternal Christ came to share our form and make possible our glorious transformation.

"Glory" never can be achieved by human effort; the old hymn, "O That Will Be Glory for Me," trivializes Paul's significant meditation on the glory of Jesus Christ. Jesus reveals and mediates glory. The knowledge of glory is discovered in Jesus (2 Cor. 4:6). The saving deeds of Jesus make known the mystery of Glory, hidden from the ages past, to all the nations (Rom. 9:23). Incorporation into Christ transfers glory to the believer. In other words, God invites our participation in the divine life. Paul characterizes the pneumatic life of transformation into the resurrection likeness/image of Christ as a metamorphosis of glory (2 Cor. 3:18).[20]

It is much easier for us to desire to share in the glory of Christ as exalted one, seated with God in the heavenlies. Yet, this is not the primary way that christic glory is disclosed; rather, it is cruciform. In the words of Simone Weil, the true glory of Christianity is found in the cry of absolute despair, "*Eli, Eli, lama sabachthani!*"[21] which solidified Jesus' identity with our own suffering and abandonment. Becoming like him, attaining resurrection from the dead, must follow the pathway of voluntary displacement which does not eschew the close proximity of sacredness and vulnerability. We recall with what perceptive insight Mother Theresa spoke of encountering the Christ in the distressing presence of the "poorest of the poor." While not yet seeing face to face, this beholding both deepens and clarifies the mystery of *Deus absconditus*,[22] "the hidden God" who is the Spirit.

Seeing Face to Face

As God's creatures, human beings are essentially free. Human freedom is understood in terms of certain constitutive relationships: the relationship to God, the relationship to the earth and its living creatures, and the relationships between persons. Spiritual formation is thus not an individualistic but a relational, communal concept.

Bearing the image of God depends on a mutual relationality with others and an abiding friendship with God. Being created in the image of the trinitarian God means, in Marjorie Suchocki's words, being "called to an existence with perforated boundaries."[23] "Perforated boundaries" speaks of an openness regarding human personhood, a willingness to experience oneself as unfinished. We do not ground our own becoming; that is the fructifying work of God's spirit as well as other humans God has given to us to form our lives. Indeed, "The image is permeable, such that the [self] is in continuous transformation through the mutuality of relation. Openness to the other affects the primary identity formation of [the self]."[24]

God's being as trinitarian communion is the ontological ground of human personhood in community. As John Zizioulas argues, human beings in communion with God are transformed into a new mode of existence that allows persons to transcend the "boundaries of the self" in order to be free to become fully personal as well as a genuine expression of ecstasies toward communion.[25]

Biblical theology speaks of "seeing face to face" as delighting in the fullness of presence, God's and our own. Such clarity of vision and communion occurs after a lifetime of learning to pay attention to the mode of God's presence, however elusive. It will not occur otherwise, because as Simone Weil claimed, "Attention is the only faculty of the soul that gives us access to God."

Wendy Wright reminds us that the life of contemplation (a life of sustained attention) is "that radical and risky opening of self to be changed by and, in some way, *into* God's own self. It is a formative life; it changes us and our perceptions."[26] It is a life of continual dying, of being stripped over and over again of the comfortable and familiar ... a life of letting go and allowing a reality beyond our own to shape us. According to our reading from Psalm 32, God wants to assist in this as gently as possible. And this is how the spirit works in our lives.

Gregory of Nyssa's vision of the Christian life, in keeping with the fourth-century ethos of his time, was a vision of moving from "glory" to "glory." According to him, humankind was created to be ... made one with God. Human life was a progressive movement toward God-likeness, a concentration on and unification with the divine. This was effected in stages of spiritual growth, a sort of perpetual recreation, a constant beginning again at ever more transformed levels of being. One never "arrived" in this process but plunged deeper and deeper into divine darkness, the mystery of God; each "glory" or stage of the journey, when reached, gave way to the next "glory" which rose up beyond.[27] The spirit was the efficient cause of this transformation.

When is our presence "finished?" Traditional eschatology has followed the Johannine epistle: "When he appears we shall be like him, for we shall see him as he is" (1 John 3:2). Thus, our lives, hid with Christ in God, finally reflect the glory that is ours by the work of the spirit, who fits us to participate in the divine community of overflowing grace, in which we are fully at home.

And so we at last may sing with all Christians the words of the ninth-century hymn:

Bring us with your saints to behold your great beauty,
There to see you, Christ our God, throned in great glory;
There to possess heaven's peace and joy, your truth and love.
For endless ages of ages, world without end.[28] Amen.

NOTES

1. This information is drawn from the brief note "Giving the World a Peek," in *U.S. News & World Report*, June 9, 1997, p. 14.

2. Recently Donald L. Alexander has edited a collection, *Christian Spirituality: Five Views of Sanctification* (Downers Grove, Ill.: InterVarsity Press, 1988), which offers a comparative view of the differing ecclesial views of sanctification.

3. This memorable phrase is from Bill J. Leonard, but I do not recall when or where I first hear him use it.

4. Mark S. Burrows, "'There the Dance Is': The Dynamics of Spirituality in a Turning World," *American Baptist Quarterly* 16 (March 1997): 6.

5. See A. M. Fairweather, ed. and trans., *Nature and Grace, Selections from the Summa Theologica of Thomas Aquinas* (Philadelphia: Westminster Press, 1954), pp. 35–49.

6. Colin E. Gunton, *The One, the Tree, and the Many: God, Creation, and the Culture of Modernity* (Cambridge: Cambridge University Press, 1993), p. 182.

7. Margaret R. Miles, *Practicing Christianity: Critical Perspectives for an Embodied Spirituality* (New York: Crossroad, 1990), p. 75.

8. Scholars of the "Christ Hymn" of Philippians 2 have long commented upon the contrast between the action of our human parents in grasping what was forbidden and relinquishing (refusing to grasp, giving up, or clinging to) what was naturally the possession of the eternal Son. See especially the magisterial work of Ralph P. Martin, *Carmen-Christi: Philippians 2:5-11 in Recent Interpretation and in the Setting of Early Christian Worship*, rev. ed. (Grand Rapids: Eerdmans, 1983).

9. See Miroslav Volf's significant new work, *Exclusion and Embrace: A Theological Exploration of Identity, Otherness, and Reconciliation* (Nashville: Abingdon, 1996), which challenges humanity's propensity to resist and exclude "otherness" as contrary to the Gospel.

10. St. Augustine, *Enchiridion* 117, trans. Henry Paolucci (Chicago: Henry Regnery, 1961), p. 135.

11. Blaise Pascal, *Pensees* (1660), trans. A. J. Krailshelmer (New York: Penguin Classics, 1979), p. 586.

12. Samuel Terrien's insightful study, *The Elusive Presence: Toward a New Biblical Theology*, Religious Perspectives, vol. 26 (San Francisco: Harper and Row, 1978), sketches the contradictions of the biblical presentation of the presence and absence of God.

13. Exod. 33:20.

14. Stephanie Paulsell, "Honoring the Body," in *Practicing our Faith*, ed. Dorothy C. Bass (San Francisco: Jossey-Bass Publishers, 1997), p. 15.

15. See Martin Luther, *Heidelberg Theses* (1518), W, I, 361–63.

16. Annie Dillard, *Pilgrim at Tinker Creek* (New York: Harper & Row, 1974), p. 205.

17. My own theological formation is indelibly stamped by the constructive insights of Dr. John A. T. Robinson of Trinity College, Cambridge University. Of course this phrase comes from his Christology, *The Human Face of God* (Philadelphia: Westminster Press, 1973).

18. Simone Weil, *Waiting for God* (New York: Capricorn Books, 1951), p. 36.

19. Joseph Sittler, *Gravity and Grace: Reflections and Provocations*, ed. Linda-Marie Delloff (Minneapolis: Augsburg Publishing House, 1986), p. 16. Wendy Wright, in "Living into the Image," *Weavings* 12, no. 1 (January/February 1997): 15, writes: "To gaze is to open our mind and, even more deeply, our heart, to the evocative symbolism, the continually self-revealing forms of the icon and the deep trusts encoded there."

20. Helpful to this analysis has been the study of Carey C. Newman, *Paul's Glory-Christology: Tradition and Rhetoric* (Leiden: E. J. Brill, 1992).

21. Weil, *Waiting for God*, p. 5.

22. This term is based on Isa. 45:15, often used by Martin Luther to indicate that a knowledge of God can only come through God's self-revelation, since God is "hidden" from our reason by human finitude and sin.

23. Marjorie Suchocki, "Theological Foundations for Ethnic and Gender Diversity in Faculties or Excellence and the Motley Crew," *Theological Education* 26 (1990): 43.

24. Ibid.

25. See John Zizioulas, *Being as Communion* (Crestwood, N.Y.: St. Vladimir's Seminary Press, 1985), pp. 41, 43, 53–65.

26. Wendy M. Wright, "Contemplation in Time of War," *Weavings* 7, no. 4 (July/August 1992): 22.

27. Gregory of Nyssa, *From Glory to Glory: Texts from Gregory of Nyssa's Mystical Writings*, intro. by Jean Danielou (Crestwood, N.Y.: St. Vladimir's Seminary Press, 1979), p. 29.

28. *Ubi Caritas*, Latin text, 9th c., Richard Proulx, trans. (GIA Publications, Inc.).

PART IV
FREEDOM OF CONSCIENCE IN THE PUBLIC ARENA

Issues pertaining to politics are among the most divisive and controversial on the contemporary scene. For conference participants, the question is not whether Christians and humanists should be active in the political process, but the *terms on which* they should be involved. What standards, theological commitments, or moral action guides should serve as norms for political strategies, goals, and attitudes that permeate our participation in a pluralistic society?

When posed in these terms, Baptists and humanists find a great deal of common ground both as warrants for participation and as grounds for criticizing the actions and attitudes of groups and/or individuals who are deeply involved in the pursuit of political advantage. As the late theologian Reinhold Niebuhr reminded Americans, "the temper and integrity with which the political fight is waged is more important for the health of society than any particular policy."

George Smith explores the always controversial theme of polygamy. He notes that Anabaptists practiced polygamy, as do the Mormons, which is his own tradition. While not advocating public policy accepting plural marriages, Smith nonetheless takes seriously the reasons why the phenomenon persists, among which are the stories of the patriarchs. The current expression of polygamy is often referred to as serial monogamy because of the institution of divorce.

David McKenzie wonders whether the widely discussed book by

Stephen Carter actually gets the question right. Does American law and politics actually trivialize religion, as Carter charges? Is America actually a "culture of disbelief?" Or is Carter confusing protections *from* religious zealotry with a negativism about religion as such? McKenzie thinks Carter is too much the apologist for a paranoid style in religion that sees legitimate criticism as the persecution of the faithful. There are some types of aggressive religious witness and political activity that are offensive to good taste and insulting to good sense. Rejecting them as norms for political morality is not to reject religion but certain problematic strategies, goals, or conduct.

My essay argues that commitments to religious liberty should be an important guideline in politics and the shaping of policy that affects particular groups or persons. For instance, First Amendment protections are important for public policy regarding abortion. My contention is that the religious commitments and/or moral beliefs of the woman seeking an abortion are not sufficiently protected.

The closing chapter of the book is the joint declaration "In Defense of Freedom of Conscience," with the names of twenty-one scholars who give general but genuinely heartfelt support to the vision and commitments it expresses.

CHAPTER 16

STRANGE BEDFELLOWS
Mormon Polygamy and Baptist History
George D. Smith

This gathering of Baptists and humanists at the University of Richmond continues a series of dialogues which this association of humanists has held with Jews, Muslims, Evangelicals, and Mormons for the purpose of seeking common ground and understanding.

A MORMON CONNECTION TO BAPTIST HISTORY

I became interested in Baptist history by way of my research into antecedents of Mormon polygamy, which led me to polygamous sixteenth-century Anabaptists in Münster, Germany, and the seventeenth-century separatists in England who were named after them. Baptists and Mormons do share some common traditions, such as the idea that a church should be a voluntary association, not a state institution, and beliefs in voluntary baptism, universal salvation, and aggressive missionary efforts. Each community was identified initially by a pejorative nickname, which each came eventually to accept.

The English separatists who established the first Baptist churches practiced adult baptism and certain other Anabaptist beliefs, although not the doctrine of polygamy. To disparage their ideas, detractors called them "Baptists," a shortened form of "Anabaptists" (rebaptizers), the radical group which had fallen into spiritual disrepute years earlier.

I sought to discover why plural marriage came into the Mormon Church, and into earlier religious groups such as the Münster Anabaptists. Named for the Book of Mormon, which adherents believe to be an ancient narrative of Old Testament migrations from early Jerusalem to America, the Mormon Church was founded in 1830 by New York seer and translator Joseph Smith. Claiming to restore the ancient kingdom of Israel, Smith and his followers taught that Jesus was present in the Old Testament and was in fact the creator in the Genesis account. Hence, Smith appealed to both Old and New Testaments when he established the Church of Jesus Christ of Latter-day Saints.

RESTORATION OF OLD TESTAMENT POLYGAMY

Mormon polygamists were not just taking extra wives to double and triple their connubial bliss; they were seeking to emulate the practice of the Hebrew patriarchs. On July 12, 1843, Joseph Smith dictated a ten-page revelation which restored the practice of "Moses, Abraham, David and Solomon having many wives and concubines... a new and everlasting covenant." Smith said that, "if any man espouse a virgin... [or] ten virgins... he cannot commit adultery, for they belong to him."[1]

Just when Mormon polygamy began is conjectural, but it had clearly commenced by April 5, 1841, the date of Joseph Smith's first plural marriage acknowledged by the church, two years before the official revelation. In a ceremony beside the Mississippi River, the thirty-five year-old father of five took twenty-six year-old Louisa Beaman as a second wife, disguised in a man's hat and coat. The marriage was performed by Louisa's brother-in-law, using words dictated by Smith. During the next two-and-one-half years the prophet took as many as forty-two plural wives, one or two at a time. Smith also introduced polygamy secretly to about thirty close associates in Nauvoo, Illinois, a Mormon frontier town by the Mississippi. After his death the practice in Illinois expanded to about 150 husbands and 600 wives, and comprised about 10 percent of the population before the community moved from Illinois to Utah. Plural marriage was publicly acknowledged in Utah in 1852 and the numbers increased dramatically over the next forty years.[2] Today, tens of thousands of "fundamentalist Mormons" continue to practice polygamy.

Within the Mormon community, resistance to plural marriage culminated in the publication of an exposé in a newspaper, which the prophet then had destroyed. Subsequently arrested by the state of Illinois, Joseph Smith was killed in prison. Thus, polygamy contributed to events which resulted in the Mormon prophet's death.

A LARGER CONTEXT OF POLYGAMY

Where did Joseph Smith get the idea to introduce polygamy to his followers? The Mormon practice of plural marriage was not unique. Polygamy has been found in many parts of the world: in India, Nepal, China, the Middle East, Africa, Indonesia, Australia, in early Germanic tribes, among certain Indian societies of the Americas and, at times, among Eskimos of the Arctic. In fact, polygamy has been practiced at some time within about 80 percent of 853 cultures on record.[3]

Before the Mormons, other American groups had reexamined and reinvented traditional marriage customs. Discussion of polygamy can be found in the records of early New England churches, both in sermons and within the congregations. One John Miner was excommunicated for advocating polygamy in 1780 at the Norfolk, Connecticut, village church. Beginning in 1817, about a decade before Joseph Smith founded the Mormon church, utopian Jacob Cochran taught a "spiritual matrimony" to communities in Maine and New Hampshire; it was "sanctioned by a ceremony of his own, within which any man or woman, already married or unmarried, might enter into choosing at pleasure a spiritual wife or spiritual husband." From the 1830s, John Humphrey Noyes and his Perfectionists practiced another form of group marriage over a period of nearly a half-century. Settling in Oneida, New York, in 1847, and convinced that the millennium had begun, more than five hundred men and women shared land, clothes, sex partners, and children.

Support for polygamy came from unlikely sources, such as the seventeenth-century English poet John Milton. In 1823, Milton's *Treatise on Christian Doctrine* was discovered and it was published in 1825. In that work Milton argued that the Bible allowed for polygamy as an alternative to divorce. Unhappily married, Milton had a personal reason to be interested in polygamy. When his wife Mary left him in 1642 he tried to convince both his close friend, a Miss Davis, and civil authorities that bigamy would be lawful. Milton recalled Paul's comments in 1 Cor. 7:15 as rationale for plural marriage: "A person deserted, which is something lesse than divorc't, may lawfully marry again." Milton also argued that polygamy was of necessity a form of true marriage; otherwise, Abraham and other Old Testament patriarchs with more than one wife would have been fornicators and adulterers, and their offspring, bastards (Deut. 23:2). Miss Davis rejected the idea of a bigamist relationship, and Milton's wife returned.[4]

Deemed too sensitive to publish when Milton wrote it, the *Treatise on Christian Doctrine* had been suppressed for 150 years. In 1826 in the *Christian Examiner and Theological Review*[5] published in both London and

Boston, Unitarian social critic William Ellery Channing praised Milton's biblical scholarship, as did Macaulay,[6] though not all responses were so positive. Since it came from the same renowned poet whose *Paradise Lost* had elaborated the Garden of Eden account into a detailed narrative that was preached from the pulpit in Europe and America, Milton's treatise was widely reviewed in over fifty periodicals in Britain and New England.[7] Milton's argument favoring polygamy was discussed throughout the theological community at the same time that Joseph Smith was conceptualizing his teachings.

Joseph Smith's ideas on plural marriage may have reflected Milton's, or they may have echoed the plural marriage controversy of a hundred years before Milton during the Protestant Reformation. Between the advent of Christianity and its reformation, monogamy had been the norm through Europe. Under the influence of Christianity, which emerged as the primary religion of the Roman Empire in the fourth century, bigamy became a criminal offence. While the Gospels of the New Testament say little of Jesus' views about sex, the letters of Saint Paul conceived that the world would soon end and urged Christians to eschew earthly concerns, including sex—either illicit or marital.[8]

The Protestant Reformation initiated a major shift away from papal authority toward individual interpretation of the Bible. Now, with Scripture in hand, new leaders sought to reform their church in light of the teachings of Christ, and the Old Testament as well. Marriage and divorce were pertinent issues. Even though some Protestant reformers had removed marriage from the sacraments, they continued the long-standing church ban on divorce and remarriage, condemning the practice as adultery. However, as stories of the numerous wives of Old Testament patriarchs, such as Jacob, David, and Solomon, became more familiar, polygamy emerged as a possible alternative to divorce for sixteenth-century Christians. After all, neither Christ nor influential church fathers such as Augustine and Jerome had explicitly forbidden plural marriage.

In 1526, when Landgrave Philip of Hesse, the powerful ruler over one of the first Lutheran German states, wanted a male heir, he asked Martin Luther if he might follow the example of Old Testament patriarchs and take a second wife. Luther answered on November 28, 1526, that Christians especially should not have more than one wife, although he acknowledged that some of the patriarchs like Abraham and Jacob "inherited the wives of their friends under Moses' law and had many wives." A decade later, when Philip wanted to marry 17-year-old Margaretha von der Saal, Luther and other Protestant leaders gave their private consent.[9]

England's King Henry VIII had also been granted permission for a second wife. Before he was able to arrange an annulment of his marriage to Catherine of Aragon, who had borne no male heirs to the throne, Henry appealed for years to Catholic and Protestant leaders for approval to marry Anne Boleyn. On September 3, 1531, Luther reasoned that although the Bible opposed divorce, "it permits the king to marry a second queen, by the example of the patriarchs, who had many wives even before the law."[10]

MÜNSTER POLYGAMISTS: LATTER-DAY SAINTS OF SIXTEENTH-CENTURY GERMANY

With an eye to the apocalyptic biblical texts of Daniel and Revelation, some radical Christians sought to reform the Protestant reformers, whom they saw as exercising control as autocratic as the Roman Church. The Anabaptists, adult "rebaptizers," advocated baptism as a freely chosen Christian covenant rather than an institutional ritual imposed on individuals too young to exercise this rational choice. Some radical Anabaptists gathered in Münster, Germany, which they perceived to be the holy city of God—the New Jerusalem that was promised survival from the apocalypse in Rev. 3:8. These "latter-day saints" faced Catholic armies and civil punishment in Holland, Switzerland, and Germany; their fellow Anabaptists and other Protestants also shunned them. In Münster they prepared for the millennium by adopting a strict primitivism religion, which included a restoration of Old Testament polygamy.

In 1534, John Bockelson, a Dutch tailor who had come to Münster from Leyden, Holland, led the Anabaptists as they awaited the apocalypse. He "purified" the town of ten thousand of all infidels—Catholics and Lutherans—so that it might become the New Jerusalem. Bockelson urged faithful Anabaptists everywhere to come to Münster. "I do not simply tell you about it, but command you in the name of the Lord to obey without delay." Some fourteen-to-sixteen thousand pilgrims came from Holland and Germany; many of them were intercepted and killed on their way to Münster.[11]

Claiming the authority of a prophet, Bockelson declared that a man might take to wife as many women as he wanted. Bockelson's followers proclaimed him to be king, and he took sixteen wives who were considered "queens." Fourteen-year-old males and twelve-year-old females were deemed to be of marriageable age and were ordered to marry. Unmarried women had to accept as husband the first man who asked them, a practice which led to a disorderly competition for the most wives.[12] Married Anabaptist women found additional wives for their husbands, as Sarah had done for Abraham in biblical times, and Mormon wives would do for their husbands in the 1800s. Similarities between the Münster Anabaptists and nineteenth-century "Latter-day Saints," the Mormons, have been discussed by several scholars.[13]

In Münster, Anabaptist theologian Bernhard Rothmann justified polygamy by the Lord's exhortation in Gen. 1:28 to Adam and Eve to "be fruitful and multiply." He advised that "if a man is so richly blessed that he is able to fructify more than one woman he is free" to do so. Besides, if a man is sexually dependent on one wife, she leads him about "like a bear on a rope." Rothmann argued that women "who everywhere have been getting the upper hand," should submit to men as man to Christ, and Christ to God.

As with the Mormons, polygamy among the Anabaptists met resistance both within and outside the community. Within the community, forced cohabitation led to dissension. Bockelson jailed and even executed prominent members who refused to cooperate. Moreover, the surrounding German community found the practices of these polygamous religious rebels to be intolerable. Late in 1535, Catholic Bishop Franz von Waldeck and his forces invaded the fortified city and put the Anabaptist leaders to death. Surrounded by Protestant communities, Münster has remained predominantly Catholic ever since.

ANABAPTISTS AND BAPTISTS

Although plural marriage was never a Baptist doctrine, twentieth-century Baptists and Mormons share some important core beliefs with sixteenth-century Anabaptists. Both Baptists and Mormons embrace the conviction that a meaningful covenant to accept Christian beliefs, to follow the continuing leadership of Jesus, and to commit to living a certain lifestyle must be made as a conscious act of free will. Because they believe that only adults can exercise this volition, Anabaptists, and later Baptists, rejected infant baptism practiced by the Roman Catholic Church and some mainline Protestant churches. While Catholics maintain that "revealed data of faith" force them to conclude that infants dying without baptism still have original sin on their souls and cannot enter heaven, Baptist, Anabaptist, and also Mormon traditions consider children to be innocent of sin up to an "age of accountability," after which they are encouraged to make a free-will commitment to accept Christian covenants, which are expressed in the ritual of baptism.

As divisive as the issue of infant baptism was during the Reformation, the broader tradition of baptism links not only Anabaptists, Baptists, and Mormons, but other more ancient groups, as well. Baptismal traditions in late Judaism and Christianity can be traced to ritual purification rites in Jewish washing and bathing; early antecedents are found in the sacred baths of Hellenistic and Persian mystery cults. Mithraic ceremonies in which initiates were temporarily buried or symbolically drowned mimed death and resurrection. River baths of India (in the Ganges), Babylonia (in the Euphrates), and Egypt (in the Nile) included rites of moral cleansing and bestowal of immortality. The rabbi Jesus submitted to baptism by the Nazarite prophet John, who with his disciples formed one among several baptizing communes in the Judean desert that taught repentance in preparation for final judgment at the end of the world (John 1:32–34; Mark 1:9–11). Although Jesus apparently did not personally baptize, his disciples performed the rite (John 4:2). Christian baptism is the New Testament fulfillment and replacement of circumcision. Both signify reception into the covenant. Christian baptism has been called the "circumcision of Christ" (Col. 2:11). Baptism became the sacramental representation of the death and resurrection of Jesus. Paul presented baptism as being buried with Christ (Rom. 6:3-5; Col. 2:12). Among Baptists and Mormons, and other Christians as well, baptism remains an important part of individual acceptance of the covenant and reception into the congregation of believers.

Mormons define baptismal rites as beginning "before the foundation of the world," that is, prior to the Adam and Eve account in Genesis. Here again, Jesus, as creator of the earth, is regarded as the overseer of the rite of baptism before the creation. Like earlier associations of baptism with rebirth and immortality, Mormons regard the ordinance of baptism as an "answer to the likeness of the dead." *The Doctrine and Covenants* (*D&C*), a collection of revelations of Joseph Smith, speaks of baptism "after the manner of [Jesus'] burial, being buried in the water in his name," and "to be immersed in the water and come forth out of the water in the likeness of the resurrection of the dead in coming forth out of their graves."[14] Book of Mormon figures are described as being "buried in the water" out of which they arise (Mosiah 18:14).

Mormon doctrine extends this ritual to the dead themselves, who might have died without a knowledge of the Gospel: "[Baptism] was instituted to form a relationship with the ordinance of baptism of the dead, being in likeness of the dead. Consequently, the baptismal font was instituted as a similitude of the grave."[15] For Mormons, the biblical writers Paul and Malachi advocated baptism of the dead. Paul wrote to the Corinthians: "Else what shall they do which are baptized for the dead, if the dead rise not at all? Why are they then baptized for the dead?" (1 Cor. 15:29). In one of the revelations Smith presented to his adherents, he writes: "I will give you a quotation from one of the prophets [pertaining to] baptism for the dead; for Malachi says, last chapter, verses 5 and 6: 'Behold, I will send you Elijah the prophet before the coming of the great and dreadful day of the Lord: And he shall turn the heart of the fathers to the children, and the heart of the children to their fathers.' The Mormon doctrine of the perfectibility of humanity depends on baptism of the dead: 'For we without them cannot be made perfect.' "[16]

Mormons believe that the ordinance of baptism must be performed in this life, for the living, or by proxy for the dead. Such ordinances as marriage or baptism are performed in Mormon temples, often by family members for their ancestors whose names they have traced by extensive genealogical searches. Otherwise, temple workers perform these rituals for the dead relatives of others. Over five million baptisms for the dead are performed each year in forty-seven Mormon temples. Recent proxy baptisms of Holocaust victims in Mormon temples were angrily denounced by their Jewish relatives and the ordinances were annulled.

For Baptists in the seventeenth century, the ritual of baptizing adult believers became both a personal religious covenant and an aspect of political expression. The political and religious establishment ridiculed the English congregationalists by naming them after the outcast Anabaptists of Switzerland, Germany, and Holland. In the 1600s some of these separatists who had come to New England were still called "Anabaptists" and were threatened by legislation against that creed. Roger Williams was an exile from Puritan Massachusetts in 1636 when he bought land from the Indians which he called Rhode Island. In 1638, Williams established the first Baptist congregation in America. As with their English experience, and in the tradition of their nominal ancestors, the American Baptists proved to be revolutionaries. Baptists sided with the American Patriots in their secession from the English establishment. English and American Baptists now represent about 90 percent of all thirty million Baptists in over one hundred countries worldwide.

Baptists have always claimed independence from political and ecclesiastical control. Rejecting the territorial definition of Christian belief—Italians as Catholic, Germans and Danish as Lutheran, English as Episcopalian, Scottish as Presbyterian—they became part of political revolution in the seventeenth century. Baptists limited their membership to "true people of God," as defined by an expression of testimony before a local (not national) congregation. Members accepted the discipline of that local congregation, conceived to be directly guided by Jesus.

This dialogue between Baptists and humanists at the University of

Richmond, a Baptist school, signals the continuing effort by Baptists to exercise free agency at the local level. Within the university, issues of academic freedom and open inquiry define contemporary struggles to secure ideals that both Baptists and humanists historically share.

NOTES

1. *Doctrine & Covenants*, 132:4, 61, 62. (Hereafter cited as *D&C*.)
2. Andrew Jenson, "Plural Marriage," *The Historical Record* 6 (May 1887): 219-40; Fawn Brodie, *No Man knows My History: The Life of Joseph Smith*, 2d ed. (New York: Knopf, 1971), pp. 457-88; Daniel W. Bachman, "A Study of the Mormon Practice of Plural Marriage Before the Death of Joseph Smith" (master's thesis, Purdue University, 1975); George D. Smith, "Nauvoo Roots of Mormon Polygamy, 1841-46: A Preliminary Demographic Report," *Dialogue: A Journal of Mormon Thought* 27 (spring, 1994): 1-72.
3. Delta Willis, *The Hominid Gang: Behind the Scenes in Searching for Human Origins* (New York: Viking, 1989), p. 259; George P. Murdock and Douglas R. White, "Standard Cross-Cultural Sample," *Ethnology* 8 (October 1969): 329-69.
4. John Milton, *De Doctrina Christiana*, trans. and ed. Charles Sumner (Cambridge: Cambridge Univ. Press, 1825), reproduced in "Two Books of Investigations into Christian Doctrine Drawn from the Sacred Scriptures Alone," (ca. 1658-ca. 1660) in Geoffrey Cumberlege, ed., *Complete Prose Works of John Milton* (New Haven: Yale Univ. Press, 1973), vol. 1, p. 3; vol. 6. pp. 126-850. See also John Milton's *Doctrines of Discipline and Divorce* (August 1, 1643); vol. 2, pp. 137-58, 217-356; vol. 6, pp. 762-63; Leo Miller, trans., *John Milton Among the Polygamophiles* (New York: Loewental Press, 1974), p. 8.
5. *Christian Examiner and Theological Review* 3 (1826): 57-77.
6. *Edinburgh Review* 42 (1825) 304-46.
7. See reviews of *De Doctrina* in Europe and America: *Complete Prose Works*, I:3-10; James G. Nelson, *The Sublime Puritan: Milton and the Victorians* (Westport, Conn.: Greenwood Press, 1974), p. 176, n. 54.
8. James A. Brundage, *Law, Sex, and Christian Society in Medieval Europe* (Chicago: University of Chicago Press, 1987), pp. 1-9, 37-50, 57-76.
9. *Dr. Martin Luthers Werke* (Weimar, 1933), vol. 4, p. 140, letter 1056; vol. 8, pp. 628-44; Miller, *John Milton Among the Polygamophiles*, pp. 14-15, 21-22.
10. Miller cites Ernst L. Enders, *Dr. Martin Luther's Sämmtliche Werke* (Frankfort, 1903) vol. 9, p. 80; Miller, *John Milton Among the Polygamophiles*, p. 21.
11. James M. Stayer, *Anabaptists and the Sword* (Lawrence: University of Kansas, 1976), p. 374.
12. George H. Williams, *The Radical Reformation* (Philadelphia: Westminster, 1962), pp. 371-78, 505-17.

13. See Cornelius Krahn, *Dutch Anabaptism* (The Hague: Martinus Nijhoff, 1968); William E. Juhnke, "Anabaptists and Mormons," *John Whitmer Historical Association Journal* 2 (1982); David B. Davis, "The New England Origins of Mormonism," *New England Quarterly* (June 1953); and D. Michael Quinn, "Socioreligious Radicalism of the Mormon Church: A Parallel to the Anabaptists," *New Views of Mormon History*, ed. Bitton and Beecher (Salt Lake City, 1987).

14. *D&C*, 124:51, 128:12.

15. Ibid., 128:17–18.

16. Ibid.

CHAPTER 17

STEPHEN CARTER, THE CHRISTIAN COALITION, AND THE CIVIL RIGHTS ANALOGY

David McKenzie

Stephen Carter's *The Culture of Disbelief* has justifiably attracted a great deal of academic and public attention. The response is caused in part by the novelty of the project—an African American Episcopalian and professor of law at Yale University writes to encourage a larger role for religion in the public square. But more importantly, the response stems from the work's arguments themselves. Carter takes on many of the basic assumptions of liberal democracy regarding the proper public role of religion. He argues against the Supreme Court, for instance, that the first prong of the *Lemon* test—secular purpose—is dysfunctional. He rejects the Rawlsian assumption that distinctively religious views are not permissible in public debate, insisting instead that religious opinion is urgently needed in many areas today where secular arguments are at a standstill. And he argues against the liberal establishment's view that activities of political organizations such as the Christian Coalition violate church-state separation, maintaining rather that such activities are not significantly different from earlier political involvement of African American churches on behalf of racial justice.

The Carter text has much to commend it. The author's mastery of church-state legal history is obvious throughout, and the fact that he can

---

This article was first published in *Journal of Church and State* 38, no. 2 (spring 1996): 297–319. Copyright © 1996 by J. M Dawson Center for Church-State Studies, Waco, Texas. Used by permission.

speak from a religious tradition of active political involvement adds practical credibility to the work's theoretical concerns. Carter's attention to the legal disfranchisement of Native American and other minority religious faiths is especially welcome, as is the effort, seen most notably in his analysis of the school prayer and Bible reading cases, to avoid establishment while encouraging religious participation in public life.

Nevertheless, some of the work's arguments are troubling, especially when considered in light of the Christian Coalition's activities in the recent midterm elections and the role played by conservative religious groups in the American abortion wars. In this essay, it will be argued that in many respects Carter goes too far in his effort to rehabilitate the religious voice, that in fact he sanctions a degree of influence by religion which violates the Establishment Clause. The essay focuses on the analogy between the activities of the Christian Coalition today and those of the civil rights activists thirty years ago. More directly, it focuses on the pro-life abortion argument as an analog for protest of racial injustice.

A NEW LIBERAL RELIGIOUS VIEW

It should come as no surprise that some conservative thinkers criticize Carter for not going far enough in his effort to accommodate religious contributions. Richard John Neuhaus, for instance, argues that Carter is really just circulating traditional liberalism in a new form.[1] Others have pointed out that although Carter invites conservative Christians to the public square, he really does not consider the possibility that they might win the argument and implement a policy deemed correct because it is the "will of God." Given that after much debate Carter himself seems always to adopt the position of liberal academics (on school prayer, creationism, and abortion cases, for example), he appears to welcome conservative Christians only insofar as one can be sure that they are in the minority and their arguments are faulty.[2]

These conservative critiques certainly have merit. It is, indeed, a curious feature of the text that Carter almost always sides with liberal outcomes. One may argue, however, that although he obviously speaks from a liberal academic and religious tradition, in many respects Carter does break new ground by occupying positions most other liberal Christian thinkers would reject. Though the examples are numerous, this essay will address only a few of the most important of Carter's positions, which are:

- Throughout the work, Carter consistently interprets the Establishment Clause to mean only that government should not control the church, not that the church is prohibited from influencing government decisions. In his words, "Simply put, the metaphorical separation of church and state originated in an effort to protect religion from the state, not the state from religion."[3] Most liberal thinkers would prefer a symmetrical relation.

• Regarding private schools, Carter is not yet ready to endorse a voucher system, but he does occupy the position that if such a system is approved then it should also extend to religious schools. Not to do so, in his opinion, would compromise government neutrality toward religious belief in that it would punish parents for selecting a religious over a secular private school.[4] Again, liberal Christian thought generally opposes a voucher program specifically because it would allocate government funds for sectarian schools.

• In his treatment both of school prayer and creationism cases, Carter explicitly rejects the first prong of the *Lemon* test as a violation of government neutrality, arguing that it contributes preferential treatment to secular as opposed to religious interests. In his view, the motivation for legislative bills requiring the teaching of creationism or a moment of silence is irrelevant. The Court has decided both kinds of cases, however, by appeal to the *Lemon* test, holding in *Edwards* v. *Aguillard*[5] that "creation science" was really an attempt to smuggle religious doctrine into the classroom, and that the "moment of silence" for Alabama classrooms in *Wallace* v. *Jaffree*[6] was a similar effort to get sectarian prayer in place. Carter argues against strict separationists and the Court that these proposals must be decided on the basis of their content, not the purposes behind the bills.[7] He argues that all kinds of interests, after all, lie behind any bill. Thus, for the Court to allow any kind of interest except those of a religious nature demonstrates a bias against religion.

These few examples show that Carter is moving beyond traditional liberalism in his argument that religion should be accommodated. This essay argues that he goes too far. It begins by demonstrating two problems in Carter's treatment of the civil rights analogy. Then it explores each of these problems in detail, arguing first that recent activities of the Christian Coalition violate restrictions of the Internal Revenue Code that are meant to encourage church-state separation, and that these violations should constitute the basis for removal of its tax-exempt status; and second, that the virtual absence of secular, egalitarian arguments for the pro-life abortion stance demonstrates that such a position violates credible requirements for participation in the arena of public reason, and that efforts to write this position into law constitute a violation of the Establishment Clause.

THE CIVIL RIGHTS ANALOGY

Throughout his book, Carter employs the analogy between civil rights activism by church leaders in the 1950s and 1960s and the political activity of the Christian Coalition and other religious groups in the 1990s.[8] He argues that there is no significant difference, indeed, that there is great irony in the fact that liberals promoted church-related support of civil rights but today condemn conservative political activity. In his view, conservatives have presently as much right to such activism as the liberals did earlier.

The civil rights parallel is indeed instructive, but Carter's appeal suffers from two grave mistakes. First, he argues correctly that the earlier movement operated in and through churches at least as much as the Religious Right today and, therefore, that if one is legitimate so is the other. But on this point he overlooks another option, namely, that *neither* should be construed as legitimate, which is the position this author wishes to defend. Second, he does not notice the profound difference in the level of secular support for these two movements. Here the analogy breaks down in that the civil rights movement was widely supported by secular, egalitarian moral arguments. But making "pro-life" a political priority, as the religious right does, has scarcely any support at all from secular ethics. The impetus for pro-life is essentially and distinctively religious. The same is not true of civil rights.

On the nature of the activism in both cases, it is important to make a distinction that Carter overlooks, and that is the difference between the statement of a position on public and social issues and the direct endorsement of a candidate or use of the church as a locus of political activity. The former has never been found problematic by the Supreme Court. There are Sunday School lessons, sermons, tracts, theological works, special emphasis Sundays (the Southern Baptist Convention's "Sanctity of Human Life" Sunday is a good example),[9] and official church statements such as the American Catholic Bishops' various pronouncements on peace, economic justice, and many other concerns. Almost all ministers preach sermons that contain arguments of a scriptural or theological sort regarding social issues. Indeed, it is virtually impossible not to, given the normal theological links among scripture, tradition, morality, and society. Such public influence is what Christian ethics is all about.

It is one thing to engage in such legally sanctioned activities, but quite another to promote or demonize a candidate, to have various political figures speak in the churches in support of their campaigns, and to organize political action committees and run campaigns within the churches.

There is no question that the civil rights movement went far beyond the simple statement of its position or sermons preached in support of such. As John Noonan and others point out, the movement was centered in churches and the various leading organizations were directly religious. Martin Luther King himself, of course, was a minister and his motivation was theological from the beginning. Almost all of the officers of the Southern Christian Leadership Conference (SCLC) were ordained ministers, as were the leaders of other civil rights organizations. The members of SCLC were churches, and its financial support came primarily from church offerings. Demonstrations were planned within churches and orchestrated from a church base. King's "Letter from a Birmingham Jail" was a direct religious appeal addressed to "fellow clergymen," and had a circulation, according to Andrew Young, of nearly one million copies by the time its author was released.[10]

Looking back, it might be argued that the reason why no charges of church-state violations were made against the African American churches was that civil libertarians strongly favored the policies being advocated from the pulpit. Conservatives did not have the firepower to bring such charges at that time. Had it been attempted, it is arguable that the effort would have been defeated as racist.

From its inception in 1989 to its recent activities in the midterm 1994 elections, and under the leadership and political cunning of Pat Robertson and Ralph Reed, the Christian Coalition has similarly gone far beyond a simple statement of its positions. It has operated with the direct involvement and leadership of clergy and has carried out its activities through churches. Activists are using the pulpit today to advance conservative causes, most notably the elimination of abortion. Religious support for the relevant positions on public issues has been rallied through sermons, church school classes, and denominational literature. Specific support for or opposition to various political figures has been a central part of the rhetoric (for instance, materials vilifying President Bill Clinton for his "anti-Christian" positions on abortion, gun control, and gays in the military).

Looking at the present situation, it is arguable that the Coalition has not been vigorously opposed on a church-state basis for three reasons: because of the practical difficulties in bringing such charges, a point to be developed later; because intellectuals such as Stephen Carter are hamstrung by their need to accept both church-state separation and civil rights church involvement; and because of the widespread academic interest in a more communitarian role for religious belief in the contemporary period.

On the disanalogy between the civil rights movement and abortion protest, we should distinguish positions taken by religious organizations that are supported also by egalitarian moral arguments and those that are taken on the basis of divine authority as sectarian revelations without egalitarian support. It is the ethics of moral equality, worked out by utilitarian and rational ethicists, and more recently in the newly invigorated moral-sense approach, that undergirds a system of human rights and various rights documents such as the American Bill of Rights and the UN International Declaration of Human Rights. Communitarian philosopher Philip Selznick refers to this approach as the ethics of "civility," in contrast to the ethics of "piety," the latter reflecting more particular interest such as religious traditions, filial obligations, and patriotism.[11]

Applying the distinction to Carter's analogy, it becomes clear that in its civil rights activity the church was supporting for theological reasons a position with strong support from egalitarian ethics as well.[12] And it is not just that the position benefited from the political rhetoric of both church leaders and moral philosophers. Rather, there are good arguments from both perspectives. Here the church embodied in a superlative way its most appropriate democratic social function—to provide the theological basis and spiritual encouragement for actions, programs, and policies that are morally required by secular arguments that all can agree to no matter what their religious beliefs.

But in its opposition to abortion, along with many other Christian Coalition positions, the church is asserting a moral point of view by divine authority which is either inconsistent with egalitarian ethics or goes far beyond what might be sanctioned by a consensus of secular ethicists. It is, after all, a matter of debate whether a fetus is a person. Egalitarian ethicists rather uniformly argue that it is not, and that even if at some point in fetal development it becomes appropriate to associate personhood with the fetus, the rights of the mother still outweigh those of the unborn.[13] Indeed, the American public remains divided on the personhood of the fetus, as the recent sociological analysis by James Davison Hunter and Carl Bowman shows,[14] and this after twenty years of propagandizing by conservative religious organizations.

Given the lack of consensus supporting fetal personhood and the general opposition to such a view by secular ethicists, religious leaders who want the society to eliminate abortion must rely primarily on revelatory authority for their position. Thus, although the Bible itself is silent on abortion, fundamentalists will argue that certain passages such as Jeremiah's confession that God "knew" him while he was still in the womb give biblical support to the pro-life position. This argument, however, is purely theological, it rests on the supposed revelatory authority of the Bible, and it is very debatable even within that context. For instance, it is easily arguable that Jeremiah was writing poetically of his sense of calling, saying, in effect, that from the beginning God had destined him for his prophetic ministry. On this interpretation, the passage has absolutely nothing to do with fetal rights.

Similarly, Catholic leaders will argue from the authority of church tradition that ensoulment occurs at conception. Sometimes the church's doctrine is further defended by appeal to historical natural law theories or contemporary philosophical arguments based in natural human reason, unaided by revelation. As such, the Catholic pro-life argument is not inherently problematic for church-state concerns, but neither is it very convincing as an argument. Appeals to natural law seem obscure outside the context of Catholic theology, and the various contemporary philosophical arguments for a pro-life position do not command a consensus either among the community of bioethicists continually at work on the issue, or within the society at large. On a more popular level and in the framework of Catholic pro-life activism, support for the view that ensoulment occurs at conception is again purely theological, resting on the supposed revelational authority of the church. Against such an appeal to church tradition, it should be pointed out that the church has fluctuated in its views of fetal personhood through the centuries, coming to its present identification of ensoulment and conception only in 1869.[15] Also, a *reductio ad absurdum* is immediately at hand. If ensoulment occurs at conception, then God is incredibly wasteful with souls since at least one in three zygotes/embryos will naturally abort.

Even though the arguments are weak in their own context, they are put forward with great authority by religious zealots. Their pamphlets distributed for Sunday School use in Baptist churches, for instance, portray abortion as against the will of God, or even make the claim that "God says" abortion is wrong. In their desperation to make sure that the government illegalized abortion to conform with their sectarian religious views, and in the light of their obvious inability to win the moral argument, many pro-life advocates resort now to force in the effort to put their view in place. This is evidenced, of course, by abortion clinic blockades and bombings, intimidation of women seeking abortions, harassment of abortion clinic personnel, and the murder of abortion doctors. Though official denominational statements have generally condemned the violence, the most fervent pro-life clergy and their followers have supported it. Here the church reveals itself at its worst, imposing views by supposed divine authority on society by any means necessary.

By Carter's account, secular theorists are divided on the questions of life and personhood, and society thus needs uniquely religious perspectives. But this view is almost certainly wrong. Although there are all kinds of divisions among secular thinkers on the question of when the fetus achieves personhood, by and large a secular approach will endorse some form of the pro-choice position. The basic division is not among secular thinkers, but between secular and religious thinkers.

Carter's work with the civil rights analogy, therefore, is problematic in two ways. First, he overlooks the possibility that both civil rights activism and Christian Coalition activism violate church-state separation; and second, he ignores the important disanalogy arising from differences in the level of secular, egalitarian support for the two kinds of involvement. At this point, we need to explore each of these problems in greater detail.

TAX EXEMPTION AND RELIGIOUS INVOLVEMENT IN POLITICS

The Christian Coalition qualifies as a tax exempt religious lobby under section 501(c)(4) of the Internal Revenue Codes, and the churches through which it operates are exempt on the basis of section 501(c)(3). The difference between these two sections is that the latter includes both an exemption from taxes on income and a tax deduction for contributions. The former, in contrast, allows only the income-tax exemption.[16] The lobbying groups with tax exempt status under section 501 (c)(4) may discuss issues and put forward positions but *cannot* endorse or urge support for a particular candidate.[17] Further, such religious lobbies are not required to report large donations, whereas federal election laws require such reporting from nonexempt lobbies.[18] Nonprofit religious organizations are exempt from taxation under section 501 (c)(3) so long as they do not devote a "substantial" part of their activities to propaganda or other efforts to influence legislation.[19] Furthermore, these exempted organizations are not permitted to participate in political campaigns either directly or indirectly. They are specifically prohibited from endorsing a candidate. They may publish voter guides as long as they do not contain a "bias" in their presentation of positions or candidates.[20]

It is important to be clear about why religious tax exemptions exist and why there are restrictions imposed regarding the political activity of exempted religious organizations. The exemptions are not in place just because of long-standing traditions in American tax law, but also because of the perceived social as well as moral and spiritual benefit of such organizations. Humanist critique and the threat of abuse in the name of God notwithstanding, religious belief is generally seen in America as a good for society.

Various restrictions on political activity apply to all tax-exempt organizations, but the application of these restrictions to religious organizations and lobbies is particularly important. Against the suggestion of Carter's book, they are restricted specifically to limit religious control over the government. Even with the constitutional safeguards of American politics and the pluralism of American religion, it is still possible that a particular church or religious faction would grow large and powerful, organize essentially as a political party, elect its candidates, and enact legislation embodying its theological doctrines. Restrictions on the political activity of tax exempt religious organizations and lobbies mitigate against such a violation of the Establishment Clause.

Both the Christian Coalition and its supportive churches have routinely violated the requirements for tax exempt status. In the 1994 midterm elections, as well as the 1992 presidential race, conservative Christians mounted an "in-your-face" political effort in which numerous candidates were vilified and others openly endorsed. The Coalition has attempted to circumvent the federal requirement through its voter guides, but they are a sham. According to Coalition literature, some thirty-three million guides were distributed on election Sunday.[21] They were put in church bulletins, handed out at the end of services, distributed in church vestibules, and put on the windshields of cars in church parking lots.

The voter guides made little pretense to objectivity. Positions of Democratic candidates all over the country were misrepresented and the issues were stated in such a way as to discredit opponents of Coalition candidates. A typical example was the issue described as "Government Control of Healthcare." Any candidate who supported the Clinton healthcare proposal was said to "favor" such "control." Logically, of course, the issue was put in a slanted way. Supporters of Clinton did not favor government "control" as in complete government administration of the program. The Clinton plan left ample room for the private sector through its ideal of "managed competition." Indeed, the actual providing of healthcare was to be left largely in private hands.

Virtually every line on the voter guides was slanted in a similar way. Democrats who supported Clinton's Crime Bill, for instance, were said to "support" the "banning" of private gun ownership, again as though it were universal, whereas the bill itself involved only a limited ban on certain semiautomatic weapons. Candidates who favored continued government support for public radio and television programming were said to favor instead "government support for pornography," as though all public programs were pornographic and ignoring the fact that the vast majority of these funds subsidize serious literary and artistic presentations utterly bereft of pornographic content. The guides were full of such half-truths and loaded terms. They were nothing if not biased.

Democratic and moderate Republican candidates have complained bitterly about the treatment they received from the Religious Right. The midterm elections were notable even in American politics as among the dirtiest ever, and it is ironic that "Christians" were so vicious in their attacks against Coalition opponents. There was certainly a holy war mentality about the approach. No matter how immoral, unchristian, or even illegal, the strategies of vilification were justified, it appears, as necessary means to electing "Christian" candidates.

Various formal complaints and suits have been filed in protest against these activities. Thus, the Democratic Congressional Campaign Committee filed a complaint with the Federal Election Committee accusing the Christian Coalition of carrying out "shadow" campaigns for Republican candidates.[22] And in Florida, moderate Republican and successful school board candidate Tom Chapman filed suit in September 1994 against the Coalition in Orlando, accusing the group of "totally misrepresenting" his position and launching "malicious lies" against his campaign.[23] Like many others vilified by the Coalition, Chapman is himself a practicing Christian (Methodist) who wishes to protect the separation of church and state.

The problem with these legal responses is that they take too long and, in the final analysis, seem to accomplish little. Losing candidates, knowing that the race is over and that a suit will require several years for settlement, do not feel the compulsion and often do not have the funds to take formal action. Winning candidates have little motivation for pursuing the issue either, preferring instead to focus attention on mending fences within their constituencies and dealing with the legislative issues at hand.

The time factor is problematic enough for most. Indeed, as new offenses occurred in the 1994 elections, the FEC was still handling older complaints, primarily Coalition activities in the 1990 campaign of Senator Jesse Helms and the Christian Action Network's (CAN) opposition to Clinton in the 1992 presidential election.

In the Helms case, the charge is that distribution of voter guides in North Carolina on election Sunday 1990 was carried out in response to a request for help by Helms, a practice in violation of federal tax codes for exempt organizations such as the Coalition.[24] In the CAN case, the FEC sued the Network for its overt opposition to Clinton in the 1992 presidential election, again in violation of the tax code, which explicitly prohibits organizations such as CAN from advocating the election or defeat of specific candidates.[25] These conservative Christian groups, in fact, have done everything possible to vilify President Clinton and to associate various targeted candidates with him.

It may be that the Coalition will be able to defend itself against such charges by hiding behind the supposed objectivity of their voter guides. Even if their clever counsel blocks legal sanctions, however, there are still moral and theological problems with the nature of their political activity. Coalition leaders justify their use of half-truths, innuendo, misrepresentation, and labeling on the basis that everyone does it in political campaigns. Then having asserted the common practice, they portray the Coalition as victim of social prejudice by arguing that there are complaints only when conservative Christians do what other groups have done all along.

Common practice is a weak justification, of course, but beyond the obvious logical fallacy there is the additional culpability stemming from the "Christian" identity of the organization. At the very least we should expect that those who bring the name of Christ into the political arena would remember basic Christian virtues such as honesty and integrity. But in the midterm elections, highly slanted political rhetoric and pamphleteering was employed in an unrelenting crusade against Coalition opponents, all in the name of God.

Perhaps the church-state issue could be downplayed in this case if Coalition candidates had routinely lost; if, in other words, the organization had no significant impact on the election. But that, of course, was not the result. According to its own statements, the Coalition spent approximately $2 million to distribute its voter guides in sixty thousand churches.[26] Leaders of People for the American Way say that 60 percent of the six hundred candidates associated with the Religious Right won their races, and the Coalition claims to have provided the swing vote in fifty important races.[27] Former Executive Director Ralph Reed boasts that Coalition exit polls showed that one-third of voters could be identified as "white, evangelical, born-agains,"[28] and almost 70 percent of these chose Republican candidates.[29]

An analysis of election returns reveals that the so-called Republican Revolution was actually voted into place by only about 20 percent of the voters. Fewer than 39 percent of registered voters actually cast a ballot, and the total nationwide vote was much closer than the results would indicate. In House races, for instance, where Republicans gained sixty-two seats, the total vote was almost exactly split, with Republicans receiving 51 percent and Democrats 49 percent. The necessary majorities for Republican victory, in fact, did come from white males, according to an exit poll taken by Voter News Service. Indeed, the majority of women and most Blacks voted for Democrats.[30] With such results, it is arguable that the Coalition provided the swing vote for the Republican "landslide." In this case, Carter's politically involved Christians have by all means had an impact. They won the election.

Here the Coalition and the churches through which it operates are obviously partisan in their politics: They are endorsing a candidate or program, they use their church donations to provide the basis for such support, and as political advocacy organizations they should lose their tax exemptions.

EGALITARIAN ETHICS, PUBLIC REASON, AND SECTARIAN REVELATION

Carter is directly opposing the liberal requirement that legislative action and court decisions appeal to secular reasons. One of the most troubling aspects of Carter's position is his claim that religious arguments need not be translated into secular terms to be incorporated as a basis for judicial decision and legislative action, a view he expresses throughout the text.

He employs legal theorist Michael Perry's concern that such a policy requires citizens to "bracket" religious convictions, in effect, to split off an essential part of their identity in order to participate in public debate.[31] In his response to various liberal theorists who require such a secular justification alongside religious motivation, he says,

> What is needed is not a requirement that the religiously devout choose a form of dialogue that liberalism accepts, but that liberalism develop a politics that accepts whatever form of dialogue a member of the public offers.[32]

In relation to the abortion issue, Carter's predictable move is to decry the notion "that the definitions of life offered by many in the pro-life movement are out of bounds because they are drawn from the religious tradition."[33] He is particularly concerned about Justice Stevens' dissenting opinion in *Webster v. Reproductive Services* (1988), in which Stevens argued that the preamble for Missouri's abortion statute violates the Establishment Clause in defining conception as the beginning of life.[34] In opposition to Stevens, Carter makes the dubious claim that "there are atheists and agnostics aplenty in the pro-life movement," and complains that Stevens's reasoning would "force the religiously devout to bracket their religious selves before they may enter politics."[35] Such bracketing, of course, is exactly what traditional liberal theory requires. A brief review of salient contributions by Thomas Nagel, Bruce Ackerman, John Rawls, and Kent Greenawalt will clearly show the bases for such a requirement, as well as the problematic nature of Carter's objection to it.

Thomas Nagel gives two requirements for "public justification" of policy. It requires first, he says, "preparedness to submit one's reasons to the criticism of others," in which context there is "the exercise of a common critical rationality and consideration of evidence that can be shared."[36] This procedure is not possible, he argues, if the source is "personal faith or revelation."[37] Second, public justification requires that if others are thought to be wrong, there is, at least in principle, an explanation of their error which is not circular, that is, which does not assert simply that "they do not believe the truth."[38] Religious appeals, in Nagel's view, do not satisfy these requirements, and amount instead to attempts to use state power to make others conform to one's own beliefs.[39]

Similarly, Bruce Ackerman advances two general principles of rationality and neutrality as fundamental to the liberal state. The first is that the legitimacy of anyone's assumption of power must be defended by good reason in a dialogical setting.[40] The second principle is that a good reason must exhibit the feature of neutrality, meaning that no assertion is acceptable if it implies that the one with power has a "conception of the good" that is "better than that asserted by any of his fellow citizens," or that the power holder is somehow "intrinsically superior" to others.[41]

Ackerman is a strong proponent of the translation requirement that Carter rejects:

> A liberal state is nothing more than a collection of individuals who can participate in a dialogue in which all aspects of their power position may be justified in a certain way; to participate in such a dialogue of justification, actors must be intelligible to one another; to be intelligible, one's utterances must be translatable into a language comprehensible to other would-be participants.[42]

References to disembodied spirits, along with the belief that one has received a communication from such, are perfectly legitimate expressions of religious freedom and belief systems voluntarily assumed. But given that we do not know whether such spirits exist or how they wish to communicate to us, any assertion of a special revelation from them violates the principle of neutrality, giving someone an arbitrary authority in the public domain, and legitimating such by a language inaccessible to others.[43]

The work of John Rawls, of course, is pivotal for the entire tradition of liberal political thought. In *A Theory of Justice*, he provides a strictly secular basis for the liberal state. In the past several years, however, he has been taken to task by a host of communitarian thinkers, all complaining basically that Rawlsian egalitarian thought overlooks the normative and constitutive role of traditional institutions such as religion in providing for the life of a community. His recent work, *Political Liberalism*, is an attempt to address these criticisms, and especially to portray religion in a more favorable light. To that end, he speaks now of the importance of "comprehensive doctrines," a category meant to include philosophical, moral, political, and religious commitments of great diversity. Such doctrines possess their own internal rationality, and are legitimately brought together to form an "overlapping consensus" in the public arena.[44]

Alongside this rehabilitation of religious traditions, however, Rawls is still careful to make several moves which severely restrict the role of religion in public discourse. First, he places religious belief, as it should be, behind the veil of ignorance in the original position. Just as with positions of wealth and political power, no one knows at the outset whether he or she will be a part of the religious majority or minority. And ignorance in the original condition has an obvious implication:

> The fact that we affirm a particular religious, philosophical, or moral comprehensive doctrine with its associated conception of the good is not a reason for us to propose, or to expect others to accept, a conception of justice that favors those of that persuasion.[45]

Second, he requires that the comprehensive doctrines themselves be reasonable if they are to brought into the arena of public reason. To be reasonable, such a doctrine should provide "a consistent and coherent" account of our experience of reality; it should also designate certain values as particularly important and work out a way to deal with value conflict; and last, it should represent a relatively stable tradition of discourse and thought.[46] Rawls is at pains to distinguish his concern at this point from customary philosophical arguments regarding skepticism. In requiring these reasonable doctrines, he says, the point is not to disqualify belief in God on epistemological grounds, as many liberal theorists would. Rather, it is to point out the practical difficulty of ever achieving consensus among competing, comprehensive doctrines without the criteria mentioned above.[47]

Third, Rawls disallows the use of political power by proponents of any one of the comprehensive doctrines "to repress comprehensive views that are ... different from their own."[48] The problem here again is typically Rawlsian. Given "reasonable pluralism," there is no objective decision procedure for determining true or false comprehensive beliefs. Thus, those who attempt to use state power to enforce their beliefs seem to others simply to be insisting on their own way.[49]

In his recent *Christian Century* review of *Political Liberalism*, David

Hoekema vigorously attacks Rawls for the last qualification. It shows, he complains, that Rawls is really saying again that it is unreasonable "to dissent from liberal pluralism."[50] By such a move, Rawls has disenfranchised those whose creeds endorse "coercive power" in the interest of achieving a goal deemed higher than political freedom. Hoekema puzzles over "closed and controlled communities" such a Jonestown or Waco, and theological creeds such as the Muslim Shari'a and the Christian view of theonomy, both of which would make the will of God also the law of the land. By what standard, he asks, are such approaches "unreasonable?" It is especially frivolous to eliminate the Muslim and Christian theonomies from public discourse, in Hoekema's view, since they exhibit most of the features Rawls associates with reasonable comprehensive systems. Hoekema charges Rawls with a circular argument. Approaches endorsing coercive power on behalf of goals higher than political freedom are off-limits, he says, essentially because they oppose "liberal toleration."[51]

Hoekema's response is an important one, not only because it addresses a possible weakness in the revised version of Rawlsian liberalism, but also because it suggests the move that Carter makes to rehabilitate the conservative religious voice. Against Hoekema, however, and thus also indirectly against Carter, two arguments should be made immediately. First, Hoekema overlooks the fact that it is specifically through political liberalism that groups advocating theocracy are granted the religious freedom to practice their faith. They can build churches, publish books, and flood the radio frequencies and television channels with religious programming. It is a false dichotomy to suppose that such groups are socially dismissed. It is only that their rhetoric will not be permitted as part of the public reason, given its rejection of liberal democracy. Second, both Hoekema and Carter seem to picture such groups as minorities only. The question to be asked is what would happen if they became majorities in a liberal democracy operating in accord with standard voting practices. The answer is easy. Those who are victims of the fundamentalist takeover in the Southern Baptist Convention during the past fifteen years know it well. Theonomists will use the public discourse and its participatorial privileges to gain power. And when they achieve a majority, democracy will be replaced with theocracy. This outcome may be difficult to achieve in a constitutional democracy, but it should be remembered that even constitutions can be changed. Hoekema is asking the impossible, and Carter is engaging in wishful thinking if he supposes such participation does not immediately introduce the possible destruction of public reason.

What Hoekema seems to miss is that Rawls has set out the conditions for the *liberal* state. One of these conditions is that public reason does not include the voice of theonomists, given that in the right setting such a voice would use coercive power to destroy the liberal state. Hoekema seems to want the description to include somehow the ideals of the illiberal state. But these are other ideals. That they are not included shows that Rawls is consistent, not that he has argued in a circle.

The most sensitive work to date on political participation by religious groups is that of Kent Greenawalt. In his 1988 work, *Religious Conviction and Political Choice*, and his recent article in *Journal of Church and State*, he generally defends a Rawlsian rationalist approach to liberal democracy, focusing specifically on "shared premises" and "publicly accessible reasons" as the requirements for participation.[52] He maintains that religious belief should be construed as outside the domain of public reason, given that it is highly personal and that many intelligent members of society find *all* religious arguments unconvincing.[53] He assumes nonsupportive separation, and with certain qualifications recommends that religious arguments be translated into secular terms to fit the public domain:

> The common currency of political discourse is nonreligious argument about human welfare. Public discourse about political issues with those who do not share religious premises should be cast in other than religious terms.[54]

Support of particular legislative proposals by religious leaders, he allows, is often appropriate, but he advises against the direct support of candidates and parties for many reasons. There is, he says, "the disturbing quality of an overall evaluation of a party or candidate as being more in tune with the religiously correct view," and there is also the debt incurred by political figures to the relevant religious lobbies who supported them. "When churches play this role, they may come too close to running the government."[55]

Of the many ways in which Greenawalt develops his argument beyond Rawls, two are of the most interest. First, he calls attention to the complexity of distinguishing religious and secular motivations. And second, he argues, as does Carter, that on many issues secular reason is at a standstill, and distinctively religious ideals may be of great service to the society. In this context, he also works specifically with the abortion issue.

As to the former—the difficulty of isolating religious motivation—Greenawalt argues that for believers, it is often impossible to disentangle religious and secular support for particular belief; that there are frequently religious origins now forgotten for moral rules thought to be purely secular; and that courts especially would find it nearly impossible to make such distinctions between the sacred and the secular.[56]

In response, however, it should be noted that despite these practical difficulties, the Supreme Court has been able to employ the *Lemon* tests over the past twenty years and in over thirty decisions.[57] And the first of the three prongs of the *Lemon* test—secular purpose—directly concerns religious motivation. Often the motivations are obvious, despite all efforts by religionists to hide them, as in the case of scientific creationism.

As to the latter—issues at a standstill in the arena of secular reason—Greenawalt develops a masterful treatment of the abortion issue, arguing as does Carter that here we have the perfect example of the need for religion in the public domain. "Shared premises and publicly accessible reason cannot resolve the points at which a fetus is entitled to particular degrees of moral consideration."[58] But if this is so, he reasons, we must employ grounds that go beyond secular bases, and the believer has a "powerful argument" for relying on religious reasons.[59]

What Greenawalt overlooks, however, is the possibility that our liberal democracy has done exactly what careful secular arguments indicate should be done on the issue of abortion, and that is to compromise, as was done in *Roe v. Wade*. Greenawalt's own analysis is essentially like that of *Roe*, identifying the late-term fetus as more like a real person than the first-term fetus, and thus more deserving of protection. Where shared premises and publicly accessible reasons run aground, there is no need to settle a public issue by appealing to religious belief. It is settled in a secular way by suspending judgment or working out a compromise. Use of an explicit religious basis will both constitute an establishment of religion and alienate a portion of the citizenry.

The upshot of these reflections on participation in political activity by religious groups is that Nagel, Ackerman, and Rawls provide a strong theoretical basis for excluding distinctively religious arguments, dependent on divine revelation and church tradition, from the domain of public reason. Greenawalt argues for a more inclusive though carefully nuanced approach, but this brief analysis of his work on the issue of abortion as an example of secular reasoning run aground shows that even here the need to resort to religious arguments is not so obvious.

In summary, liberals exclude untranslated religious argument from public discourse for several reasons: (1) religious arguments give the one who offers them an arbitrary authority by appeal to God, an external source of truth, and are not subject to lay and professional scrutiny for their truth value; (2) religious arguments are apt to make an overlapping consensus impossible; (3) religious arguments violate the requirements of a common language for public reason; (4) religious arguments may empower a majority to deny minority religious freedom.

Stephen Carter is certainly aware of these kinds of arguments. He refers briefly to the approaches of Ackerman, Rawls, Nagel, Greenawalt, and several others, but dismisses their arguments with little discussion, insisting that the solution to the problem about religious involvement "lies in another direction."[60] He makes an effort at a general response to liberal concerns by engaging in a brief discussion of certain epistemological issues.[61] The point of his work in this context is to deal with a skeptical argument along the lines of Ackerman and Nagel by which revelatory appeals are said to be off-limits because of the impossibility of theological knowledge. In order to level the terrain, Carter calls attention to our increasing doubts about knowledge in all areas, then points out that what is deemed by secular thinkers "inaccessible" in terms of starting point and method is not seen as such by conservative religious belief. The logic of fundamentalists, for instance, is clear: "They are informed by God's revelation."[62] Thus, on creationism, "based on the interpretive tool of literal biblical inerrancy, evolution theory is *demonstrably* false."[63] Or on moral issues, facts and values are not separated for the devoutly religious as they are in a secular worldview. Morals are based in divine command, and assume again the facts of revelation.[64]

These responses, however, are problematic in two ways. One, it is hard to say how serious Carter is in his antifoundationalist gesture, because even in light of his stated appreciation for the way conservative Christians see the "facts" of reality, he still argues that creationism should be rejected (against revelatory claims) as bad science; and he still uses egalitarian concerns (against revelatory claims) to opt for a liberal position on abortion. And two, on a more theoretical basis we should remember that just because we acknowledge antifoundationalist concerns, we are not reduced to a complete leveling of the epistemological playing field. It still must be shown that revelatory claims to factual knowledge have the same standing as observational or theoretical claims in science, or that divine command ethics has the same moral standing as secular, egalitarian ethical theories. The theological appeal, no matter how much it constitutes reality for those who accept it, is transcendental in nature. It appeals to premises that are not shared, and it uses reasons that are not accessible.

These reflections show Carter's encouragement of the religious voice to be misplaced. Winston Davis, in his *Christian Century* review of *The Culture of Disbelief*, makes a similar point. He concedes that the discourse of politics in a liberal democracy is not essentially more rational than that of theology, but maintains all the same a "qualitative difference" between the two. The distinction, in agreement with the liberal position, is that "political discourse is vulnerable to a wider range of public criticism than is religious proclamation."[65] Politicians may personally hold themselves accountable to God. Whether or not they do, they are in fact accountable to the public, and indeed to "professional scrutiny" by legal historians, statisticians, and policy experts. Their opinions must be tested against the information and methodologies available to the public. For the sake of consensus, some of the "depth or comprehensiveness" of their religious doctrines may be lost. They will have to defend positions without the authority of their particular religious narrative, text, or dogma, and apart from the language of "conviction, proclamation and celebration." This, however, is the price paid for a liberal democracy.[66]

Davis points out that Carter works with a false dichotomy when he makes the supposition that removal of religion from government privatizes it. He overlooks the discourse of what Davis refers to as "civil society," that is, media proclamations, university forums, or even street-corner preaching. Our society is really a "free-for-all" in regard to religious and philosophical claims. Carter consistently downplays this enormous power of religion in American society. But in a pluralistic society, "secular political civility" must bracket the "untranslated oracles of religion." It is not that a liberal establishment "imposes" such on religious individuals, who are then the victims of prejudice as described by Carter. Rather, "civility in the public realm" requires that all participants engage in a "common public discourse."[67]

CONCLUSION

Given the disanalogy between the civil rights movement and the activities of the Christian Coalition, and the difference in secular support for civil rights and abortion protest arguments, it may be seen that the lobbying activity of the Christian Coalition through churches and the abortion protests of pro-life groups constitute outright efforts to establish a religious position through participation in the public arena. Thousands of churches around the country receive exemption from property taxes and deductions for contributions while putting forward a political agenda based on sectarian revelational authority. This seems an obvious threat to the separation of church and state.

Religious conservatives might object to his argument by pointing out that in the case of the Christian Coalition, no denomination is asking to be recognized as a state church. Rather, the churches are merely supporting various candidates and policies consistent with their doctrines. But this is really a "distinction without a difference." Sociologists of religion say that this is a period of religious realignment, that the old denominational loyalties are no longer meaningful for most church members, and that the more significant religious entities are the cross-denominational activist groups such as the Christian Coalition.[68] In this situation, in other words, we need not be concerned about a state church, but we should be concerned about an organization representing Christians from many different denominations bound together by common conservative doctrinal commitments and seeking political power an organization that desires the status, though not the official position, of the established churches in the colonial period.

The subtitle of Carter's book, "How American Law and Politics Trivialize Religious Devotion," is terribly misleading. Perhaps it is true in a few ivory tower academic settings, but it is not true in public life. Religion is alive and well in American society. Gallup Polls show consistently that over 90 percent of Americans believe in God, that approximately three in four believe in an afterlife, that two-thirds are members of a church or synagogue (and there is a rapidly growing Muslim community as well), and that on any Sunday morning over 40 percent will be in church.[69] Private religious schools and fundamentalist homeschooling are growing by leaps and bounds. Religious broadcasters permeate the cable television channels, religious book publishers have a booming industry, and contemporary Christian music rivals secular fads for the devotion of the nation's youth. Churches already receive enormous subsidies from the exemption of their property from taxes and from deductions for members' donations. And the Christian Coalition experienced sweeping midterm electoral victories in 1994. Organized religion in America does not need any more help from the government. It has received quite enough already. Those who worry about church-state issues should be concerned about the legally sanctioned power of religion in America, not its disenfranchisement.

NOTES

1. Richard John Neuhaus, "The Culture of the Public Square," *First Things* 38 (December 1993): 66–68.

2. Tocqueville scholars Joe Knippenberg and Peter Lawler developed these critiques in lectures at Berry College. Knippenberg characterized Carter as a "Tocquevillian liberal" who, despite appearances to the contrary, will not finally accept divine authority for policy decisions; and Lawler refers to Carter as a "Progressive-Orthodox" Christian thinker whose basic commitments coincide with those of liberal academics (Contemporary Thought Seminar, Berry College, fall 1994).

3. Stephen Carter, *The Culture of Disbelief* (New York: Anchor Books, 1994), p. 105.

4. Ibid., p. 199.
5. *Edwards v. Aguillard*, 482 U.S. 578 (1987).
6. *Wallace v. Jaffree*, 472 U.S. 38 (1985).
7. Carter, *Culture of Disbelief*, pp. 157–62, 184–92.
8. Ibid., pp. 48, 63, 227–29.
9. "Sanctity of Human Life" Sunday found its way into the calendar of the Southern Baptist Convention in June 1985 as a result of the fundamentalist takeover of the convention.
10. John T. Noonan Jr., *The Believer and the Powers that Are* (New York: Macmillan Company, 1987), pp. 450–51. Noonan notes that the first meeting of the SCLC, held in January 1957, "was held at the call of four black ministers and one layman" who met at the Ebenezer Baptist Church in Atlanta. Aldon Morris, *The Origins of the Civil Rights Movement* (New York: Free Press) p. 265–66, quotes the Young figure of "close to a million" copies. The circulation itself was directed by the American Friends Service Committee.
11. Philip Selznick, *The Moral Commonwealth: Social Theory and the Promise of Community* (Berkeley: University of California Press, 1992), pp. 387–409.
12. It might be objected that there were, after all, opposing arguments arising from segregationists; but these were not based on a solid egalitarian footing, relying instead on pseudoreasoning tactics such as spite and indignation.
13. Judith Jarvis Thomson, of course, gave the classic statement of this position in her article, "A Defense of Abortion," originally published in *Philosophy and Public Affairs* 1 (fall 1971): 47–66.
14. James Davison Hunter, *Before the Shooting Starts* (New York: Free Press, 1994), pp. 85–121, esp. 92–95. Carl Bowman was coauthor of chap. 4, "The Anatomy of Ambivalence: What Americans Really Believe."
15. Those acquainted with the history of dogma know that the Church's position on zygote personhood is a relatively recent change of its more historic position. See, for instance, Stephen Asma, "Abortion and the Embarrassing Saint," *Humanist* 54 (May/June 1994): 30–33.
16. Noonan, *Believer and the Powers that Are*, p. 461; also, "Christian Action Network Faces Fine," *Christian Century* (July 13–20, 1994): 675–76.
17. "Christian Action Network," p. 676.
18. Christopher John Farley, "Prodding Voters to the Right," *Time* 144 (November 21, 1994): 62.
19. The term "substantial," is obviously vague, and as such, it has been the focus of much discussion. A good treatment of the difficulties in applying the substantiality criterion may be found in James E. Wood Jr., "Tax Exemption of Religion and the Separation of Church and State," *Review and Expositor* 83 (spring 1986): 241–43.
20. Noonan, *Believer and the Powers that Are*, p. 461.
21. Farley, "Prodding Voters," p. 62.
22. Ibid.
23. Rob Boston, "Failed Crusade," *Church and State* (November 1994):

9–11. Chapman was part of a successful moderate challenge to fundamentalist control of the local school board.

24. "FEC Looking into Christian Coalition's Role in Helms Campaign," *Church and State* (July/August 1994): 17.

25. "Federal Election Commission Sues," *Church and State* (December 1994): 3; also, "Christian Action Network Faces Fine," pp. 675–76.

26. Farley, "Prodding Voters," p. 62.

27. Ibid. Also, Gayle White, "The Right's Might," *Atlanta Journal*, January 15, 1995, p. A8.

28. News Section, "Rightward, Christian Soldiers," *Christian Century* (November 23–30, 1994): 1103.

29. White, "The Right's Might," A8.

30. "Victory by the Numbers," *Time* 144 (November 21, 1994): 64.

31. Michael J. Perry, *Morality, Politics, and Law: A Bicentennial Essay* (New York: Oxford University Press, 1988), pp. 72–73; cited by Carter, *Culture of Disbelief*, p. 56.

32. Carter, *Culture of Disbelief*, p. 230.

33. Ibid., p. 253.

34. Ibid., p. 254.

35. Ibid., p. 255.

36. Thomas Nagel, "Moral Conflict and Political Legitimacy," *Philosophy and Public Affairs* 16 (summer 1987): 232.

37. Ibid.

38. Ibid.

39. Ibid., p. 231.

40. Bruce Ackerman, *Social Justice in the Liberal State* (New Haven: Yale University Press, 1980), pp. 4–10.

41. Ibid., pp. 10–11.

42. Ibid., p. 72.

43. Ibid., p. 111.

44. John Rawls, *Political Liberalism* (New York: Columbia University, 1993), pp. 35–40.

45. Ibid., p. 24.

46. Ibid., p. 59.

47. Ibid., pp. 62–63. This argument is traceable to Rawls's basic commitments, such as ontological relativity and the method of wide reflective equilibrium rather than deductive rationality in ethics.

48. Ibid., p. 60.

49. Ibid., p. 61.

50. David Hoekema, "Liberalism Revisited: Religion, Reason, Diversity," *Christian Century* (October 19, 1994): 959.

51. Ibid., pp. 959–61.

52. Kent Greenawalt, *Religious Convictions and Political Choice* (New York: Oxford University Press, 1988), p. 57.

53. Ibid., p. 75; also, Kent Greenawalt, "The Role of Religion in a Liberal

Democracy: Dilemmas and Possible Resolutions," *Journal of Church and State* 35 (summer 1993): 517.

54. Greenawalt, *Religious Convictions*, p. 217.

55. Ibid., p. 160; also, Kent Greenawalt, "The Participation of Religious Groups in Political Advocacy," *Journal of Church and State* 36 (winter 1994): 155–60.

56. Greenawalt, *Religious Convictions*, pp. 156–69, 254.

57. *Board of Education of Kiryas Joel Village School District v. Grumet*, 114 S. Ct. 2481 (1994) (Blackmun, J., concurring).

58. Greenawalt, *Religious Convictions*, p. 126.

59. Ibid., p. 137.

60. Carter, *Culture of Disbelief*, pp. 55, 230.

61. Ibid., chap. 11.

62. Ibid., p. 217.

63. Ibid., p. 216.

64. Ibid., p. 233.

65. Winston Davis, "Translating God-Talk: Church, State and the Practice of Civility," *Christian Century* (April 20, 1994): 418.

66. Ibid.

67. Ibid.

68. Hunter and Bowman, for instance, use the broad groupings, "Evangelical Protestants," "Mainline Protestants," and so on, as better predictors than specific denominations. These are, they say, "communities of moral conversation," Hunter and Bowman, *Before the Shooting Starts*, pp. 101–102.

69. George Gallup Jr. and Jim Castelli, *The People's Religion* (New York: Macmillan, 1989), p. 14, 58, 132; also, George Gallup Jr., *The Gallup Poll Public Opinion 1993* (Wilmington, Del.: Scholarly Resources, 1994), p. 72.

CHAPTER 18

RELIGIOUS LIBERTY AND ABORTION POLICY
Casey As Catch-22
Paul D. Simmons

Like the hapless Yossarian and his fellow GIs in the closing days of world War II, women facing abortion regulations face a frustrating and often humiliating Catch-22.[1] The movie version of the novel made the phrase an unforgettable and telling part of the American vocabulary. Joseph Heller movingly portrayed the trap of the permission/denial syndrome—what is given with one order is taken away with another—in a way that Everywoman facing an abortion can understand. Recent Supreme Court decisions regarding abortion have left women facing the classic dilemma captured so memorably by Heller's antiheroes. The dilemma goes to the heart of First Amendment concerns regarding abortion and public policy.

Arguments concerning religious liberty have for years been a significant part of the abortion debate, of course. The contention is both that public policy should not be based upon narrowly construed sectarian perspectives, and that religious groups should not seek to impose their moral or theological belief upon others who hold equally personal and sacred beliefs and commitments. The first is a concern that First Amendment protections be guarded by the courts and Congress; the second that religious groups and/or leaders be faithful to the social contract of tolerance toward pluralistic religious views.

This article first appeared in *Journal of Church and State* 42, no. 1 (winter 2000). Copyright © 2000 by J. M Dawson Center for Church-State Studies, Waco, Texas. Used by permission.

The wisdom of that approach seems increasingly evident as the heat of the debate has intensified over the past three decades. The deep investment in the issue by various faith communities has led to acrimonious and divisive rhetoric and heavy-handed actions that threaten the cohesion of the social fabric. The civility that is necessary to maintain tolerance among and for all religious groups in a free and open society is profoundly lacking.

Recent Supreme Court decisions about abortion have raised substantive religious liberty issues without addressing them directly. Just how First Amendment interests might affect the shape of public policy is the concern of this essay. The aim is not to deal with abortion as a *moral* problem, but to explore the meaning(s) of religious liberty and the implications of the Supreme Court decision in *Casey* for First Amendment concerns. My thesis is that *Casey* amounts to a Catch-22 for women confronting abortion and public policy. The dilemma cries out for attention from the Supreme Court, which has thus far refused to deal with the religious liberty issues at stake.

DEFINING THE RELIGIOUS ISSUE

Locating or defining the religious nature of the abortion debate is of central importance. The campaign to ban abortion contends that no religious issue is involved since there are atheists as well as believers (Catholics, Jews, Baptists, and so on) who oppose abortion as the killing of innocent human life.

Another contention is that abortion is merely a political or moral issue to be settled by the politics of majority rule.[2] The argument is that democratic processes, that is, establishing public policy through elected officials or majority rule, is the way all issues are to be settled.

A further problem is that the Supreme Court has not dealt with abortion in terms of First Amendment concerns, which some take to mean there are none involved. *Roe v. Wade* evaded the question, even while recognizing the philosophical/religious conundrum in the notion of fetal personhood. Justice Stevens raised the establishment issue in *Webster*, and both he and Blackmun alluded to religious liberty concerns in *Casey*. To this point, notions of the "right to privacy" and "personal liberties" assured under the Fourteenth Amendment have been used to encompass abortion decisions. These concepts are sufficiently broad to encompass religious liberty concerns, in my judgment, which has mitigated the need for direct address by the Court. Even so, the issue has considerable importance and thus the need for clarifying the concerns at stake.

We know however that there are certain things which are *not* violations of the First Amendment in the abortion debate. First, *the issue is not whether religious leaders may address issues of moral import in the public arena.* At this level, the mandates of theology and First Amendment liberties come together. Freedom *for* religion means that religious people have every right to engage in the democratic process of shaping public policy.

Second, *a simple coincidence between religious doctrine and certain laws or regulations does not necessarily violate the First Amendment.* The charge that a sectarian *doctrine* lies behind public policy restricting access to abortion[3] fails to prove entanglement or favoritism amounting to religious establishment.[4]

Even so, I believe *both establishment and free exercise issues are at stake in the abortion debate.* First Amendment issues can be seen in efforts to establish protections for the pregnant woman, the attempt to attribute personhood to gestating life, the constraints imposed upon women seeking abortions, and the latitude permitted religious groups who seek legislative power through political processes. Of special concern are those proposals regarding fetal personhood that rest on abstract metaphysical opinion, and the actions of various religious groups whose determination to shape policy results in actions which infringe upon the religious liberties of others.

The abortion debate has expended enormous energies on the question of the fetus as person. The issue for public policy, of course, is a definition of personhood that is appropriate in and for a pluralistic society. To be sure, any legal definition will more nearly approximate one religious opinion than another. The *question is whether the definition is reasonable or logically problematic, and whether it enhances or restricts protected personal liberties.* The first principle of religious liberty is that laws will not be based upon abstract metaphysical speculation, but will be fashioned through democratic processes in which every perspective is subject to critical analysis. Any proposal must be open either to revision or rejection. There are some "religious" definitions far more consistent with reason and amenable to pluralism and democratic discussion than others.

Part of the genius of *Roe v. Wade* (now affirmed by *Casey*) was the distinction in fetal value that should be recognized and protected at law at the gestational stage of viability. By definition, viability is that stage of development at which the fetus has sufficient neurological and physiological maturation to survive outside the womb. Prior to that stage of development, the fetus simply is not sufficiently developed to speak meaningfully of it as an independent being deserving and requiring the full protection of the law, that is, a person. The notion of viability correlates biological maturation with personal identity in a way that can be recognized and accepted by reasonable people. It violates no group's religious teachings nor any premise of logic to provide protections for a viable fetus.

The same can hardly be said for those efforts to establish moral and legal parity between a zygote (fertilized ovum) and a woman. For equally powerful and valid reasons rooted in common sense, religious beliefs, and tradition, many take offense at the imposition of laws and regulations that reflect problematic logic or abstract metaphysical opinion. The dogmatic approach to public policy adopted by the National Council of Catholic Bishops and the Religious Right[5] poses substantive First Amendment issues.

The first is the claim to special knowledge. The proposal to ban abortion legally is based on a claim that a pre-embryo is a person, *whether other people believe it or not*. As John Finnis put it: "When philosophers discuss natural law, they are talking about the fact that there is a reality which is what it is whether one personally likes it or not."[6] In other words, no matter what ordinary logic might indicate, the (philosophical) opinion of the theologian is really the truth. Those who disagree are either misguided, uninformed, or willfully ignorant. At issue is the argument that the conceptus is a person deserving the full range of constitutional protections assured any citizen of the country. This assumption is the grounding for actions that attempt to shape public policy in a way that presupposes a basic parity in value and legal standing between a woman and the fetus.[7]

The Catholic dogma which holds that abortion is the taking of innocent human life is regarded as a principle of natural law.[8] Natural law is a construct employed by theologians that attempts to bridge the worlds of religion and reason, or of revelation and nature. It has roots in Greek philosophy but was wedded to Christian moral thought most systematically in the works of Thomas Aquinas. Basic to his approach was the notion that the laws of God permeate nature and may be discerned by human reason. No special disclosure by God is necessary since all people are endowed by reason, he argued. The divine logos permeates all of creation and provides a link between the divine and human mind; the very structures of nature are available universally and embody the absolute moral law of God. It is thus held to be true for all people. Since it is available to and by reason, which all people have, and since it permeates nature, which everyone might observe, every person, whether believer or unbeliever, is obligated to obey the moral law. This type of logic lies behind the Catholic ban on contraception, believing that it is an absolute evil for anyone willfully to interfere with the generative process.

A second feature of this approach is the contention that such moral premises are not sectarian or religious in nature. The argument is that neither nature nor reason is the special monopoly of the religious. Secularists or atheists are also capable of discerning the divine mandate—it requires no special revelation. The advantage of the church is that it is devoted to the God of the universe and has the special calling and divine appointment to carry God's authority to teach the truth by which all people are to live. The moral rule can thus claim both religious and nonreligious meanings and attempt to win the allegiance of both believers and nonbelievers. Thus Bernard Nathanson claimed in "The Silent Scream" that he once regarded a conceptus as a human being as an article of faith, but now holds it as a simple assertion of fact.[9] He was trained as a Catholic priest in natural law theory. Now that he is an atheist, however, he argues that the same premise and ethical construct are secular in nature. Such an argument allows the contention to be made that efforts to prohibit or severely limit abortion are not being made on the basis of religious or sectarian dogma and thus pose no First Amendment problems. The natural law construct makes that contention possible, but it is hardly persuasive.

The final step is from morality to law. When the truth of God is made obvious, the laws of the state should be made to conform. Thus, the strict moral rule against abortion articulated by clergy should be implemented by civil law. The relation between the moral and the civil law is one that underscores the "duty of the public authority to insure that the civil law is regulated according to the fundamental norms of the moral law in matters concerning human rights, human life and the institution of the family."[10]

What seems obvious and convincing to the natural-law theorist often appears unconvincing, if not ludicrous, to the critic, however. To claim a monopoly on truth on both secular and religious ground is self-serving in the extreme. It fits well in the scheme of the sectarian claim to be the final arbiter of all truth and the embodiment of divine revelation, that is, to claim an absolute grounding for conclusions supposedly based on human reason. The ultimate outcome of that line of thought was found in the *Syllabus of Errors*,[11] which claimed, among other things, that error has no rights. The Inquisition itself had been conducted on the fervent belief that the church was doing heretics a favor by saving them from the damnation to which their false beliefs would most certainly lead.

The absolutist attitude against abortion claimed by evangelicals of the New Right makes similar arguments but appeals to the authority of Scripture instead of to natural-law theory. The fact that scholars equally committed to biblical authority do not agree with fundamentalist or evangelical interpretations does not deter them from the claim that the

Bible teaches that zygotes are persons and that abortion is murder. They also claim a type of "special knowledge," though its roots are ostensibly in revelation, not reason. Their intolerance toward people with different opinions reflects assumptions about the special nature of their calling and the particularly offensive nature of elective abortion.

The fact that Inquisitions and heresy hunts are now more subtle than those of the pre-Reformation era often conceals the fact that the same structure of thought and authority is still at work. When religious authorities make absolute pronouncements as if they were patently true and obviously obligatory for all people, whether acknowledged as a faith commitment or not, an authoritarian claim is laid bare that is inimical to democratic processes and undermines respect for differing religious beliefs. The clear message is that those who disagree are to be corrected or coerced to conform, since their opinions have no right to moral standing and thus are not to be respected in the court of conscience or, finally, even by civil law.

The appeal to privileged knowledge that is available only to those within a special circle but is somehow mandatory for everyone is especially problematic. The assertions of religious authorities must finally be submitted to the critical scrutiny of common sense and reason in a secular or pluralist society.[12] Whether or not a zygote is a person is a question for reflective analysis by jurists, theologians, philosophers, sociologists, embryologists,[13] and a host of other people, almost all of whom are interested both in good public policy, solid morals, and family values.

CASEY AND ABORTION RIGHTS

Casey took a positive step in the direction of clarifying an important establishment question at this point. It began by rightly affirming the "essential holding" of *Roe*[14] protecting the right of a woman to choose to have an abortion before viability.[15] It also affirmed the state's power to restrict abortions after viability as long as there are provisions to protect the woman's life and health. But the Court created a quagmire of logical and practical problems when it affirmed (without recognizing any contradiction) the legitimacy of state interests throughout the pregnancy in protecting the life of the fetus that may become a child.[16]

Rejecting Abstract Metaphysics As Law

The most significant finding of the Court from a religious liberty perspective is that the woman is *the* person whose constitutional rights are to be protected.[17] The Court found two important lines of precedent for affirming the right to an abortion. The first relates to procreative rights—a "recognized protection accorded to the liberty relating to intimate relationships, the family, and decisions about whether to beget or bear a child."[18] The second is the limits "on government power to mandate medical treatment or its rejection," as in the *Cruzan* ruling. "*Roe*," said the Court, "may be seen not only as an exemplar of Griswold liberty but as a rule ... of personal autonomy and bodily integrity...."[19]

Antiabortion groups have attempted to overturn *Roe* and outlaw abortion based on the belief that a fetus is a person with constitutional protections.[20] Certain states had enacted legislation protecting "the unborn from the moment of conception."[21] The preamble to the Missouri statute declares that "the life of each human being begins at conception" and that "[u]nborn children have protectable interests in life, health and well-being."[22]

Casey amounted to a strong affirmation of the woman as unquestionably *the person* whose rights are at stake in the abortion debate.[23] Whatever "rights" a fetus may have are subsidiary to those of the woman.[24] A fetus—at any stage of gestation—is not to be protected at the expense of the woman. The Court said emphatically that states may not outlaw abortion, in effect rejecting the underlying presupposition of fetal personhood as a basis for law.

That many people believe strongly that a zygote is a person is by now well established. The First Amendment allows people to believe as they will as a matter of conscience or religious belief. That is a matter of freedom *of* religion. But as a definition of personhood for constitutional protections in a pluralistic society, the zygote-as-person rationale is untenable in the extreme.

As John Rawls put it, definitions for public policy "must be supported by ordinary observation and modes of thought ... which are generally recognized as correct."[25] Abstract metaphysical speculation has its rightful place in theology; but it must finally be rejected as inappropriate to the logic necessary for democratic rule. The appropriate ground for abortion regulations, said *Casey*, is "reasoned judgment," the "boundaries [of which] are not susceptible of expression as a simple rule."[26] In a passage reminiscent of *Roe*, the majority questioned whether

> the State can resolve [the questions revolving around the profound moral and spiritual implications of terminating a pregnancy, even in its earliest stage] in such a definitive way that a woman lacks all choice in the matter, except perhaps in those rare circumstances in which the pregnancy is itself a danger to her own life or health, or is the result of rape or incest.[27]

Justice Blackmun put it strongly in saying that an abortion is not "the termination of life entitled to Fourteenth Amendment protection. Accordingly, a State's interest in protecting fetal life is not grounded in the Constitution. Nor, consistent with our Establishment Clause, can it be a theological or sectarian interest."[28]

A second prong of the metaphysical argument rejected by the Court concerned the nature and role of the woman as woman. The prohibition of abortion argument is typically a corollary of the notion that women are created to be child-bearers and nurturers. Choosing abortion thus denies a woman's "essential being" and allowing abortion legally contradicts the nature of the good and just society, by this construct. But, as *Casey* rightly held, to impose such abstract visions of woman-as-she-is-created-to-be upon all women through public policy is to violate constitutional rights. Considered phenomenologically, for instance, not all women consider themselves "created" or intended to be mothers. Their own sense of being is therefore contradicted and denigrated when a contrary notion is imposed through law.

Other religious liberty considerations stem from the fact that some religious traditions stress individualism and calling in a way that emphasizes voluntarism and variety in the response of faith. Forbidding the abortion option is thus to foreclose an alternative based in what some women regard as religious, moral, or spiritual mandates.

The Court therefore rejected the notion that public policy should define the woman's role. "The liberty of the woman is at stake in a sense unique to the human condition and so unique to the law," said *Casey*. "Her suffering is too intimate and personal for the State to insist, without more, upon its own vision of the woman's role, however dominant that vision has been in the course of our history and our culture." Her decision is to be based upon the "right to define one's own concept of existence, of meaning, of the universe, and of the mystery of human life." Her own destiny "must be shaped to a large extent on her own conception of her spiritual imperatives and her place in society."[29] The Court has said strongly that the decision about abortion belongs basically to that zone of conscience and belief unique to the woman as a person. It is her liberty that is uniquely at stake, limiting (though not absolutely) the ability of the State to impose its own views of the woman's role.[30]

By affirming the woman's rights, *Casey* went beyond *Roe*, which had made abortion a matter of decision between the woman *and her physician*. *Roe* emphasized the right of the physician to practice medicine without interference from the law. But *Casey* focused on patient autonomy—the uniqueness of the decision *for the woman*: it is her "anxieties," "physical constraints," and "pain" that give prominence to her judgment.[31] That women have been willing to make "sacrifices" to bear and nurture children does not mean that the state can impose those roles upon them.

The concurring opinion by Justice Blackmun explicitly spoke to the issue of "gender equality."[32] By limiting abortion, he said, the state "conscripts women's bodies into its service, forcing women to continue their pregnancies, suffer the pains of childbirth, and in most instances, provide years of maternal care," all of which goes uncompensated.[33] It is simply assumed to be a duty she owes the state. The Court rightly held that both good ethics and equal protection require that pregnancy and childbirth be voluntary and not coerced.

Abortion and Male Authority

Casey also struck down provisions requiring spousal notification,[34] which had the effect of maintaining male authority over the woman.[35] Any physician who induced an abortion for a married woman without certain assurances would be subject to having one's license suspended and liability for damages to the husband. The physician was thus an agent of the state to enforce the paternal rule.

The Court held that such a statutory requirement would pose an "undue burden" on actions permitted under *Roe* and thus were invalid. "Women do not lose their constitutionally protected liberty when they marry," it said. "The Constitution protects all individuals, male or female, married or unmarried, from the abuse of governmental power, even where that power is employed for the supposed benefit of a member of the individual's family."[36]

Casey thus amounts to a further step in the realization of women's rights in America. That women have been relegated to second-class citizenship and often regarded as having rights only secondary to those of men has been substantially documented.[37] The abortion debate has furthered the awareness that both the personhood of women and their exercise of procreative rights are uniquely at stake in pregnancy. While men typically share the burden of pregnancy and childbirth in certain ways, they do not know personally or experientially the threat and burden of an unwanted pregnancy. Thus, when consensus in the marriage breaks down, the woman is the final arbiter in the abortion decision.

RESCUERS AND *BRAY*

The strong affirmation of the woman's prerogatives and the uniqueness of her role in abortion decisions caused many to anticipate that the

Court would support the use of the "Ku Klux Klan" law against antiabortion efforts to prevent access to abortion clinics.[38] The Reconstruction-era law bars conspiracies to deprive "any person or class of persons" of the equal protection of the law. Oddly, the Court held that the 1871 law could not be applied by federal judges to the disruptive tactics of Operation Rescue.[39] Attorneys for women's groups had argued that demonstrations intended to shut down abortion clinics constituted a type of discrimination against women as a class, since only women have abortions.

Justice Scalia, writing for the 6–3 majority, argued that both women and men can be found on both sides of the abortion debate, thus negating the "class" argument.[40] "Whatever one thinks of abortion," he said, "it cannot be denied that there are common and respectable reasons for opposing it, other than hatred of or condescension toward . . . women as a class."[41]

Both Justices Stevens and O'Connor took issue with Scalia. The test under the law, Stevens argued, is not hostility toward women, but whether it is "aimed at conduct that only members of the protected class have the capacity to perform."[42] The aim, he said, was "to deny every woman the opportunity to exercise a constitutional right that only women possess."[43] Pointing both to "massive defiance of the law" and "violent obstruction of the constitutional rights of their fellow citizens," Stevens argued that the protesters' strategy "represents a paradigm of the kind of conduct that the statute was intended to cover."[44]

In spite of the coherent and plausible arguments of both Stevens and O'Conner, those of Scalia prevailed. Scalia happens to embrace the notion that all issues in a democratic society should be settled by majority vote and thus has little patience for constitutional protections accorded minorities.[45] His religious commitments have also been shaped by a tradition that is profoundly and strongly opposed to the legal availability of abortion. The primary problem, however, is that there was no attention to the special category of people at issue in the clinic demonstrations. They were women who had reasons rooted in experience, moral perspectives, personal values, and religious commitments that supported their decision to terminate a pregnancy. As such, they deserved protection based on First Amendment considerations, none of which were raised.

The message from the Supreme Court regarding abortion is thus ambiguous, if not contradictory. *Casey* says strongly that women are the citizens at issue in the abortion dilemma. It is *the woman's* conscientious judgment that is to be protected. But in the *Bray* decision, the Court reverted to a paradigm that assumed abortion rights could be exercised only if the woman can win out in a pushing contest with those trying to prevent her from doing so. Scalia's comment that people differ about the morality or legal acceptability of the issue is simply to state the obvious. In no way does that characteristic of the political process alter the fact that only women (whose religious beliefs and moral framework allow abortion) are those whose rights are at stake. The *Bray* decision allows women to be subjected to the hostile opinion and actions of those who are strongly opposed to abortion, that is, to her moral and religious values. The "vote" includes the moral judgment of men, none of whom will ever be pregnant, and of women who are conscientiously opposed to abortion and thus feel no deprivation of *their* constitutional rights.

Several reasons seem to lie behind the reasoning of the Court majority. First, is the *Court's deference to what it perceives as the ambivalence in American public opinion toward abortion*. Scalia believes strongly that public opinion, not the Court, should settle public policy toward abortion (cf. *Webster*). Polls seem to show that Americans do not like abortion, but they want it legally available.[46] But how might that be translated into a finding to shape public policy?

At one level, such an opinion reflects a becoming reticence to deal with matters which are sensitive and often upsetting, much as polite company does not like to talk about the gory details of surgery or bodily functions. At another level, the perception is that good morals mandate compelling reasons to justify an abortion. Such reasons seem not to be present in a large number of elective abortions. That understandable and laudatory attitude on the part of thinking people shows the need for "disapproving" abortion, that is, not being simply indifferent toward what appears to be a calloused attitude toward ending a problem pregnancy. The other side of that ambivalence is that Americans want abortion to be legally available. That is the basic meaning of being "pro-choice." No one I know of is "for" abortion if that means being enthusiastic about or indifferent toward pregnancy terminations. Most everyone I know, on the other hand, can think of circumstances under which good and moral women might reasonably and justifiably choose to terminate a pregnancy and be supported in doing so by the moral community. At a minimum, that means good morals requires the legal availability of abortion, as *Casey* affirms.

Second, *the Court seems concerned to protect liberties associated with religious beliefs, free speech, and public assembly*. Thus it is reluctant severely to curtail the actions of even the most militant and aggressive antiabortion groups.[47] In *Schenck*, the Court rejected the notion that a "buffer zone" should protect women entering an abortion clinic to shield them from the harsh rhetoric and intimidating, often injurious handling by antiabortion protesters.[48] The decision followed the Court's earlier comments in *Madsen* that a protective zone around a clinic "burdened more speech than necessary to serve a significant governmental interest."[49] The general principle, said the Court, is that "citizens must tolerate insulting, and even outrageous speech in order to provide adequate breathing space to the freedoms protected by the First Admendment."[50] The bottom line is that rights regarding free speech have greater protection than those regarding First Amendment rights regarding the free exercise of religion.

The most generous interpretation of the *Schenck* and *Madsen* decisions is that they tend to underscore the Court's commitment to protecting the freedoms of speech associated with religious and moral beliefs. That it is also protecting the most egregious forms of civil disturbances seems an irony requiring further attention. The strategies of brutal rhetoric and bodily assault employed by Rescuers seem to constitute harassment of those exercising legitimate constitutional protections, as Justice Kennedy's comments seem to admit.[51] Such actions might be construed either as violating the woman's bodily integrity or as limiting a woman's free exercise of liberties premised on religious commitments. The abortion clinic becomes a battleground over religious liberties; but only one party is attempting to coerce the other. At what point is religious intolerance to be restrained?

LIMITING THE ABORTION OPTION

A final reason the Court may have had in mind was that protecting those who demonstrate against abortion providers is one way to *allow certain limitations to be imposed on the right to abortion*. That interpretation would be consistent with *Webster*, which allowed states to provide incentives for childbirth (such as providing financial support), while instituting various impediments to securing an abortion. Thus states could ban abortion in hospitals receiving public funds, refuse to pay for the procedure, and forbid any public personnel from discussing abortion with a client.

Neither *Casey* nor *Bray* endorsed the heavy-handed measures of Rescuers as a way to discourage abortion. Even so, *Bray* gives strong encouragement to activists in the private sector. One way a state may now create hindrances to procuring an abortion is to be lenient toward disruptive demonstrations against women entering clinics.[52]

The consistency between *Webster* and *Casey* is certainly no virtue. It compromises both internal logic and basic constitutional rights. What is granted the woman with one hand is taken from her with the other; she is caught in a legal Catch-22. The rationale behind permitting limits, said *Casey*, is that the decision is "more than a philosophical exercise," which had been admitted as basic to the woman's choice. The Court went on to say:

> Abortion is a unique act. It is fraught with consequences for others; for the woman who must live with the implications of her decision; for the persons who perform and assist in the procedure; for the spouse, family and society which must confront the knowledge that these procedures exist, procedures some deem nothing short of an act of violence against innocent human life; and, depending on one's beliefs, for the life or potential life that is aborted.[53]

In short, it is an action about which others have strong feelings and vested interests which, in the mind of the Court, constitute grounds for limiting the woman's choice! The religious and moral sensibilities of the woman contemplating abortion may be submitted to the tribunal of people holding profoundly different religious opinions.

A Contest of Religious Conviction

The woman's situation is exacerbated by the fact that *Casey* also affirmed requirements for informed consent followed by a twenty-four-hour waiting period.[54] Abortion providers may be required to inform women contemplating abortion concerning gestational development, arguments against elective abortion, and alternatives to abortion such as adoption. The woman then must wait a day while further considering her choice.

The Pennsylvania statute was apparently accepted as a general corollary to the doctrine of informed consent which prevails in medical ethics.[55] The problem for religious liberty concerns lies not so much with informed consent as with the types of information that might be given, and the ways in which it is imparted to the woman. There are types of "information" and styles of giving "information" that are more like insults, harassment, and intimidation than providing crucial data for responsible decision making. The now somewhat dated saying that one had rather study Marxism under a Christian than Christian doctrine under a Marxist makes the point. The style and loyalties/beliefs of the instructor are all-important.

The Court admitted that the abortion decision belongs to "the zone of conscience and belief," but then allowed the conscientious convictions of another party to prevail in determining not only the information to be covered but the style in which it is delivered. Those familiar with the tactics of "pregnancy counseling centers" know only too well that women are badgered and harangued by antiabortion militants.[56] The badgering can take place even while insisting that abortion is still an option the woman may choose. The scenario conjured up is that of a Court-approved equivalent of the grand inquisitor in the medical context.

Limiting abortion by inducing shame is a major strategy of the antiabortion movement, as admitted by Gary Bauer, head of the ultraconservative Family Research Council. Domestic policy advisor to former President Reagan, Bauer noted that "legal or illegal, ... abortion will be seen as a matter of shame and something to be avoided."[57] The aim is to institute "informed consent" procedures that result in a woman's being cajoled, shamed, humiliated, and badgered so as to deter her choosing an abortion, or, if she does, she will be miserable emotionally for years to come. Such actions on the part of zealous religious ideologues seems a form of legalized abuse of a citizen attempting to exercise a constitutional right.

Even the choice of terminology when speaking of an abortion signals the posture of the speaker. Neutral or scientific terms like conceptus, zygote, embryo, or fetus will likely be used by sympathetic counselors when speaking of the entity in the uterus. And the procedure will likely be spoken of as removal, suctioning, or vacuuming. Loaded words like baby, unborn child, or infant will be used by those committed to deterring women from abortion. And the procedure will be spoken of as killing, murder, dismembering, or destroying. Such freighted terminology is hardly "a scientifically impeccable choice of terms."[58] It is an explicit but deniable attempt to manipulate the woman by inducing guilt and shame.

The Court should be interested not only in informed consent, therefore, but also in the protection of the woman's religious and personal dignity. A significant part of the concerns for the health of the woman undergoing an abortion is that of her mental and spiritual well-being. If she is treated as a pariah, problems of guilt and remorse will be exacerbated, if not actually induced. If she is treated with courtesy and accorded respect and dignity (as in Japan, where women undergoing abortion are shown great deference),[59] whatever elements of remorse are present will be negligible or manageable. As the comment by Bauer admits, the critical variable between the experience of women who wind up with profound guilt and those who see the experience more favorably may well be the type of informed-consent process to which they have been subjected.

The Concern for Conscience

Casey's emphasis on conscientious belief as the grounds for personal liberty and bodily integrity is consistent with *Roe*'s concern for privacy as encompassing procreative decisions. Both notions somewhat capture the religious liberty concern for the respect due a person's moral commitments based upon ground-of-meaning beliefs. "Privacy" is not just a matter done in private; it is another name for conscience or the interiority of compelling beliefs, whether defined in religious or philosophical terms.[60] The concern for conscience is a corollary of the protections accorded under the First Amendment.

Casey thus dealt with important religious liberty concerns, without ever saying so.[61] Holding that the basic questions regarding abortion are rooted in "one's own concept of existence, of meaning, of the universe, and of the mystery of human life," the Court acknowledged the role of ground-of-meaning beliefs in defining fetal value and/or the moral acceptability of terminating an unwanted pregnancy. These, said the Court, are shaped by the woman's own "conception of her spiritual imperatives and her place in society." The question of abortion takes place in an arena in which the strong moral beliefs of the individual citizen *and not others* ought to prevail.

The Court thus seemed to settle an important establishment question in the abortion debate. Declaring that states may not ban abortion, the Court in effect rejected the dogma of a zygote-as-person which would be a basic presupposition for a legal ban. States like Guam, Utah, Louisiana, and Missouri had tried to prohibit abortion based on the belief that one is a person "from the moment of conception." That many people believe that a zygote is a person does not alter the fact that the attribution of personhood to a zygote is based on metaphysical speculation, not scientific fact. Appeal must be made to "special metaphysical, e.g. religious, premises," says Thomas Boles. The facts "provide no empirical basis for the thesis that the person of the child which the zygote will become is already present in the zygote."[62] In effect, to ban abortion is to base law on religious or sectarian opinion contrary to the guarantees against establishment of religion.[63]

The second part of the religious liberty issue, however, deals with "free exercise." In this area, *Casey* seems less sensitive to the protection of conscientious judgments. Allowing states to implement procedures to discourage the practice is to permit others to harass and cajole those women whose religious scruples and teachings (conscience) permit abortion as a moral option. Women whose conscience is formed *against* abortion are in no way required to terminate a pregnancy, of course, and thus never encounter the problem of harassment as a violation of conscientiously held convictions. Those who choose to abort may well encounter a hostile environment of opinion and action based on religious or moral viewpoints contrary to their own. They may well be humiliated and denigrated unless there are safeguards for the free and open exercise of their own profoundly held beliefs.

Abortion As Free Exercise

In sum, the establishment issue is focused in whether the fetus is a person protected as are all citizens under the Constitution; the free exercise issue pertains to access to abortion services. The Supreme Court has approached abortion policy in precisely that sequence. We can confidently say that abortion *as such* is not a question of religious liberty on the grounds of free exercise.[64] Were it possible to establish that a fetus (from whatever stage of gestation) is a person, elective abortion would not be a legal option, certainly not on the basis of an appeal to the free exercise of religion.

Anything can be believed, but not just anything can be done in the name of religion. Human sacrifice, for instance, whether of a child or an adult, would not be tolerated no matter how venerated such a practice might be among certain religious groups. Nor can such matters as child or spousal abuse be excused in the name of religious belief. Were the Court convinced the fetus is a person, abortion would be banned either as homicide or child abuse.

In all cases, the free exercise of religion is limited by the parameters established by the rights to life and liberty of other persons under the law. Arguing that abortion is related to free exercise is hardly an "anything-goes-in-the-name-of-religion" argument. Even the most fervent religious belief cannot circumvent the protections accorded other persons. Rabid antichoice voters understand this point and thus have worked feverishly to have embryos or fetuses (depending on the stage of gestation chosen) declared persons under the Constitution. If they are persons they are protected. Rights are to be exercised by persons who come under the umbrella of protections from constitutional guarantees.[65]

Privacy is one of those rights and it includes decisions regarding procreative choice from contraceptives (*Griswold*) to abortion (*Roe* and *Casey*). No state may ban abortion as if embryos or fetuses are persons. The appeal to the free exercise of one's religious beliefs and affections is thus quite simply to be able to make choices consistent with one's religious tradition regarding a constitutionally protected right. The decision to terminate a pregnancy is not a matter of killing a child. Elective abortion belongs to that arena of choice that has to do with the woman's pursuit of a meaningful life consistent with her own moral and personal values and religious beliefs, as *Casey* said so strongly and rightly.[66]

Free exercise also requires that such a choice must be without undue coercion. At one level, this standard requires that no woman is to be coerced to terminate a pregnancy. Those women who believe strongly that a fetus is an "unborn child" are protected from religious beliefs that run contrary to that opinion. Having a child is a basic freedom or entitlement in America, as one of those protected liberties that women may exercise without undue interference from others.

The other side of the free exercise coin is that women who choose to terminate a pregnancy are doing so out of equally powerful ground-of-meaning beliefs that permit or allow her to abort. She is exercising the religious convictions that help to shape her own sense of meaning about life and her sense of calling in life. Whether and/or when to become a mother is a decision fraught with heavy parental responsibility and thus must be done only after due consideration of consequences and personal commitments.

Those women whose consciences are formed against abortion for any reason have every right to appeal to the protection of the law against those who would injuriously cajole, criticize, or otherwise attempt to coerce her to abort. That is in spite of the fact that a strong argument could be made that there are numerous people who are hardly responsible enough to become parents and/or whose decisions are hardly in the best interests of the child-to-be. One could argue on eugenics grounds, for instance, that the common good should be protected against having children born who are known to have severe physical or neurological deficits. But such arguments do not prevail against the prerogatives rooted in the religious and moral commitments of the pregnant woman. Her rights against coercion are protected.

The parallel to women on the other side of the argument should be reasonably obvious. Women who decide not to bring a pregnancy to term should have equal protection from harassment, injury, and coercion. The paradigm case of the religious liberty issues at stake is that Rabbi Shira Stern, who decided along with her husband, Rabbi Donald Weber, to terminate a pregnancy in the fifth month of gestation. Tests showed the fetus was affected by Tay Sachs, a lethal genetic disease. Their decision to abort had the full support of their religious tradition and the community of which they were a part. But while she was lying on her hospital bed, a television program carried a strongly-worded antiabortion message by then-president Ronald Reagan. He declared abortion to be "this nation's number one moral problem" and that he would press for legislation to outlaw "the murder of unborn children."[67]

Rabbi Stern's free exercise of religion was at stake. But she could have become the object of intimidation and humiliation under the Court's ruling. Had the "information" some states require to be given a woman prior to abortion been written or provided by a person with the moral or religious convictions of President Reagan, for instance, Rabbi Stern would have been subjected to severe verbal abuse and personal humiliation. The conflict between speaker and hearer would have been at the ground-of-meaning level of foundational beliefs regarding fetal "personhood" and the moral acceptability of terminating a problem pregnancy. It would have been a clash of religious convictions. The one in a position of power and authority (for example, information provider, health care professional) would have been able to harass and intimidate, to cajole and badger the one who was vulnerable and dependent—a pregnant woman who had decided to terminate a pregnancy.

The law now allows "informed consent" procedures which seem more humiliating than helpful, and abortion protesters to engage in egregious acts of rhetoric and efforts to impede the woman's decision to abort. Such actions are consistent with the Court's statements in *Webster*, which allowed "hindrances" or "impediments" to be placed in the path of women seeking abortions, and *Schenk*, which allowed verbal and emotional harassment.[68] One can only imagine the type of information made available in states that had previously banned abortion.

The provision regarding informed consent is thus not as benign as it might otherwise appear. Under the rubric of a perfectly acceptable doctrine in medical ethics (that is, informed consent), the Court is apparently willing to turn a blind eye and deaf ear to extensive infringements of one's "free exercise" of religious liberty.

At this level, the *Casey* decision has a glaring inconsistency. It speaks of conscience and moral beliefs as prevailing in decisions regarding abortion, but it allows a clash of opposite opinions to prevail in the clinic or delivery room. Such a scenario is neither good morals, good medicine, good law, nor good religion. Those who are concerned with the total well-being of the woman will work for assurances that the informed-consent process assures respect and support for the woman. The reception or operating room should not become a forum for profoundly divisive and competing religious and moral visions. A vulnerable patient should not have to give account to a judgmental team of care providers.

The contradiction around which *Casey* was fashioned goes to the heart of First Amendment concerns. Denying that pre-embryos have constitutional rights at one level seems implied or presupposed—however tentatively—at another. If, as Blackmun noted in his dissent, "a State's interest in protecting fetal life is not grounded in the Constitution," then why might women be "discouraged" or hindered from exercising the option of abortion, certainly in the early stages of pregnancy? To say that others disagree is only to state the obvious. It hardly provides a justification or gives substantive reasons for allowing egregious hindrances. If she has already considered the data, examined the issues at stake, considered her circumstances, weighed her alternatives, and reached a conscientious decision, she may well discover the "informed-consent process" to be a humiliating and degrading experience.

Casey thus perpetuated the Catch-22 allowed by *Webster*. Women seeking abortion are protected from the imposition of alien and odious opinions in one area; but they are subjected to injurious and abusive insults in another arena governed by contrary religious beliefs and practices.

CONCLUSION

Casey has therefore clarified important points *and* left a great deal to be desired and done in its response to the abortion debate, from the perspective of religious liberty concerns. Each state has enormous work to do in clarifying its approach to abortion within the permissible parameters allowed by *Casey*. Fortunately, no state may ban abortion; unfortunately, hindrances to procure an abortion may be instituted in a variety of ways. The stage is set for a continuation of belligerent confrontations based on deeply held religious opinions regarding the morality of abortion.

At a minimum, justice concerns for women's health underscores the moral mandate to assure competency in medical assistance as well as an environment of compassion and support during this highly personal procedure. Americans committed to the pursuit of both good medicine and good morals will work to assure that state regulations provide optimum care for women facing problem pregnancies. *Casey* rightly affirmed the right to an abortion, but it wrongly accepted hindrances and harassments as if they are neutral in the impact on the well-being of women.

The High Court would do well to examine abortion as an issue of religious liberty and First Amendment guarantees. It has done reasonably well in ferreting out what amounts to establishment issues; it would do well also to protect the free exercise of the woman's conscientious (that is, religious) judgment.

NOTES

1. Joseph Heller, *Catch-22* (New York: Simon and Schuster, 1955).
2. D. J. Horan et al., eds., *Abortion and the Constitution: Reversing* Roe v. Wade *Through the Courts* (Washington: Georgetown University, 1987), p. xiv.
3. See, for instance, John Swomley, "Supreme Court's Abortion Decision Parallels Roman Catholic Bishop's Position," *Churchman's Human Quest* (September–October 1989): 16–17.
4. Both *Harris v. McRae* and *Casey* said the issue is not the coincidence

between law and doctrine but whether a protected liberty is infringed. See *Casey* 2807.

5. "The Religious Right" refers to a coalition of ultraconservative, primarily evangelical Protestant groups who have become politically active for right-wing causes. Pat Robertson's Christian Coalition is now the titular leader, though Jerry Falwell's Moral Majority campaign led during the eighties. James Dobson of Focus on the Family, Ralph Reed, Gary Bauer, and Phyllis Schlafly are other leaders. For a list of leaders and groups and a description of their aims and strategies, see Robert Boston, *Why the Religious Right is Wrong About Separation of Church and State* (Amherst, N.Y.: Prometheus Books, 1993).

6. See his comments in Horan, *Abortion and the Constitution*, p. 116.

7. T. H. Stahel, "Cardinal Bernardin on the 'Forgotten Factor'and other Gaps in the Abortion Debate," *America*, April 7, 1990, p. 577.

8. There are other versions of natural law theory that are found among both Protestant and Roman Catholic theologians. The absolute ban on abortion among traditional Catholics typically appeal to the type here outlined. For another approach see Beverly W. Harrison, *Our Right to Choose* (Boston: Beacon Press, 1983).

9. See also Bernard Nathanson, "Operation Rescue: Domestic Terrorism or Legitimate Civil Rights Protest?" *Hastings Center Report* (November–December 1989): 28–32.

10. Joseph Cardinal Ratzinger, *Instruction on Respect for Human Life in its Origin and on the Dignity of Procreation: Replies to Certain Questions of the Day.* Congregation for the Doctrine of the Faith (Rome: Vatican, 1988), part 3.

11. Pope Pius IX, *Syllabus of Errors*, 1864.

12. See Peter S. Wenz, *Abortion Rights as Religious Freedom* (Philadelphia: Temple University Press, 1992), p. 112. Wenz contends the question is whether beliefs can be "supported cogently with arguments or demonstrations whose premises include only secular beliefs." The issue, he says, is a matter of "epistemology," that is, the way in which knowledge is gained or claims are supported.

13. See Charles A. Gardner, "Is an Embryo a Person?" in *Abortion, Medicine and the Law*, 4th ed., ed. J. D. Butler and D. F. Walbert (New York: Facts on File, 1992), pp. 453–56.

14. See *Casey* at 2804 (I.5) and Stevens' dissent, 2844 (I.1).

15. Ibid., 2804 (I.6[1][2][3]).

16. Ibid. See also Rehnquist at 2867.

17. Ibid., 2812 at 5, and 2816 at [15].

18. Ibid., 2810 [11], and 2830 [37] citing *Eisenstadt v. Baird*, 405 U.S., at 453, 92 S.Ct., at 1038.

19. Ibid, 2810 [11, par. 3].

20. D. J. Horan and T. J. Balch, "*Roe v. Wade*: No Justification in History, Law or Logic," in *Abortion and the Constitution*, p. 76.

21. Guam, Utah, and Louisiana, for instance. See Rebunfeld, "On the Legal Status of the Proposition that 'Life Begins at Conception'," 43 *Stanford Law Review*, 599 (1991).

22. See *Webster v. Reproductive Health Services* (1997). Fetal personhood was not at issue in the Pennsylvania law which sought only to regulate the availability of abortion.

23. *Casey*, 2816 at [16].

24. Ibid., 2818; see also Stevens' comments at 2839.

25. John A. Rawls, *A Theory of Justice* (Cambridge: Harvard University Press, 1971), p. 213.

26. *Casey*, 2806.

27. Ibid.

28. Justice Stevens concurring in ibid., at 2188, citing *Thornburgh*, 476 U.S., at 778, 106 S.Ct.

29. Ibid., II.[6], par. 6 (2807).

30. Ibid., [19].

31. Ibid, 2807; see also Blackmun's comments.

32. Ibid., II.A.

33. Ibid.

34. Ibid., [35].

35. Pennsylvania barred a physician from performing an abortion for a married woman unless there was: (1) a signed statement from the woman that she had notified her spouse; (2) her certification that her husband was not the man who had impregnated her; (3) that her husband could not be located; (4) that the pregnancy resulted from spousal sexual assault which she had reported; or (5) that the woman believed notifying her husband would result in serious bodily harm to herself.

36. Ibid., 2831.

37. Catherine MacKinnon, "Reflections on Sex Equality under Law," 100 *Yale Law Journal*, 1281, 1309–10 (1991).

38. *Bray v. Alexandrian Women's Health Clinic, et al.* 90-915, S.Ct. Jan 13, 1993.

39. See ibid., dissent by O'Connor, Par. I.

40. Ibid., opinion by Scalia, I.A.3.

41. Ibid., I.A.5.

42. Ibid., dissent by Stevens, V.6.

43. Ibid., V.7.

44. Ibid., V.8.

45. *Oregon v. Smith* (1990). Also see Wenz, *Abortion Rights as Religious Freedom*, pp. 246 ff.

46. "Whose Life is it?" *Time*, May 1, 1989, p. 21. The poll for CNN and *Time* by Yankelovich Clancy Shulman indicated that, while half those questioned believe abortion is wrong, fully 67 percent believe the decision should be left to the woman in consultation with her doctor. *Roe* is supported by 54 percent and 62 percent of all respondents opposed any limits on abortion in the first three months of pregnancy.

47. See *Time*, May 4, 1992, 27 ff.

48. *Schenck v. Pro-Choice of Western New York*, 95-1065 (1997).

49. *Madsen v. Women's Health Center, Inc.*, 512 U.S. 753 (1994) at 774.
50. Citing *Boos v. Barry*, 485 U.S. [312, 322 (1988)].
51. See *Bray*, concurring opinion by Kennedy, as in par. 3.
52. Justice Kennedy's comments in his concurring opinion in *Bray* seem to admit as such. See "Abortion! The Future is Already Here," *Time*, May 4, 1992, pp. 27 ff.
53. *Casey*, opinion by O'Connor, I.[6].3.
54. *Casey*, V.B.
55. Ibid., V.B. [34]. See T. L. Beauchamp and J. F. Childress, *Principles of Biomedical Ethics*, 3d ed. (New York: Oxford University Press, 1989), p. 74, for a treatment of the importance and place of informed consent.
56. See "Crusading Against the Pro-Choice Movement," *Time*, October 21, 1991, p. 26.
57. Quoted in *Time*, May 4, 1992, p. 28.
58. B. J. George Jr, "State Legislatures Versus the Supreme Court: Abortion Legislation into the 1990s," in *Abortion, Medicine and the Law*, p. 4.
59. See Daniel Callahan, "Abortion; Some Ethical Issues," in *Abortion, Medicine and the Law*, p. 697; also see, p. 278, n.19.
60. *U.S. v. Seeger*, 380, U.S., 163, 165 (1965). *Seeger* clarified the question as to whether one had to be a person committed to a distinctive community or tradition of belief in order to qualify for the constitutional protections accorded the "religious." The answer was "no." All Americans may qualify as having profound beliefs which are the equivalent to what religious traditions and communities inculcate in their followers and which constitute ultimate concerns.
61. Justice Blackmun did refer to the establishment provision of the First Amendment, but the amendment was not itself the focus of the deliberation by the Court and did not figure in the decision of the majority. Cf. Blackmun in *Casey*, II.B.6 (2849).
62. Thomas Boles, "Zygotes, Souls, Substances and Persons," *Journal of Medicine and Philosophy* 15 (December 1990): 648.
63. P. D. Simmons, "Religious Liberty and the Abortion Debate," *Journal of Church and State* (summer 1990): 567–84.
64. *Harris v. McRae*, U.S. 79-1268 (1980), considered whether indigent women seeking an abortion had a right to public funding. The Court rejected the argument that government's refusal to pay for this medical procedure violated either the Establishment Clause of the First Amendment or the equal protection guarantees of the Fifth Amendment. Quite properly, no argument was advanced concerning the free exercise of religion. *United States Law Week*, 48:50 (June 24, 1980), Syllabus, 1(b) and 4, 48 LW 4942.
65. The argument frequently heard that the Supreme Court declared that African Americans were not persons in its infamous *Dred Scot* decision is hardly true. The Court did not deal with the issue of personhood, but questions of property. African Americans are persons when measured by any basic norms of human personhood. The same can hardly be said for an embryo or fetus. The fatal error in reasoning from racism to abortion can also be found in George

McKenna's article, "On Abortion: A Lincolnian Position," *Atlantic Monthly* (September 1995): 51–68. McKenna dodges the issue of personhood by saying the question is a matter of "the stilling of heartbeats and brains" (p. 68). His radical reductionism allows him to regard embryos as persons.

66. See *Casey* at II.[6], par. 6 (2807).
67. *New York Times*, May 22, 1985.
68. As in *Schenck* and *Madsen*, supra, notes 48 and 49.

CHAPTER 19

IN DEFENSE OF FREEDOM OF CONSCIENCE

A Cooperative Baptist/Secular Humanist Declaration

Joint Statement

At a historic dialogue convened on October 6 and 7, 1995, at the University of Richmond, Virginia, Baptist and secular humanist scholars came together to find some common ground.

For many years both Baptists and humanists have been embroiled in heated controversy in the public square. Fundamentalist Baptists in particular have leveled strong charges against humanists, especially secular humanists, accusing them of undermining the moral and social fabric of America. And secular humanists have in turn accused some Baptists of betraying democracy and working to establish theocracy.

The dialogue focused on the following areas of concern: (1) Academic Freedom; (2) Biblical Scholarship; (3) Separation of Church and State; and (4) Pluralistic Democracy. This declaration presents a consensus statement. Although not necessarily agreeing with every detail in the declaration, those who endorse it accept its general terms and are committed to further cooperation.

ACADEMIC FREEDOM

First, the principle of academic freedom is widely accepted in American higher education and at colleges and universities throughout the world. Recently, many Baptist schools and seminaries have undergone a major assault on the academic freedom of their faculties. As a result of this campaign by boards of trustees and administrators, leading scholars and professors have been dismissed or forced out by intimidation and harassment.

A college or university is first and foremost a center dedicated to the search for truth. A school of higher education belongs to a grand tradition that passes onto each new generation some of the lessons and intellectual skills of its forebears. *The search for greater understanding, wisdom, and truth thrives best in a setting of academic challenge free of intimidation and repression.*

To maintain its integrity, an institution of higher learning must operate by the rules and regulations that enhance rather than hinder the primary goal of inducting students into the joys and rigors of the learning process. Objectivity in inquiry is not conducted by a mind free of all biases but a community achievement whereby various biases, theories, views, doctrines, and interpretations are explicated and examined. Accuracy and fairness of presentation are high academic ideals. Without them, education becomes mere propaganda. While indoctrination may be the necessary beginning point of education, it cannot be its goal. In objective inquiry, the various relevant doctrines and interpretations are subjected to rigorous analysis and criticism. It is partly through critical inquiry that the interpretations and theories are tested, refined, improved, and sometimes exchanged for more promising ones. Without the testing process, higher education is impossible.

Academic freedom entails (1) *protection from* all the external forces that threaten objective inquiry, and (2) *access to* the tools and resources that make the academic process a concrete reality rather than an abstraction. Various interests tempt scholars to sacrifice their objectivity of inquiry both in the classroom and in research and publications. The academic life of searching for truth and of seeking to solve the problems raised in experience and research will not survive unless scholars, teachers, and the friends of education fight diligently against the temptations and threats.

Some professional schools have the responsibility of inculcating the students in a specific tradition or body of information, skills, interpretations, and doctrines. A theological seminary is a professional school designed to equip students for the various branches of the ministry. There are two competing models of the seminary. The first is designed to indoctrinate the students in a body of beliefs and to train them to serve and defend those doctrines. Within that model are varying degrees of latitude in providing students with the history and development of those beliefs.

According to the second model of seminary education, the training of students for various avenues of the ministry includes, in addition the goal of higher education, namely, the search for greater truth and understanding. The emphasis is on the search and the adventure. On this model, much is expected of research. Seminary training is viewed as analogous to the medical training that prepares students for medical practice. Good medical schools are also research centers where the medical students are expected to learn some of the results of the latest research. Research carries a certain risk, as does all objective inquiry. Unlike indoctrination alone, objective research at the seminary level encourages students not only to learn and appreciate their heritage, but also to examine its doctrines and to try to test them by comparative, historical, and critical analyses. A denominational seminary has the added responsibility of exposing its students to the denomination's rich and diverse history.

The trustees and administrators of a seminary have a moral duty to communicate clearly which of these two models they expect the newly appointed faculty to follow. There is also the moral duty not to shift from one model to another abruptly and without regard for the faculty's advice and counsel.

In each of the models of seminary training, instructors have a professional and moral duty regarding rival views. If they choose to present those views, the instructors' duty is to represent them accurately and clearly. To misrepresent and distort is dishonest. To present a view or doctrine accurately, instructors must show why or how it is regarded as meaningful *to those who embrace it*. This practice does not prevent criticism, however; for criticism without accuracy in presentation will always be superficial.

BIBLICAL SCHOLARSHIP

Second, *we believe that it is essential that objective biblical scholarship be encouraged*. There is already a rich tradition of scholarly work, one that uses rigorous standards of historical and scientific inquiry. Dogma is no substitute for rigorous research and the integrity of inquiry must take precedence over demands for doctrinal conformity or censorship. The students in schools and seminaries have a right to know, and the faculty, to teach. They—as well as the public at large—should be made aware of the tradition and they also should be exposed to the intellectual debates about the Old and New Testaments. Scholars should not be compelled to adopt a simple literal or inerrant interpretation, but need to draw upon the best linguistic, literary, archeological, and historical research that is available. They should be familiar with the works of critics; for it is only by the free give-and-take of ideas that truth can be more nearly achieved.

The humanism of the Renaissance stressed the "return to antiquity."

The ancient texts were seen as sources of enlightenment and wisdom. Among these texts were Hebrew Scripture and Christian Scripture. Renaissance humanism generated a new sense of inquiry into the past, and inquiry that evolved eventually into historical criticism. As a part of this movement, the Dutch Christian humanist Desiderius Erasmus (1466–1536) brought together what he regarded as the most reliable ancient manuscripts to produce his *Novum Testamentum*, a critical edition of the Greek New Testament. Thirty years later, Martin Luther translated the Bible into German. This, too, was a part of the Renaissance drive to go back to the ancient sources for enlightenment.

One result of the quest for the authentic sources was that of exposing documentary falsification and false attribution. Humanism's fundamental concern for historical accuracy helped bring about the Enlightenment, which sowed the seeds of a more sophisticated historical criticism and source criticism in the study of Scripture. In the nineteenth and twentieth centuries, biblical scholarship went in search of not only the most reliable texts of Scripture, but the prior sources that fed into the texts. Form criticism joined source criticism in enriching the field of biblical scholarship.

The latter quarter of the twentieth century has spawned a version of literary criticism that is becoming increasingly sensitive to the diversity of literary styles and genres in the Bible. Historical criticism's drive to uncover, if possible, the actual events of biblical times is joined by a new and equally powerful drive. The new literary criticism boldly claims that the authors and traditions producing the biblical texts harbored deep theological, more aesthetic, and literary interests that permitted them to reshape and even invent putative historical events. Furthermore, the new literary criticism has taken a fresh look at biblical myths to discover their power, value, and limitations.

Currently, biblical scholarship has exploded into a rich array of literary orbits—rhetoric criticism, narrative criticism, and redaction or editor criticism. In addition, there has emerged the sociology and anthropology of the early communities in which the biblical texts possibly came into being. Added to this study is canon criticism, or stories of the selection and function of religious texts in the centuries after their composition. Such Baptist scholars as Dan O. Via Jr., T. C. Smith, Edgar McKnight, and R. Alan Culpepper have contributed to the thriving biblical scholarship of the second half of the twentieth century. Secular humanists like R. Joseph Hoffmann, Morton Smith, and G. A. Wells have made notable contributions to New Testament studies.

Contemporary humanists in particular—both secular and religious—have explored in depth the humanness of the biblical texts. They have opened up new opportunities for modern readers to find profound kinship with the ancients and their human struggles. Archaeologists, and Old Testament scholar Gerald A. Larue in particular, have stressed the humanity of the ancients. They have explored new vistas enabling Christians, Jews, secular humanists, Hindus, Muslims, and others to see that while they do not share the same views on God or gods, they as readers of the various Scriptures can appreciate the human conditions, sufferings, and tragedies embodied in the texts.

SEPARATION OF CHURCH AND STATE

Third, the Baptist/secular humanist dialogue made it abundantly clear that both traditions supported freedom of conscience, and this enlists both religious liberty and the right of unbelief. *This means that we are vigorously opposed to any effort by the state to establish a religion, legislate conviction, or erode the cherished principle of separation of church and state embodied in the U.S. Constitution.*

Humanism is a wide and deep river of certain ideals and values fed by numerous traditions. No one tradition can regard itself as the sole tributary. One of the more fascinating tributaries that both secular writers and the Religious Right have yet to appreciate fully is the early seventeenth-century Baptist and seeker, Roger Williams. For over half a century, this undaunted defender of liberty of conscience and freedom of publication fought against those who insisted on using the state to propagate religion. With characteristic boldness, he proclaimed that liberty of conscience must not only include freedom to believe in a given religion, but freedom to disbelieve. Against Massachusetts Governor John Winthrop and other theocrats, Williams argued that a religion that depends on the state either to intimidate putative heretics or to give preferential treatment to religious believers and institutions will succeed not in building up faith and righteousness but in increasing hypocrisy and deceit.

As a religious humanist, Williams denounced the Puritans for their claim that the Native Americans were the Canaanites of the New World. He charged that both the New England Puritans and King Charles I of England had stolen the land that rightfully belonged to the natives. In addition, he not only protested the enslavement of the defeated natives, but invited Anne Hutchinson to live in Rhode Island when the Massachusetts Bay Colony banished her for expressing her unorthodox beliefs in her own house.

Roger Williams contributed to the Enlightenment's later emphasis on individual human dignity. Immanuel Kant (1724–1804) gave perhaps the most succinct expression of this belief in dignity when he wrote that individuals everywhere ought to be treated as ends in themselves and never as means only. Kant's contemporaries Thomas Paine, James Madison, and Thomas Jefferson spoke openly of human rights and believed that no religion could call itself worthy of human commitment unless it paid more than lip service to the Golden Rule.

The First Amendment of the U.S. Constitution reflects the influence of both the early Baptists and deistic humanists. Thomas Jefferson was a natural ally of eighteenth-century Baptists. This is nowhere more evident than in correspondence between Jefferson and the Danbury Baptist Association. Those Connecticut Baptists wrote a letter to President Jefferson in 1801. They had little theological common ground, but they shared a belief in the importance of human freedom.

The letter opened by expressing "our great satisfaction in your appointment to the chief Magistracy in the United States." They continued,

> Our Sentiments are uniformly on the side of Religious Liberty—That Religion is at all times and places a matter between God and individuals—That the legitimate Power of civil government extends no further than to punish the man who works ill to his neighbor. . . ." With strong words they affirmed, "Our hopes are strong that the sentiments of our beloved President, which have had such genial affect already, like the radiant beams of the Sun, will shine and prevail through all these States and all the world till Hierarchy and Tyranny be destroyed from the Earth.

Jefferson replied,

> Believing with you that religion is a matter which lies solely between man and his God, that he owes account to none other for his faith or his worship, that the legislative powers of government reach actions only, and not opinions, I contemplate with sovereign reverence that act of the whole American people which declared that their legislature should "make no law respecting an establishment of religion, or prohibiting the free exercise thereof," thus building a wall of separation between Church and State.

In *Revolution Within the Revolution*, Baptist historian William R. Estep has traced out the fruitful exchange between Madison and some of the early Baptists, an exchange reflected in Madison's noted defense of the wall of separation between church and state entitled *A Memorial and Remonstrance*. Secular humanists are strongly committed to religious liberty—for both believers and unbelievers. The free mind is thus the cardinal principle of humanism. It is embodied in the words of Thomas Jefferson when he declares his opposition to "any tyranny over the mind of man" and in James Madison's defense of religious liberty and the First Amendment. *As Baptists and humanists we share this devotion to freedom of conscience and separation of church and state.*

PLURALISTIC DEMOCRACY

Fourth, we recognize the pluralistic character of American life and the fact that there are different conceptions of morality and different systems of faith and belief. We respect that men and women may practice alternative styles of life and express different visions of the good life. In America there are often radically different religious eupraxophies and secular worldviews; Christian and humanist, Muslim and Jew, Buddhist and Hindu; and there are multiplicities of denominations and associations. We realize that theists may differ with humanists about the nature of ultimate reality; at the same time it is possible for both believer and unbelievers to participate in American life in a responsible way. Moreover, Americans—whether people of faith or not—may believe in and practice the common moral decencies and basic virtues, respect human rights, and share common values.

As Christians and humanists, we call for tolerance and mutual respect for alternative religions and philosophies and we pledge ourselves to rational dialogue and the negotiation and settlement of differences. We share our commitment to our pluralistic democratic American heritage.

The Baptist/Secular Humanist Declaration was drafted by Paul Kurtz, Joe E. Barnhart, and Robert S. Alley. It is endorsed by the following individuals:

Norm Allen, executive director, African-Americans for Humanism
Robert Alley, professor emeritus of humanities, University of Richmond
Edward Joe Barnhart, professor of philosophy, North Texas State University
David Burhans, chaplain, University of Richmond
Bernard Cochran, professor of religion, Meredith College
Frank Eakin, chairman, department of religion, University of Richmond
Bernard Farr, director of academic programmes and head of the school of theology, Westminster College, Oxford University
Thomas W. Flynn, senior editor, *Free Inquiry*

James Hall, professor of philosophy, University of Richmond

Stan Hastey, executive director, Alliance of Baptists

Glenn Hinson, professor emeritus of church history, Baptist Theological Seminary, Richmond

R. Joseph Hoffmann, senior lecturer and research fellow, Westminster College, Oxford

Paul Kurtz, editor, *Free Inquiry*; professor emeritus of philosophy State University of New York at Buffalo

Gerald Larue, professor emeritus of biblical archaeology, University Southern California

Timothy J. Madigan, executive editor, *Free Inquiry*

Lois Porter, associate editor, *Free Inquiry*

George Shriver, professor of history, Georgia Southern University

Paul D. Simmons, clinical professor, University of Louisville School of Medicine

George Smith, president, Signature Books

Dan O. Via, professor emeritus of New Testament, Duke Divinity School

Edward O. Wilson, professor of entomology, Harvard University

CONTRIBUTORS

ROBERT S. ALLEY, B.D., Ph.D., is professor of humanities, emeritus, at the University of Richmond, where he has taught since 1963. He also served on the faculty at William Jewell College and was visiting professor at the University of Virginia. Honors include being the first recipient of the Virginia ACLU Bill of Rights Award in 1994. He is a trustee of Americans United for Separation of Church and State. He has written fourteen books, numerous articles, and has produced a number of films. His *Love is All Around* is an analysis of the *Mary Tyler Moore Show*.

JOE EDWARD BARNHART, M.Div., Ph.D., is chair of the Department of Philosophy and Religion Studies, University of North Texas, Denton, where he has taught since 1967. Joe is a prolific writer with special interests in literature and religion. His latest book is *Dostoevsky on Evil and Atonement*, with L. L. Kraeger. He is now completing a novel he hopes to be the sequel to *The Brothers Karamazov*. He has also completed a book on Roger Williams and John Winthrop.

VERN BULLOUGH, M.A., Ph.D., B.S.N., has served as dean of Natural and Social Sciences at SUNY College, Buffalo, and is a SUNY Distinguished Professor. Since 1993 he has been visiting professor at the University of Southern California. He now writes especially in the area of healthcare but has published widely on topics ranging from sex and gender issues to medieval and modern science and medicine. Several of his books have been coauthored by his wife. He has been a member of the American Humanitarian Association since 1948 and is one of the founders of the Council for Secular Humanism.

BERNARD FARR, B.D., Ph.D., is director of International Masters Programmes, Oxford Center for Mission Studies. He is former head of the School of Theology and director of Research and Academic Programmes at Westminster College, Oxford University. His work involves helping two-thirds world theological institutions develop postgraduate masters degree programs with U.K. university validation. His travels take him to Eastern Europe, Africa, Asia, and Latin America, as well as the United States.

E. GLENN HINSON, M.Div., Ph.D., D.Phil., is professor of spirituality and worship and is John Loftis Professor of Church History at the Baptist Theological Seminary at Richmond, Virginia. He has also taught at the Southern Baptist Theological Seminary, Louisville, Kentucky, and Wake Forest University, Winston-Salem, North Carolina. He has served as Visiting Professor at St. John's University, Catholic University of America, and the University of Notre Dame. He is author of seventeen books and numerous scholarly articles, and has served as editor of *Review and Expositor* and *Baptist Peacemaker*.

PAUL KURTZ, Ph.D., is professor emeritus of philosophy at the State University of New York at Buffalo. He is also president of Prometheus Books and founder and editor of *Free Inquiry*, a magazine published by the Council for Secular Humanism. Dr. Kurtz was the founding chairman of the Committee for the Scientific Investigation of Claims of the Paranormal, and has served as copresident of the International Humanist and Ethical Union. He is author of numerous books, especially in the area of ethics and the paranormal, and humanist critique of religion. He is an internationally recognized authority on secular humanism and a popular speaker on a wide range of topics.

MOLLY MARSHALL, Ph.D., M.Div., is professor of spirituality and worship at Central Baptist Theological Seminary, Kansas City, Kansas. She also taught Christian theology at the Southern Baptist Theological Seminary, Louisville. Molly is an ordained Baptist minister and the author of *What it Means to be Human*. She has also written numerous articles for professional journals. She is an engaging speaker and travels widely as a preacher and conference leader.

Contributors

DAVID MCKENZIE, B.D., M.A., Ph.D., is chair, Department of Religion and Philosophy at Berry College, Mount Berry, Georgia, where he has served on faculty since 1978. He is author of a book on Wolfhart Pannenberg and has contributed articles for scholarly journals such as *Journal of Church and State*. He is also pastor of the Rehoboth Baptist Church, Cave Springs, Georgia.

ROBERT M. PRICE, Ph.D., holds doctoral degrees both in New Testament and systematic theology. He is adjunct instructor in philosophy and religion at Montclair State University and also serves on the faculty at the Center for Inquiry Institute in Amherst, New York, and as editor of the *Journal of Higher Criticism*. He has also served as pastor at the First Baptist Church, Montclair, New Jersey. Price is a prolific writer with numerous scholarly articles and three books to his credit, including *Mystic Rhythms: The Philosophical Vision of RUSH*. A study in biblical authority is forthcoming.

GEORGE H. SHRIVER, B.D., Ph.D., is professor of church history at Georgia Southern University, where he has taught since 1973. He has also taught at Southeastern Baptist Seminary (1959–1973), and, as visiting professor, at Meredith College and Duke University. He is author of six books and a contributor to books and journals. He is now writing a history of First Baptist Church, Savannah, Georgia. He also served as women's tennis coach, leading the Georgia team to the nationals three years and producing four All-Americans.

PAUL D. SIMMONS, B.D., Th.M., Ph.D., is clinical professor, Department of Family & Community Medicine, and adjunct professor, Department of Philosophy, University of Louisville. He taught Christian ethics at the Southern Baptist Theological Seminary, Louisville, 1970–1993. He has written three books and contributed to eighteen books in addition to articles written for journals and magazines. Simmons also serves as a trustee for Americans United for Separation of Church and State and on several hospital ethics committees. His special interests are in medical ethics and the intersection of religion and science, morality and public policy. He was named the first recipient of the Dr. David Gunn Award by the Kentucky Religious Coalition for Reproductive Rights.

ARTHUR JOE SLAVIN, Ph.D., has been Justin Bier Distinguished Professor and chair, Department of Religion and Humanities at the University of Louisville since 1977. Prior to that, he held appointments as dean of Arts and Sciences at U of L, professor at UCLA, and Regents Distinguished

Visiting Professor of History at Arizona State University. He is the author, coauthor, and editor of fifteen books and numerous articles and chapters in books. Most recently he served as editor of a special number of the *Huntington Library Quarterly* (Summer 1998), which includes his major essay "On Understanding Tudor Politics: Games and Dramas." Joe has held numerous fellowships and is Life Fellow of the Royal Historical Society of Great Britain. A Festschrift, "State, Sovereigns and Society: Essays on Early Modern England in Honor of A. J. Slavin," was presented to him in 1998. He is now working on a book on Ibsen.

GEORGE D. SMITH, Ph.D., is president of Signature Books, San Francisco, California.

DAN O. VIA, B.D., Ph.D., after a distinguished teaching career, now makes his home in Charlottesville, Virginia. He is emeritus professor of New Testament from the Divinity School of Duke University. Prior to that he was visiting professor of New Testament at Harvard Divinity School. He has also taught in the religion department at Wake Forest University and the University of Virginia. Via has distinguished himself as a New Testament scholar and is widely known for his work on the parables of Jesus. His most recent book is *The Revelation of God And/As Human Reception*. He has also written a play about Jesus and a book on Beckett's "Waiting for Godot," in addition to numerous articles for professional journals.